Good Housekeeping

BAKING BOOK

Good Housekeeping

BAKING BOOK

DELICIOUS RECIPES FOR EVERY OCCASION

COLLINS & BROWN

First published in the United Kingdom in 2012 by
Collins & Brown
10 Southcombe Street
London
W14 0RA

An imprint of Anova Books Company Ltd

This edition published in 2012 for WHSmith

The Good Housekeeping website is
www.allboutyou.com/goodhousekeeping

10 9 8 7 6 5 4 3 2 1

ISBN 978-1-90844-943-6

A catalogue record for this book is available from the British
Library.

Reproduction by Dot Gradations Ltd, UK
Printed and bound by Craft Print, Singapore

This book can be ordered direct from the publisher at
www.anovabooks.com

PICTURE CREDITS

Photographers: Marie-Louise Avery (pages 65, 230, 239, 241, 245,
248, 253, 254, 255, 258, 259, 322L and 323); Neil Barclay (page 113);
Steve Baxter (pages 85, 141 and 203); Martin Brigdale (pages 12,
46, 154, 214 and 315); Stephen Conroy (page 175); Nicki Dowey
(pages 22, 26, 35, 36, 54, 55, 58, 75, 101, 102, 103, 104, 106, 107, 109,
112, 116, 117, 119, 120, 121, 124, 125, 126, 129, 130, 131, 136, 137, 142,
143, 144, 145, 146, 147, 149, 151, 155, 163, 180, 181, 190, 201, 210, 225,
237, 238, 249, 250, 261, 271, 276, 287, 288, 291, 292 and 309T);
William Lingwood (pages 15, 41, 49, 51, 94 and 317); Emma Lee
(page 275); Gareth Morgans (pages 16, 30, 32, 38, 47, 53, 66, 150,
152, 171, 184, 204, 219, 283 and 296); Myles New (page 208); Craig
Robertson (pages 191, 192, 193, 194, 195, 200, 211, 213, 218, 226,
300, 301, 302, 303, 304, 305, 306, 307, 309B, 311, 312, 318, 319, 320,
321, 324, 325, 326, 327, 328, 329, 330 and 331); Lucinda Symons
(pages 13, 19, 21, 24, 27, 29, 42, 43, 44, 52, 57, 70, 71, 70, 73, 74, 76, 77,
78, 79, 80, 81, 82, 83, 84, 86, 87, 88, 89, 90, 91, 92, 93, 95, 96, 97, 98,
99, 100, 105, 115, 135, 138, 157, 161, 162, 168, 172, 187, 197, 207, 217,
222, 224, 227, 231, 233, 234, 236, 242, 244, 247, 256, 263, 264, 267,
272, 284, 310, 316 and 322R); Martin Thompson (pages 11, 294 and
312B); Phillip Webb (pages 34, 59, 132, 164, 167, 279 and 280); Jon
Whitaker (page 148); Kate Whitaker (pages 18, 37, 61, 63, 64, 118,
122, 176, 179, 198, 221 and 260)

Home Economists: Joanna Farrow, Emma Jane Frost, Teresa
Goldfinch, Alice Hart, Lucy McKelvie, Kim Morphew,
Aya Nishimura, Bridget Sargeson and Mari Mererid Williams
Stylists: Tamzin Ferdinando, Wei Tang, Helen Trent
and Fanny Ward

Contents

Foreword

Baking has always had a welcome place in people's hearts. It promises not only a house filled with tantalising aromas, but also the satisfaction of feeding those you love with irresistible sweet treats — not to mention yourself! With the rise of the patisserie outlet and excellent shop-bought cakes, there's always the threat of 'the easy way out' but, good though these shop-bought cakes and bakes may be, they are not homemade.

For me, this self-madeness shows you care and it's hard not to feel a nibbling of pride when you're surrounded by munching sounds of delight. On the flip side, if a little mishap does occur and, say, your scones have not risen to the heavens, you'll know they still taste good.

In my experience, baking is what hooks most people into enjoying their kitchen — and with good reason, it's fun! Even if you haven't started at a tender age, stamping out dinosaur biscuits, there's always time to learn and to be rewarded with the huge sense of satisfaction of seeing something cooling on a wire rack.

Baking involves a delicate — scientific, even — balance, where a small change in an ingredient can have a large effect on the finished result. It's hard to 'wing it' when baking. But fear not, baking is very simple if you follow a good recipe closely — and Good Housekeeping recipes are not only excellent, but have also been triple-tested in our dedicated kitchens, so you are sure to succeed.

I hope you enjoy this book — it's filled with sweet promise.

Meike.

Meike Beck
Cookery Editor
Good Housekeeping

Everyday Cakes

Victoria Sandwich

Preparation Time
20 minutes
Cooking Time
about 25 minutes, plus cooling

- 175g (6oz) unsalted butter, softened, plus extra to grease
- 175g (6oz) caster sugar
- 3 medium eggs
- 175g (6oz) self-raising flour, sifted
- 3–4 tbsp jam (strawberry or raspberry is most traditional)
- icing or caster sugar

NUTRITIONAL INFORMATION
Per Slice 445 cals; 21g fat (of which 11g saturates); 30g carbohydrate; 0.8g salt

1 Preheat the oven to 190°C (170°C fan oven) mark 5. Grease two 18cm (7 inch) sandwich tins and base-line with greaseproof paper.

2 Put the butter and caster sugar into a large bowl and, using a hand-held electric whisk, beat together until pale and fluffy. Add the eggs one at a time, beating well after each addition – add a spoonful of the flour if the mixture looks as if it's about to curdle.

3 Once the eggs are added, use a large metal spoon to fold in the remaining flour. Divide the mixture evenly between the prepared tins and level the surface.

4 Bake in the centre of the oven for 20–25 minutes until the cakes are well risen and spring back when lightly pressed in the centre. Loosen the edges with a palette knife and leave in the tins for 10 minutes.

5 Turn out, remove the lining paper and leave to cool on a wire rack. Sandwich the two cakes together with jam and dust with icing sugar, or sprinkle the top with caster sugar. Slice and serve.

Variations
Chocolate: Replace 3 tbsp flour with sifted cocoa powder. Sandwich the cakes with vanilla or chocolate buttercream (see pages 314–15).

Coffee: Blend together 2 tsp instant coffee granules with 1 tbsp boiling water. Cool and add to the creamed mixture with the eggs. Sandwich the cakes together with vanilla or coffee buttercream (see pages 314–15).

Citrus: Add the finely grated zest of an orange, lime or lemon to the raw cake mixture. Sandwich the cakes together with orange, lime or lemon buttercream (see page 315).

Cuts into 10 slices

Chocolate Victoria Sandwich

Preparation Time
20 minutes
Cooking Time
20 minutes, plus cooling

- 175g (6oz) unsalted butter at room temperature, plus extra to grease
- 3 tbsp cocoa powder
- 175g (6oz) golden caster sugar
- 3 medium eggs, beaten
- 160g (5½oz) self-raising flour, sifted
- golden caster sugar to dredge

FILLING

- 1 tbsp cocoa powder
- 75g (3oz) unsalted butter, softened
- 175g (6oz) icing sugar, sifted
- a few drops of vanilla extract
- 1–2 tbsp milk or water

NUTRITIONAL INFORMATION
Per slice 520 cals; 30g fat (of which 19g saturates); 62g carbohydrate; 1g salt

Cuts into 8 slices

1 Preheat the oven to 190°C (170°C fan oven) mark 5. Grease two 18cm (7 inch) sandwich tins and base-line with baking parchment. Blend the cocoa powder with 3 tbsp hot water to make a smooth paste, then leave to cool.

2 Using a freestanding mixer or hand-held electric whisk, cream the butter and sugar together until pale and fluffy. Add the cooled cocoa mixture and beat until evenly blended.

3 Add the beaten eggs, a little at a time, beating well after each addition. Using a metal spoon or large spatula, fold in half the flour, then carefully fold in the rest. Divide the mixture evenly between the prepared tins and level the surface.

4 Bake both cakes on the middle shelf of the oven for about 20 minutes until well risen, springy to the touch

and beginning to shrink away from the sides of the tins. Cool in the tins for 5 minutes, then turn out on to a wire rack and leave to cool completely.

5 To make the chocolate buttercream, blend the cocoa powder with 3 tbsp boiling water and set aside to cool. Put the butter into a bowl and beat with a wooden spoon until light and fluffy. Gradually stir in the icing sugar. Add the blended cocoa, vanilla extract and milk or water and beat well until light and smooth.

6 When the cakes are cool, sandwich them together with the chocolate buttercream and sprinkle the top with caster sugar.

Whisked Sponge

Preparation Time
25 minutes
Cooking Time
about 25 minutes, plus cooling

- ◆ unsalted butter to grease
- ◆ 90g (3¼oz) plain flour, plus extra to dust
- ◆ 3 large eggs
- ◆ 125g (4oz) caster sugar

FILLING AND TOPPING
- ◆ 3–4 tbsp strawberry, raspberry or apricot jam
- ◆ 125ml (4fl oz) whipping or double cream, whipped (optional)
- ◆ icing or caster sugar

NUTRITIONAL INFORMATION
Per slice 215–160 cals; 4–3g fat (of which 0.9–0.7g saturates); 30–24g carbohydrate; 0.1g salt

Cuts into 6-8 slices

1 Preheat the oven to 190°C (170°C fan oven) mark 5. Grease and base-line two 18cm (7 inch) sandwich tins, grease the paper lightly and dust the sides with a little flour.

2 Put the eggs and caster sugar into a large heatproof bowl and, using a hand-held electric whisk, beat until well blended. Put the bowl over a pan of hot water (making sure the base of the bowl doesn't touch the water) and whisk until the mixture is pale and creamy and thick enough to leave a trail on the surface when the whisk is lifted (about 5 minutes). Remove the bowl from the pan and carry on whisking until cool.

3 Sift half the flour into the mixture and, using a large metal spoon or spatula, fold it in very lightly (trying to knock out as little air as possible). Sift in the remaining flour and repeat the folding process until combined.

4 Pour the mixture into the prepared tins, tilting the tins to spread the mixture evenly (do not bang on the surface as this will knock out valuable air). Bake in the middle of the oven for 20–25 minutes until well risen and springy to the touch when lightly pressed in the centre (do not test with a skewer, as this can cause the cake to sink).

5 Turn the cakes out on to a wire rack to cool. When completely cool, peel off the lining paper and sandwich the cakes together with jam and whipped cream, if using. Dust with icing sugar, or sprinkle the top with caster sugar. Serve in slices.

Genoese Sponge

Preparation Time
25 minutes
Cooking Time
25–30 minutes or 30–40 minutes,
plus cooling

- 40g (1½oz) unsalted butter,
  plus extra to grease
- 65g (2½oz) plain flour, plus
  extra to dust
- 3 large eggs
- 75g (3oz) caster sugar
- 1 tbsp cornflour

FILLING AND TOPPING
- 3–4 tbsp strawberry,
  raspberry or apricot jam
- 125ml (4fl oz) whipping
  cream, whipped (optional)
- icing sugar or caster sugar

NUTRITIONAL
INFORMATION
Per slice 302 cals; 17g fat (of which
9.6g saturates); 34g carbohydrate;
0.2g salt

1 Grease two 18cm (7 inch) sandwich tins or one deep 18cm (7 inch) round cake tin, base-line with greaseproof paper and dust the sides with a little flour.

2 Put the butter into a small pan and heat gently to melt, then take off the heat and leave to stand for a few minutes to cool slightly.

3 Put the eggs and sugar into a bowl and, using a hand-held electric whisk, whisk until well blended. Place the bowl over a pan of hot water (making sure the base of the bowl doesn't touch the water) and whisk until the mixture is pale and creamy and thick enough to leave a trail on the surface when the whisk is lifted (about 5 minutes). Remove the bowl from the pan and whisk until cool.

4 Preheat the oven to 180°C (160°C fan oven) mark 4. Sift the plain flour and cornflour into the egg bowl, then use a large metal spoon to carefully fold in (trying to knock out as little air as possible).

5 Pour the melted and cooled butter around the edges of the mixture, leaving any butter sediment behind in the pan. Very lightly, fold in the butter until it has been incorporated into the mixture. Pour into the prepared tin(s).

6 Bake in the oven for 25–30 minutes for the sandwich tins, or 35–40 minutes for the deep tin, until well risen and the cakes spring back when lightly pressed in the centre. Loosen the edge of the cake and leave to cool for 10 minutes. Turn out on to a wire rack and leave to cool completely.

7 When completely cool, peel off the lining paper (halve the single cake horizontally) and sandwich together with jam and whipped cream, if using. Dust with icing sugar or sprinkle the top with caster sugar. Serve in slices.

Cuts into 12 slices

Deluxe Carrot Cake

Preparation Time
30 minutes, plus cooling
Cooking Time
about 1¾ hours

- 225ml (8fl oz) sunflower oil, plus extra to grease
- 225g (8oz) light muscovado sugar
- 4 medium eggs
- 225g (8oz) self-raising flour
- 1 tsp bicarbonate of soda
- 1½ tsp each mixed spice and ground cinnamon
- 1 orange
- 150g (5oz) sultanas
- 200g (7oz) carrots, coarsely grated
- 50g (2oz) walnuts, chopped
- 50g (2oz) stem ginger, chopped

FROSTING AND DECORATION
- 600g (1lb 5oz) cream cheese
- 200g (7oz) icing sugar, sifted
- finely grated zest of 1 orange
- marzipan carrots (see right)

NUTRITIONAL INFORMATION
Per slice, without marzipan carrots 697 cals; 48g fat (of which 18g saturates); 62g carbohydrate; 0.9g salt

1 Preheat the oven to 170°C (150°C fan) mark 3. Grease the base and sides of a 20.5cm (8 inch) cake tin and line with baking parchment. Whisk the oil, sugar and eggs in a large bowl until smooth. Stir in the flour, baking soda and spices. Finely grate the zest of the orange and add to the mixture with the juice from only half the orange. Add the sultanas, carrots, walnuts and ginger and mix well.

2 Spoon the mixture into the prepared tin and bake for 30 minutes. Cover the cake with foil and bake for a further 1¼ hours or until a skewer inserted into the centre comes out clean. Leave to cool in the tin for 5 minutes, then turn out on to a wire rack and leave to cool completely.

3 To make the frosting, mix all the ingredients together in a bowl. Cut the cooled cake in two horizontally and use half the frosting to sandwich together. Spread the remaining frosting over the top and decorate with marzipan carrots.

To make marzipan carrots
Colour 75g (3oz) marzipan with orange food colouring and 15g (½oz) marzipan with green food colouring. Divide the orange marzipan into 12 pieces, then shape each piece into a cone. Using a cocktail stick, mark on ridges. Divide the green marzipan into 12 pieces, then shape each piece into a frond to resemble leaves and stick on to the carrots.

Lemon Drizzle Loaf

Preparation Time
20 minutes
Cooking Time
about 50 minutes, plus cooling

- 175g (6oz) unsalted butter, softened, plus extra to grease
- 175g (6oz) caster sugar
- 4 medium eggs, lightly beaten
- 3 lemons
- 125g (4oz) self-raising flour
- 50g (2oz) ground almonds
- 75g (3oz) sugar cubes

NUTRITIONAL INFORMATION
Per slice 424 cals; 25g fat (of which 13g saturates); 46g carbohydrate; 0.6g salt

Cuts into 8–10 slices

1 Preheat the oven to 180°C (160°C fan oven) mark 4. Grease a 900g (2lb) loaf tin and line with baking parchment.

2 Put the butter and caster sugar into a large bowl and beat together with a hand-held electric whisk until pale and fluffy (about 5 minutes). Gradually beat in the eggs, followed by the finely grated zest of two of the lemons and the juice of ½ a lemon.

3 Fold the flour and ground almonds into the butter mixture, then spoon into the prepared tin and bake for 40–50 minutes until a skewer inserted into the centre

comes out clean. Cool in the tin for 10 minutes, turn out on to a wire rack and leave to cool until just warm.

4 Meanwhile, put the sugar cubes into a small bowl with the juice of 1½ lemons and the pared zest of 1 lemon (you should have 1 un-juiced lemon left over). Soak for 5 minutes, then use the back of a spoon to roughly crush the cubes. Spoon over the warm cake and leave to cool completely before serving in slices.

Almond and Apricot Cake

Preparation Time
15 minutes
Cooking Time
15 minutes, plus cooling

- 175g (6oz) unsalted butter, softened, plus extra to grease
- 125g (4oz) caster sugar
- 4 medium eggs
- 175g (6oz) self-raising flour
- 75g (3oz) ground almonds
- finely grated zest and juice of 1 lemon

FILLING
- 250g tub mascarpone cheese
- 40g (1½oz) icing sugar, plus extra to dust
- 4 tbsp apricot compote

NUTRITIONAL INFORMATION
Per slice 325 cals; 21g fat (of which 11g saturates); 30g carbohydrate; 0.3g salt

Cuts into 12 slices

1 Preheat the oven to 200°C (180°C fan oven) mark 6. Grease two 18cm (7 inch) round sandwich tins and line with greaseproof paper.

2 Beat the butter and caster sugar together until fluffy, then beat in the eggs, one at a time, until combined. Using a metal spoon, gently fold in the flour, ground almonds, lemon zest and juice and stir until smooth.

3 Divide the mixture equally between the prepared tins, level the surface and bake for 15 minutes or until golden and a skewer inserted into the centre comes

out clean. Cool in the tins for 5 minutes, then turn out on to a wire rack and leave to cool completely.

4 To make the filling, beat the mascarpone and icing sugar together in a bowl. Spread over one of the cakes. Spoon the apricot compote evenly over the cheese mixture and put the other cake on top. Dust with icing sugar to serve.

Madeira Cake

Preparation Time
20 minutes
Cooking Time
about 50 minutes, plus cooling

- ◆ 275g (10oz) unsalted butter, softened, plus extra to grease
- ◆ 175g (6oz) plain flour
- ◆ 175g (6oz) self-raising flour
- ◆ 275g (10oz) caster sugar
- ◆ 5 medium eggs, lightly beaten
- ◆ lemon juice or milk

NUTRITIONAL INFORMATION
Per slice 260 cals; 14g fat (of which 8g saturates); 31g carbohydrate; 0.4g salt

1 Preheat the oven to 170°C (150°C fan oven) mark 3. Grease and line a deep 20.5cm (8 inch) round cake tin, then grease the paper lightly.

2 Sift the flours together. Cream the butter and sugar together in a separate bowl until pale and fluffy. Gradually add the eggs, beating well after each addition.

3 Using a large metal spoon, fold the flours into the butter mixture, adding a little lemon juice or milk if necessary to give a dropping consistency.

4 Turn the mixture into the prepared tin and level the surface. Make a slight depression in the middle of the surface of the cake to ensure that it doesn't mound/dome too much while baking. Bake in the centre of the oven for about 1½–1¾ hours until the cake springs back lightly when pressed in the centre with a finger.

5 Leave the cake to cool in the tin for 15 minutes, then turn out on to a wire rack and leave to cool completely. Wrap in clingfilm or foil and store in a cool place until required.

Cuts into 12 large slices

Traditional Rich Fruit Cake

Preparation Time
30 minutes, plus overnight soaking
Cooking Time
3½ hours, plus cooling

- 450g (1lb) currants
- 200g (7oz) sultanas
- 200g (7oz) raisins
- 150g (5oz) glacé cherries
- 75g (3oz) chopped mixed peel
- 75g (3oz) flaked almonds
- a little grated lemon zest
- 1 tbsp brandy
- 275g (10oz) unsalted butter
- 350g (12oz) plain flour
- ½ tsp mixed spice
- ½ tsp ground cinnamon
- 275g (10oz) soft brown sugar
- 5 medium eggs, beaten

NUTRITIONAL INFORMATION
Per slice 497 cals; 19g fat (of which 9.7g saturates); 80g carbohydrate; 0.4g salt

Cuts into 16 large slices

1 Put the currants, sultanas, raisins, glacé cherries, mixed peel, flaked almonds, lemon zest and brandy into a large non-aluminium bowl (glass or ceramic is best, as this won't react with the fruit). Mix well, then cover with clingfilm and leave to soak overnight in a cool place.

2 When the fruit has soaked, grease a deep 20.5cm (8 inch) round cake tin and line the base and sides with a double thickness of greaseproof paper. Grease the paper lightly. Tie a double band of brown paper around the outside of the tin (to protect the cake from burning while baking). Preheat the oven to 150°C (130°C fan oven) mark 2.

3 Sift the flour, mixed spice and cinnamon into a separate large bowl. Add the butter, sugar and eggs and, using a hand-held electric whisk, mix together until smooth and glossy (about 1 minute).

4 Using a large metal spoon or spatula, fold the soaked fruit into the flour mixture and continue folding until the fruit is evenly distributed. Spoon the mixture into the prepared tin and level the surface.

Quantities and sizes for Rich Fruit Cakes

To make a formal cake for a birthday, wedding or anniversary, use the following chart to see the quantities of ingredients required to fill the chosen cake tin or tins, whether round or square.

Note When baking large cakes, 25.5cm (10 inch) and upwards, it is advisable to reduce the oven heat to 130°C (110°C fan oven) mark 1 after two-thirds of the cooking time. The amounts of Almond Paste quoted in this chart will give a thin covering. The quantities of Royal Icing should be enough for two coats. If using ready-to-roll fondant icing, use the quantities suggested for Royal Icing as a rough guide.

Size	Square tin size	Round tin size	Ingredients	Almond Paste	Royal Icing
Size 1	12.5cm (5 inch)	15cm (6 inch)	225g (8oz) currants, 125g (4oz) each sultanas and raisins, 50g (2oz) glacé cherries, 25g (1oz) each mixed peel and flaked almonds, a little lemon zest, 175g (6oz) plain flour, 4 tsp each mixed spice and cinnamon, 150g (5oz) each softened butter and soft brown sugar, 2½ medium eggs, beaten, 1 tbsp brandy	350g (12oz)	450g (1lb)
Size 2	15cm (6 inch)	18cm (7 inch)	350g (12oz) currants, 125g (4oz) each sultanas and raisins, 75g (3oz) glacé cherries, 50g (2oz) each mixed peel and flaked almonds, a little lemon zest, 200g (7oz) plain flour, ½ tsp each mixed spice and cinnamon, 175g (6oz) each softened butter and soft brown sugar, 3 medium eggs, beaten, 1 tbsp brandy	450g (1lb)	550g (1¼lb)
Size 3	20.5cm (8 inch)	23cm (9 inch)	625g (1lb 6oz) currants, 225g (8oz) each sultanas and raisins, 175g (6oz) glacé cherries, 125g (4oz) each mixed peel and flaked almonds, zest of ¼ lemon, 400g (14oz) plain flour, 1 tsp each cinnamon and mixed spice, 350g (12oz) each softened butter and soft brown sugar, 6 medium eggs, beaten, 2 tbsp brandy	800g (1¾lb)	900g (2lb)
Size 4	23cm (9 inch)	25.5cm (10 inch)	800g (1¾lb) currants, 375g (13oz) each sultanas and raisins, 250g (9oz) glacé cherries, 150g (5oz) each mixed peel and flaked almonds, zest of ¼–½ lemon, 600g (1lb 5oz) plain flour, 1 tsp each mixed spice and cinnamon, 500g (1lb 2oz) each softened butter and soft brown sugar, 9 medium eggs, beaten, 2–3 tbsp brandy	900g (2lb)	1kg (2¼lb)
Size 5	28cm (11 inch)	30.5cm (12 inch)	1.5kg (3lb 2oz) currants, 525g (1lb 3oz) each sultanas and raisins, 350g (12oz) glacé cherries, 250g (9oz) each mixed peel and flaked almonds, zest of ½ lemon, 825g (1lb 13oz) plain flour, 2½ tsp each mixed spice and cinnamon, 800g (1¾lb) each softened butter and soft brown sugar, 14 medium eggs, beaten, 4 tbsp brandy	1.1kg (2½lb)	1.4kg 3lb)
Size 6	30.5cm (12 inch)	33cm (13 inch)	1.7kg (3lb 12oz) currants, 625g (1lb 6oz) each sultanas and raisins, 425g (15oz) glacé cherries, 275g (10oz) each mixed peel and flaked almonds, zest of 1 lemon, 1kg (2¼lb) plain flour, 2½ tsp each mixed spice and cinnamon, 950g (2lb 2oz) each softened butter and soft brown sugar, 17 medium eggs, beaten, 6 tbsp brandy	1.4kg (3lb)	1.6kg (3½lb)

Give the tin a few sharp bangs on a worksurface to remove any air pockets. Make a slight depression in the middle of the surface of the cake to ensure that it doesn't mound/dome too much while baking.

5 Put the tin on a baking sheet and cook in the middle of the oven for 3–3½ hours – cover the top with greaseproof paper after about 1½ hours – until the cake is firm to the touch and a skewer inserted into the centre comes out clean.

6 Cool completely in the tin. Once cool, take out of the tin (leaving the lining paper around the cake). Wrap the cake in a double layer of greaseproof paper, then overwrap in a double layer of foil. Leave to mature for at least a week before cutting.

Note

For an iced cake, spread the top with Apricot Glaze (see page 313), cover with a layer of purchased marzipan or Almond Paste (see page 313), and ice with ready-to-roll fondant icing or Royal Icing (see page 313).

Cuts into 16 slices

Dundee Cake

Preparation Time
20 minutes
Cooking Time
about 2 hours, plus cooling

- 225g (8oz) butter or margarine, softened, plus extra to grease
- 125g (4oz) currants
- 125g (4oz) raisins
- 50g (2oz) blanched almonds, chopped
- 125g (4oz) chopped mixed candied peel
- 300g (11oz) plain flour
- 225g (8oz) light muscovado sugar
- finely grated zest of 1 lemon
- 4 large eggs, beaten
- 75g (3oz) split almonds to decorate

NUTRITIONAL INFORMATION
Per slice 350 cals; 18g fat (of which 8g saturates); 45g carbohydrate; 0.4g salt

1 Preheat the oven to 170°C (150°C fan oven) mark 3. Grease a deep 20.5cm (8 inch) round cake tin and line with greaseproof paper. Tie a double band of brown paper around the outside of the tin (to protect the cake from burning while baking).

2 Combine the dried fruit, chopped nuts and peel in a bowl. Sift in a little flour and stir to coat the fruit.

3 Cream the butter and sugar together in a bowl until pale and fluffy, then beat in the lemon zest. Add the eggs, a little at a time, beating well after each addition. Sift in the remaining flour and fold in lightly, using a metal spoon, then fold in the fruit and nut mixture.

4 Turn the mixture into the prepared tin and, using the back of a metal spoon, make a slight depression in the middle of the surface of the cake to ensure that it doesn't mound/dome too much while baking. Arrange the split almonds on top.

5 Bake on the centre shelf of the oven for 2 hours or until a skewer inserted into the centre comes out clean. Loosely cover the top of the cake with foil if it appears to be browning too quickly. Leave in the tin for 15 minutes, then turn out on to a wire rack and leave to cool completely. Wrap in greaseproof paper and foil and leave to mature for at least a week before cutting.

Banana and Butterscotch Bread

Preparation Time
20 minutes
Cooking Time
1 hour, plus cooling

- ◆ butter to grease
- ◆ 175g (6oz) plain flour, sifted
- ◆ 2 tsp baking powder
- ◆ ½ tsp bicarbonate of soda
- ◆ ½ tsp salt
- ◆ 175g (6oz) light muscovado sugar
- ◆ 2 large eggs
- ◆ 3 medium-sized ripe bananas, peeled and mashed
- ◆ 150g carton natural yogurt
- ◆ 150g bar butterscotch chocolate, roughly chopped
- ◆ 100g (3½oz) pecan nuts, chopped
- ◆ 1–2 tbsp demerara sugar

NUTRITIONAL INFORMATION
Per slice 221 cals; 9g fat (of which 2g saturates); 34g carbohydrate; 0.2g salt

Cuts into 15 slices

---

1 Preheat the oven to 170°C (150°C fan oven) mark 3. Grease a 1.4kg (3lb) loaf tin and line with greaseproof paper.

2 Put the flour, baking powder, bicarbonate of soda and salt into a large bowl and mix together.

3 In a separate bowl, beat the muscovado sugar and eggs together with a hand-held electric whisk until pale and fluffy. Stir in the bananas, yogurt, chocolate and 50g (2oz) pecan nuts, then the flour mixture.

4 Spoon the mixture into the prepared tin and level the surface. Sprinkle with the remaining chopped pecan nuts and the demerara sugar. Bake for 1 hour or until a skewer inserted into the centre comes out clean. Leave to cool in the tin on a wire rack, then turn out and slice.

Variation
If you can't find butterscotch chocolate, use a bar of plain dark chocolate instead.

Sticky Lemon Polenta Cake

Preparation Time
10 minutes
Cooking Time
1 hour, plus cooling

- 50g (2oz) unsalted butter, softened, plus extra to grease
- 3 lemons
- 250g (9oz) golden caster sugar
- 250g (9oz) instant polenta
- 1 tsp baking powder
- 2 large eggs
- 50ml (2fl oz) semi-skimmed milk
- 2 tbsp natural yogurt
- 2 tbsp poppy seeds

NUTRITIONAL INFORMATION
Per slice 220 cals; 7g fat (of which 3g saturates); 37g carbohydrate; 0.1g salt

Cuts into 12 slices

1 Preheat the oven to 180°C (160°C fan oven) mark 4. Lightly grease a 900g (2lb) loaf tin and base-line with greaseproof paper.

2 Grate the zest of 1 lemon and put into a food processor with the butter, 200g (7oz) sugar, the polenta, baking powder, eggs, milk, yogurt and poppy seeds, then whizz until smooth. Spoon the mixture into the prepared tin and level the surface. Bake for 55 minutes–1 hour until a skewer inserted into the centre comes out clean. Leave to cool in the tin for 10 minutes.

3 Next, make a syrup. Squeeze the juice from the zested lemon plus 1 more lemon. Thinly slice the third lemon. Put the lemon juice into a pan with the remaining sugar and 150ml (¼ pint) water. Add the lemon slices, bring to the boil and bubble for about 10 minutes until syrupy. Take the pan off the heat and leave to cool for 5 minutes. Remove the lemon slices from the syrup and set aside.

4 Slide a knife around the edge of the cake and turn out on to a serving plate. Pierce the cake in several places with a skewer, spoon the syrup over it and decorate with the lemon slices.

Swiss Roll

Preparation Time
25 minutes
Cooking Time
10–12 minutes, plus cooling

- unsalted butter to grease
- 125g (4oz) caster sugar, plus extra to dust
- 125g (4oz) plain flour, plus extra to dust
- 3 large eggs

FILLING AND DECORATION
- caster sugar to sprinkle
- 125g (4oz) jam, warmed

NUTRITIONAL INFORMATION
Per slice 200 cals; 3g fat (of which 0.7g saturates); 41g carbohydrate; 0.9g salt

1 Preheat the oven to 200°C (180°C fan oven) mark 6. Grease and line a 33 x 23cm (13 x 9 inch) Swiss roll tin, then grease the paper lightly. Dust the paper with caster sugar and flour.

2 Put the eggs and sugar into a large heatproof bowl and, using a hand-held electric whisk, beat until well combined. Put the bowl over a pan of hot water (making sure the base of the bowl doesn't touch the water) and whisk until the mixture is pale and creamy and thick enough to leave a trail on the surface when the whisk is lifted (about 5 minutes). Remove the bowl from the pan and whisk until cool.

3 Sift half the flour over the mixture and, using a large metal spoon or spatula, fold it in very lightly. Sift in the remaining flour and gently fold in as before until combined. Carefully fold in 1 tbsp hot water.

4 Pour the mixture into the prepared tin and tilt the tin to spread the mixture evenly. Bake for 10–12 minutes until pale golden, risen and springy to the touch.

5 Meanwhile, put a sheet of greaseproof paper larger than the Swiss roll tin on a damp tea towel. Dredge the paper with caster sugar. Quickly invert the cake on to the paper, then remove the tin and peel off the lining paper. If needed, trim off the crusty edges of the cake to neaten. Spread the jam over the top of the cake.

6 Using the greaseproof paper to help, roll up the cake from one of the short ends. Make the first turn as tight as possible so that the cake will roll up evenly and have a good shape when finished. Once rolled, put seam-side down on a serving plate and sprinkle with caster sugar. Slice and serve.

Cuts into 10 slices

Courgette Cake

Preparation Time
30 minutes, plus cooling
Cooking Time
about 35 minutes

- 150ml (¼ pint) vegetable oil, plus extra to grease
- 250g (9oz) self-raising flour, plus extra to dust
- 50g (2oz) pistachios (shelled weight)
- 3 medium eggs
- 175g (6oz) caster sugar
- 1 tsp vanilla extract
- ½ tsp bicarbonate of soda
- 2 small courgettes, about 225g (8oz), coarsely grated

ICING
- 125g (4oz) icing sugar, sifted
- 1 tbsp roughly chopped pistachios

NUTRITIONAL INFORMATION
Per slice 359 cals; 17g fat (of which 2g saturates); 49g carbohydrate; 0.5g salt

1 Preheat the oven to 180°C (160°C fan oven) mark 4. Grease a 25.5cm (10 inch) kugelhopf or bundt tin. Lightly dust with flour and tap out the excess. Pulse the pistachios in a food processor until finely ground (or chop by hand), then set aside.

2 Whisk the oil, eggs, sugar and vanilla extract together in a large bowl. Sift in the flour and bicarbonate of soda and stir to combine. Mix in the courgettes and pistachios. Tip into the prepared tin and level the surface.

3 Bake for 35 minutes or until golden and a skewer inserted into the centre comes out clean. Leave to cool in the tin for 5 minutes, then turn out on to a wire rack and leave to cool completely.

4 To make the icing, mix the icing sugar with enough water (1½–2 tbsp) to get a smooth, fairly thick icing. Slide the cake on to a cake stand or serving plate. Drizzle the icing over it, then scatter on the chopped pistachios. Serve in slices.

Note
This cake can also be made in a deep 20.5cm (8 inch) round cake tin. Follow the recipe, baking the cake for about 55 minutes.

Lemon and Poppy Seed Buttermilk Cake

Preparation Time
25 minutes, plus cooling
Cooking Time
about 40 minutes

- 150g (5oz) unsalted butter, softened, plus extra to grease
- 175 (6oz) granulated sugar
- 3 large eggs, lightly beaten
- finely grated zest and juice of 2 lemons
- 1 tsp vanilla extract
- 125g (4oz) buttermilk
- 1 tbsp poppy seeds
- 250g (9oz) plain flour
- 2 tsp baking powder

ICING

- 150g (5oz) full-fat cream cheese, at room temperature
- 75g (3oz) unsalted butter, softened
- 2 tbsp lemon curd
- 350g (12oz) icing sugar, sifted
- crystallized rose petals (optional)

NUTRITIONAL INFORMATION
Per slice 569 cals; 29g fat (of which 17g saturates); 78g carbohydrate; 0.8g salt

1 Preheat the oven to 180°C (160°C fan oven) mark 4. Lightly grease a 20.5cm (8 inch) round cake tin and line with baking parchment. Put the butter and granulated sugar into a large bowl and, using a hand-held electric whisk, beat together until pale and fluffy (about 3 minutes). Gradually beat in the eggs, mixing constantly, followed by the lemon zest and juice, vanilla extract, buttermilk and poppy seeds.

2 Sift the flour and baking powder into the bowl, then use a large metal spoon to fold it in. Spoon the mixture into the prepared tin and bake for 40 minutes or until a skewer inserted into the centre comes out clean. Leave to cool in the tin for 5 minutes, then turn out on to a wire rack and leave to cool completely.

3 Once the cake has cooled, peel off the lining paper and transfer to a cake stand or serving plate.

4 To make the icing, put the cream cheese, softened butter and lemon curd into a food processor and whizz together until smooth (alternatively, whisk together by hand). Add the icing sugar and whizz again to combine. Spread over the top of the cake and decorate with crystallized rose petals, if you like.

Cuts into 10 slices

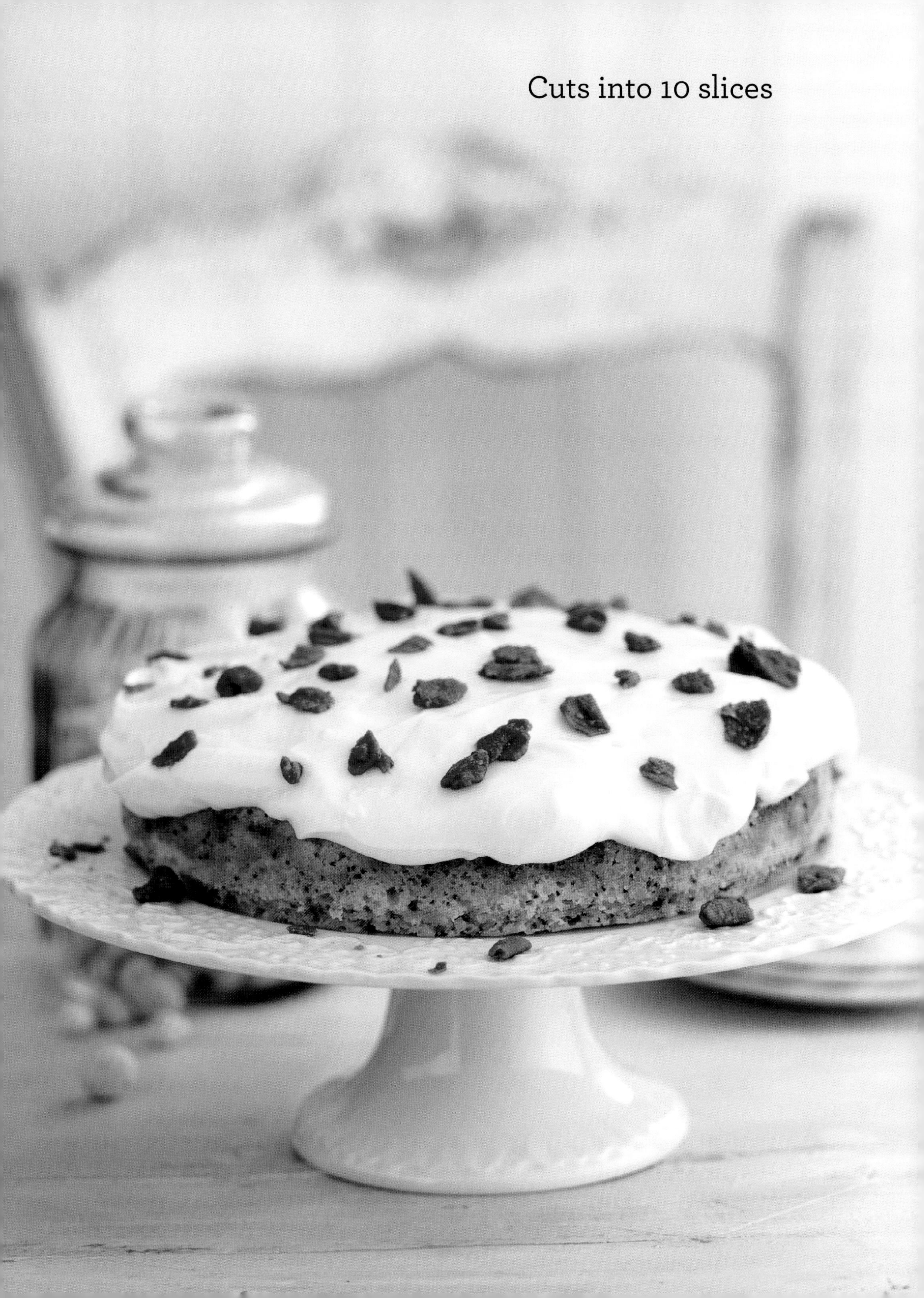

Spiced Pecan, Apple and Cranberry Cake

Preparation Time
20 minutes
Cooking Time
about 1 hour

- ◆ 175g (6oz) unsalted butter, softened, plus extra to grease
- ◆ 150g (5oz) caster sugar
- ◆ 3 medium eggs
- ◆ 1 tsp vanilla extract
- ◆ 150g (5oz) plain flour
- ◆ 1 tsp baking powder
- ◆ 2 tbsp milk
- ◆ ½ tsp ground cinnamon
- ◆ 3 Braeburn apples, peeled, cored and cut into 1cm (½ inch) cubes
- ◆ 50g (2oz) fresh cranberries, defrosted if frozen
- ◆ 75g (3oz) pecan nuts, roughly chopped
- ◆ 2–3 tbsp apricot jam

NUTRITIONAL INFORMATION
Per slice 436 cals; 28g fat (of which 13g saturates); 44g carbohydrate; 0.5g salt

Cuts into 8 slices

1 Preheat the oven to 180°C (160°C fan oven) mark 4. Grease a 20.5cm (8 inch) springform cake tin and line with baking parchment.

2 Using a freestanding mixer or hand-held electric whisk, beat 150g (5oz) butter with the sugar, eggs, vanilla extract, flour, baking powder and milk until pale and fluffy (about 5 minutes). Spoon into the prepared tin and level the surface. Bake for 10 minutes.

3 Meanwhile, heat the remaining butter in a large frying pan until foaming. Stir in the cinnamon and apples and cook for 3 minutes until almost tender. Take off the heat and stir in the cranberries and pecan nuts.

4 Carefully take the part-baked cake out of the oven and sprinkle the apple mixture over the surface. Return to the oven and bake for a further 40–50 minutes, until a skewer inserted into the centre comes out clean.

5 Leave the cake to cool in the tin for 5 minutes, then remove from the tin and peel off the lining paper. Transfer to a serving plate. Gently warm the jam in a small pan to loosen, then brush over the top of the cake. Serve the cake warm or at room temperature.

Raspberry and Peach Cake

Preparation Time
15 minutes
Cooking Time
1–1¼ hours, plus cooling

- 200g (7oz) unsalted butter, melted, plus extra to grease
- 250g (9oz) self-raising flour, sifted
- 100g (3½oz) golden caster sugar
- 4 medium eggs, beaten
- 125g (4oz) raspberries
- 2 large, almost ripe peaches or nectarines, halved, stoned and sliced
- 4 tbsp apricot jam
- juice of ½ lemon

NUTRITIONAL INFORMATION
Per slice 405 cals; 24g fat (of which 14g saturates); 44g carbohydrate; 0.8g salt

Cuts into 8 slices

1 Preheat the oven to 190°C (170°C fan oven) mark 5. Grease a 20.5cm (8 inch) springform cake tin and base-line with baking parchment.

2 Put the flour and sugar into a large bowl. Make a well in the centre and add the melted butter and the eggs. Mix well.

3 Spread half the mixture over the bottom of the prepared tin and add half the raspberries and sliced peaches or nectarines. Spoon on the remaining cake mixture, smooth over, then add the remaining raspberries and peaches or nectarines, pressing them down into the mixture slightly.

4 Bake for 1–1¼ hours until risen and golden and a skewer inserted into the centre comes out clean. Remove from the oven and leave in the tin to cool for 10 minutes.

5 Warm the jam and lemon juice together in a small pan and brush over the cake to glaze. Serve warm or at room temperature.

Fruity Teacake

Preparation Time
20 minutes, plus soaking
Cooking Time
1 hour, plus cooling

- 150ml (¼ pint) hot black tea, made with 2 Earl Grey tea bags
- 200g (7oz) sultanas
- 75g (3oz) ready-to-eat dried figs, roughly chopped
- 75g (3oz) ready-to-eat dried prunes, roughly chopped
- a little vegetable oil
- 125g (4oz) dark muscovado sugar
- 2 medium eggs, beaten
- 225g (8oz) gluten-free flour
- 2 tsp wheat-free baking powder
- 2 tsp ground mixed spice
- butter to serve (optional)

NUTRITIONAL INFORMATION
Per slice 185 cals; 1g fat (of which trace saturates); 42g carbohydrate; 0.1g salt

Cuts into 12 slices

1 Pour the tea into a bowl and add all the dried fruit. Leave to soak for 30 minutes.

2 Preheat the oven to 190°C (170°C fan oven) mark 5. Oil a 900g (2lb) loaf tin and base-line with greaseproof paper.

3 Beat the sugar and eggs together in a large bowl until pale and slightly thickened. Add the flour, baking powder, mixed spice and soaked dried fruit and tea, then mix together well. Spoon the mixture into the prepared tin and level the surface. Bake on the middle shelf of the oven for 45 minutes–1 hour. Leave to cool in the tin.

4 Serve sliced, with a little butter if you like.

Honey and Spice Loaf Cake

Preparation Time
20 minutes, plus cooling
Cooking Time
about 55 minutes

- 2 tbsp runny honey
- 200g (7oz) unsalted butter
- 80g (3¼oz) dark soft brown sugar
- 2 large eggs
- 200g (7oz) self-raising flour
- 1½ tsp mixed spice
- 100g (3½oz) icing sugar, sifted
- butter, to serve (optional)

NUTRITIONAL INFORMATION
Per slice: 393 cals; 23g fat (of which 14g saturates); 47g carbohydrate; 0.7g salt

Cuts into 8 slices

1 Put the honey, butter and brown sugar into a pan and melt together over a low heat. When the sugar has dissolved, turn up the heat and leave to bubble for 1 minute. Take off the heat and leave to cool for 15 minutes.

2 Preheat the oven to 160°C (140°C fan oven) mark 3. Line a 900g (2lb) loaf tin with baking parchment. Mix the eggs into the melted butter. Sift the flour and mixed spice into a large bowl and add the butter mixture. Mix well, then pour into the prepared tin. Bake for 40–50 minutes, until a skewer inserted into the centre comes out clean.

3 Leave the cake to cool in the tin for 5 minutes, then turn out on to a wire rack and leave to cool completely.

4 When cake is cool, peel off the lining paper and put the cake on a serving plate. To make the glaze, put the icing sugar into a bowl and whisk in just enough water to get a runny consistency. Drizzle over the cooled cake and leave to harden a little. Serve in slices, spread with butter if you like.

Cuts into 10 slices

Orange and Apricot Tea Loaf

Preparation Time
15 minutes
Cooking Time
about 1 hour 15 minutes

- 175g (6oz) butter, softened, plus extra to grease
- 175g (6oz) light soft brown sugar
- 3 large eggs, lightly beaten
- 200g (7oz) plain flour
- 1 tsp baking powder
- 100g (3½oz) mixed peel
- 100g (3½oz) finely chopped apricots
- 50g (2oz) walnuts, chopped
- zest of 1 large orange
- butter to serve (optional)

GLAZE
- 2 tbsp marmalade
- 1 tbsp runny honey

NUTRITIONAL INFORMATION
Per slice 384 cals; 20g fat (of which 10g saturates); 48g carbohydrate; 0.5g salt

1 Preheat the oven to 170°C (150°C fan oven) mark 3. Lightly grease a 900g (2lb) loaf tin and line with baking parchment. Put the butter and sugar into a bowl and, using a hand-held electric whisk, beat together until pale and fluffy. Gradually beat in the eggs.

2 Sift the flour and baking powder into the bowl, then use a large metal spoon to fold in. Stir in the dried fruit, walnuts and half the orange zest.

3 Spoon the mixture into the prepared tin and bake for 1 hour–1 hour 10 minutes, until a skewer inserted into the centre comes out clean (cover with foil if it's browning too quickly). Leave to cool in the tin for 5 minutes, then turn out on to a wire rack and leave to cool completely.

4 Peel off the lining paper and put the cake on a serving plate. To glaze, put the marmalade and honey into a small pan and heat gently until runny. Drizzle over the cooled cake and sprinkle on the remaining orange zest. Serve the cake in slices, spread with butter if you like.

Marble Cake

Preparation Time
25 minutes
Cooking Time
about 45 minutes, plus cooling
and setting

- 175g (6oz) unsalted butter, softened, plus extra to grease
- 175g (6oz) caster sugar
- 3 medium eggs, lightly beaten
- 125g (4oz) self-raising flour
- 1 tsp baking powder
- 50g (2oz) ground almonds
- 1 tbsp milk
- 2 tbsp cocoa powder, sifted

ICING

- 200g (7oz) plain dark chocolate
- 75g (3oz) butter

NUTRITIONAL INFORMATION
Per slice 579 cals; 40g fat (of which 22g saturates); 52g carbohydrate; 1g salt

1 Preheat the oven to 190°C (170°C fan oven) mark 5. Grease a 900g (2lb) loaf tin and line with greaseproof paper, then grease the paper lightly.

2 Using a hand-held electric whisk, cream the butter and sugar together until pale and fluffy. Gradually add the eggs, beating well after each addition.

3 Sift the flower and baking powder into the bowl, then add the ground almonds and milk. Using a large metal spoon, fold everything together. Spoon half the mixture into a clean bowl and fold in the sifted cocoa powder.

4 Spoon a dollop of each mixture alternately into the prepared tin until you have used up both mixtures. Bang the base of the tin once on a worksurface to level and remove any air bubbles. Draw a skewer backwards and forwards through the mixture a few times to create a marbled effect. Bake for 45 minutes–1 hour, until a skewer inserted into the centre comes out clean.

5 Leave the cake to cool for 15 minutes in the tin, then turn out on to a wire rack (leave the lining paper on) and leave to cool completely.

6 To ice, melt the chocolate and butter together in a heatproof bowl set over a pan of gently simmering water (do not let the base of the bowl touch the water). Remove the lining paper from the cake and put back on the wire rack. Pour the melted chocolate mixture over it and leave to set before serving.

Cuts into 8 slices

Brazil Nut and Clementine Cakes

Preparation Time
30 minutes
Cooking Time
1¼ hours, plus cooling

- ◆ butter to grease
- ◆ 1 lemon
- ◆ 10 clementines
- ◆ 150g (5oz) brazil nuts
- ◆ 100ml (3½fl oz) mild olive oil
- ◆ 3 medium eggs
- ◆ 275g (10oz) golden
  caster sugar
- ◆ 1 tsp baking powder
- ◆ 2 tbsp brandy

DECORATION
- ◆ mint sprigs
- ◆ icing sugar

**NUTRITIONAL
INFORMATION**
Per cake 413 cals; 26g fat
(of which 5g saturates); 41g
carbohydrate; 0.1g salt

Makes 8

1 Grease eight 150ml (¼ pint) ramekin dishes and base-line with greaseproof paper. Wash the lemon and 4 clementines and put into a pan. Cover with boiling water, reduce the heat to a gentle simmer and cook for 30 minutes or until the clementines are tender.

2 Remove the clementines with a slotted spoon and set aside. Cook the lemon for a further 10 minutes or until tender. Drain, reserving 200ml (7fl oz) liquid, and cool slightly. Halve the fruit, remove the pips and roughly chop.

3 Preheat the oven to 180°C (160°C fan oven) mark 4. Grind the nuts in a food processor until finely chopped, then tip out and set aside. Without washing the bowl, add the cooked fruit and blend to a purée.

4 Put the oil, eggs and 125g (4oz) caster sugar into a mixing bowl and whisk until slightly thick and foamy. Stir in the ground nuts, fruit purée and baking powder. Divide the mixture equally among the prepared

ramekins and put on a baking sheet. Bake for 25 minutes or until slightly risen and firm to the touch. Leave to cool in the ramekins.

5 Peel the remaining clementines, remove the pips and divide into segments, then skin each segment. Heat the remaining sugar in a small pan with 150ml (¼ pint) of the reserved cooking liquid until the sugar dissolves. Bring to the boil and cook until a pale caramel in colour. Dip the base of the pan into cold water to stop the caramel cooking further. Stir in the remaining liquid and the brandy. Return to the heat, stirring until the caramel has dissolved. Stir in the clementine segments.

6 Loosen the edges of the cakes, turn out on to individual plates and remove the lining paper. Pile the fruit segments on top and spoon the caramel over them. Decorate each with a mint sprig and a dusting of icing sugar.

Madeleines

Preparation Time
20 minutes, plus chilling
Cooking Time
10–12 minutes, plus cooling

- 125g (4oz) unsalted butter, melted and cooled until tepid
- 125g (4oz) plain flour, plus extra to dust
- 4 medium eggs
- 125g (4oz) golden caster sugar
- finely grated zest of 1 lemon
- 1 tsp baking powder
- a pinch of salt
- icing sugar to dust

NUTRITIONAL INFORMATION
Per cake 90 cals; 5g fat (of which 2g saturates); 10g carbohydrate; 0.2g salt

Makes 24

1 Brush two madeleine trays with a little of the melted butter. Leave to set, then dust with flour, shaking out any excess.

2 Using a hand-held electric whisk, beat the eggs, sugar and lemon zest together in a bowl, until the mixture is pale, creamy and thick enough to leave a trail when the whisk is lifted.

3 Sift in half the flour, together with the baking powder and salt. Carefully pour in half the melted butter around the edge of the bowl and gently fold in until evenly incorporated. Repeat with the remaining flour and butter. Cover and chill the mixture in the fridge for 45 minutes.

4 Preheat the oven to 220°C (200°C fan oven) mark 7. Two-thirds fill the madeleine moulds with the mixture and bake for 10–12 minutes until well risen and golden. Ease out of the tins, transfer to a wire rack and leave to cool. Serve dusted with icing sugar.

Notes
- Resting the sponge mixture before baking gives the madeleines their characteristic dense texture.
- If you have only one madeleine tray, then bake in two batches.

Makes 18–20

Chocolate Whoopie Pies

Preparation Time
30 minutes
Cooking Time
12 minutes

- 1 large egg
- 150g (5oz) caster sugar
- 75g (3oz) butter, melted
- 150g (5oz) crème fraîche
- 1 tsp vanilla extract
- 1½–2 tbsp milk
- 200g (7oz) plain flour
- 75g (3oz) cocoa powder
- ½ tsp bicarbonate of soda

FILLING
- 115g (3¾oz) unsalted butter, softened
- 200g (7oz) icing sugar, sifted
- 1 tsp vanilla extract
- milk (optional)

NUTRITIONAL INFORMATION
per pie 365 cals; 14g fat (of which 8g saturates); 59g carbohydrate; 0.3g salt

1 Preheat the oven to 180°C (160°C fan oven) mark 4. Line two large baking sheets with baking parchment.

2 Whisk the egg and caster sugar together until thick and light in colour. Beat in the melted butter, crème fraîche, vanilla extract and milk.

3 Sift together the flour, cocoa powder and bicarbonate of soda. Beat into the egg mixture until smooth – it will make a very thick mixture but you should be able to pipe it. Add a drop more milk if necessary.

4 Insert a large nozzle into a piping bag, then fill the bag with the mixture and pipe walnut-sized balls on the baking sheets, spacing well apart. Bake for 10–12 minutes until golden and risen. Cool on the baking sheet for 1–2 minutes until firm, then transfer to a wire rack and leave to cool completely.

5 To make the buttercream filling, cream together the butter and icing sugar until fluffy. Beat in the vanilla extract. Beat in a little milk, if necessary, to make the icing a spreadable consistency. Sandwich the whoopie halves together with the buttercream.

Black Forest Roulade

Preparation Time
35 minutes
Cooking Time
20 minutes, plus cooling and chilling

- 4 large eggs, separated
- 125g (4oz) golden caster sugar, plus extra to dust
- 125g (4oz) plain chocolate (at least 70% cocoa solids), broken into pieces, melted and left to cool a little

FILLING AND TOPPING
- 140ml (4½fl oz) whipping cream
- 1 tsp icing sugar
- 75g (3oz) Greek-style yogurt
- 2 x 425g cans morello cherries, drained, pitted and halved
- cocoa powder and icing sugar to dust
- chocolate curls to decorate (optional)

NUTRITIONAL INFORMATION
Per slice 248 cals; 12g fat (of which 7g saturates); 33g carbohydrate; 0.1g salt

Cuts into 10 slices

1 Preheat the oven to 180°C (160°C fan oven) mark 4. Line a 33 x 23cm (13 x 9 inch) Swiss roll tin with baking parchment.

2 Whisk the egg yolks with the sugar in a large bowl until thick and creamy. Whisk in the melted chocolate. Put the egg whites into a large, grease-free bowl and, using a hand-held electric whisk, whisk until stiff peaks form. Fold into the chocolate mixture. Pour into the prepared tin, level the surface and bake for 20 minutes or until firm to the touch. Leave to cool in the tin for 10–15 minutes.

3 Put a sheet of baking parchment on the worksurface and dust with caster sugar. Carefully turn out the roulade on to the parchment and peel off the lining paper. Cover with a damp cloth and leave to cool for 30 minutes.

4 To make the filling, lightly whip the cream with the icing sugar, then fold in the yogurt. Spread over the cold roulade and scatter the cherries on top. Using the baking parchment to help, roll up the roulade from one of the narrow ends. Chill for 30 minutes. Dust with cocoa powder and icing sugar, decorate with chocolate curls, if you like, and serve sliced.

Maple Pecan Meringue Roulade

Preparation Time
20 minutes, plus cooling
Cooking Time
about 25 minutes

MERINGUE
- 4 large egg whites
- 200g (7oz) caster sugar
- 1 tsp cornflour
- 1 tsp white wine vinegar
- icing sugar to dust

FILLING
- 200ml (7fl oz) double cream
- 3 tbsp maple syrup
- 75g (3oz) pecan nuts, chopped
- 2 tbsp icing sugar

NUTRITIONAL INFORMATION
Per slice 260 cals; 16g fat (of which 7g saturates); 28g carbohydrate; 0.1g salt

Cuts into 10 slices

1 Preheat the oven to 160°C (140°C fan oven) mark 3. Line a shallow 28 x 38cm (11 x 15 inch) baking tin with baking parchment.

2 Put the egg whites into a large, grease-free bowl and, using a hand-held electric whisk, whisk until stiff but not dry. Gradually add the caster sugar, whisking constantly, until the mixture becomes thick and glossy. Briefly whisk in the cornflour and vinegar.

3 Spoon the meringue into the prepared tin and spread out evenly. Bake for 25 minutes or until it has a light golden crust. Leave to cool in the tin for 5 minutes. Meanwhile, put a sheet of greaseproof paper a little larger than the baking tin on a damp tea towel. Lightly dust the paper with icing sugar. Invert the meringue on to the paper, then remove the tin, leaving the lining paper on the meringue, and leave to cool completely.

4 Whip the cream and maple syrup in a medium bowl until the cream just holds a shape. Carefully peel the lining paper off the meringue and spread the cream mixture over one side of it. Sprinkle on the pecans. Using the greaseproof paper to help, roll up the meringue from one of the short ends. Transfer to a serving plate, dust with icing sugar and serve.

Chocolate Roulade

Preparation Time
25 minutes
Cooking Time
about 15 minutes

- 150g (5oz) dark chocolate (at least 70% cocoa solids), broken into pieces
- 5 large eggs, separated
- 150g (5oz) caster sugar
- 1 tbsp cornflour
- cocoa powder to dust

TOPPING

- 125ml (4fl oz) double cream
- 75g (3oz) dark chocolate, finely chopped
- 2 tbsp golden syrup
- silver and gold balls, plus edible glitter, to decorate

FILLING

- 150ml (¼ pint) double cream
- 1 tbsp icing sugar

NUTRITIONAL INFORMATION

Per slice 480 cals; 31g fat (of which 18g saturates); 45g carbohydrate; 0.1g salt

1 Preheat the oven to 180°C (160°C fan oven) mark 4. Line a shallow 33 x 23cm (13 x 9 inch) baking tin with baking parchment. Melt the chocolate in a heatproof bowl set over a pan of barely simmering water, making sure the base of the bowl doesn't touch the water. Leave to cool.

2 Using a hand-held electric whisk, beat together the egg yolks and caster sugar in a large bowl until pale and thick (about 5 minutes). Fold in the cooled chocolate. In a separate bowl and using clean beaters, whisk the egg whites and cornflour until they form soft peaks. Using a large metal spoon, fold the whites into the chocolate mixture – be careful not to knock out too much air.

3 Spoon the mixture into the prepared tin and level the surface. Bake for 12–15 minutes, then take out of the oven and cover with a damp tea towel. Leave to cool.

4 Meanwhile, make the topping. Put the cream into a pan and bring just to the boil, then take off the heat and stir in the chopped chocolate until melted. Stir in the golden syrup and leave to cool.

5 To make the filling, lightly whip the cream and icing sugar in a bowl until the cream just holds a shape.

6 Put a sheet of greaseproof paper a little larger than the baking tin on a damp tea towel. Lightly dust the paper with cocoa powder. Invert the cake on to the paper, then remove the tin and peel off the lining paper. Spread the cream filling over the cooled cake. Using the greaseproof paper to help, roll up the cake from one of the short ends. Transfer to a platter. Spread the topping over the roulade, then using a fork, mark with ridges to resemble bark. Decorate with gold and silver balls and edible glitter. Serve.

Cuts into 8 slices

Cuts into 8 slices

White Chocolate and Raspberry Meringue Roulade

Preparation Time
20 minutes
Cooking Time
about 25 minutes

MERINGUE
- 4 large egg whites
- 200g (7oz) caster sugar
- 1 tsp cornflour
- 1 tsp lemon juice
- icing sugar to dust

FILLING
- 100g (3½oz) white chocolate, broken into pieces
- 200ml (7fl oz) double cream
- 1 tsp vanilla extract
- 25g (1oz) toasted hazelnuts, roughly chopped
- 150g (5oz) raspberries, fresh or frozen
- 2 tbsp icing sugar

RASPBERRY COULIS
- 75g (3oz) raspberries, fresh or frozen
- 2–3 tbsp icing sugar

NUTRITIONAL INFORMATION
Per slice 364 cals; 19g fat (of which 11g saturates); 40g carbohydrate; 0.1g salt

1 Preheat the oven to 160°C (140°C fan oven) mark 3. Line a shallow 33 x 23cm (13 x 9 inch) baking tin with baking parchment.

2 Put the egg whites into a large, grease-free bowl and, using a hand-held electric whisk, whisk until stiff but not dry. Gradually add the caster sugar, whisking all the time, until the mixture is thick and glossy. Beat in the cornflour and lemon juice until well combined.

3 Spoon the meringue into the prepared tin and spread out evenly. Bake for 25 minutes or until a light golden crust forms. Leave to cool in the tin for 5 minutes. Put a sheet of greaseproof paper a little larger than the baking tin on a damp tea towel. Lightly dust the paper with icing sugar, then invert the meringue on to the paper. Remove the tin, leaving the lining paper on the meringue, and leave to cool completely.

4 Meanwhile, make the filling. Melt the white chocolate in a heatproof bowl set over a pan of barely simmering water, making sure the base of the bowl doesn't touch the water. Remove from the heat and leave to cool. To make the coulis, blend the raspberries and icing sugar until smooth, then sieve into a jug. Put the cream and vanilla extract into a medium bowl and whip until the cream just holds a shape, then fold in the cooled white chocolate.

5 Peel off the lining paper from the meringue, then spread the cream mixture evenly over it and sprinkle on the hazelnuts and raspberries. Using the greaseproof paper to help, roll up the meringue from one of the short ends. Don't worry if cracks appear – they'll add to the 'log' effect.

6 Transfer to a serving plate, drizzle with the coulis, dust with icing sugar and serve.

Cardamom and Mango Cake

Preparation Time
45 minutes
Cooking Time
25–30 minutes, plus cooling and chilling

- ◆ 50g (2oz) unsalted butter, plus extra to grease
- ◆ 4 green cardamom pods, split and seeds removed
- ◆ a good pinch of saffron strands
- ◆ 4 large eggs
- ◆ 125g (4oz) caster sugar
- ◆ 100g (3½oz) plain flour

FILLING, MANGO SAUCE AND DECORATION
- ◆ 2 large, ripe mangoes
- ◆ 150ml (¼ pint) double cream
- ◆ 150g (5oz) Greek-style yogurt
- ◆ 3 tbsp icing sugar, plus extra to dust
- ◆ 4 tbsp orange juice
- ◆ orange segments

NUTRITIONAL INFORMATION
Per slice 274 cals; 16g fat (of which 9g saturates); 31g carbohydrate; 0.2g salt

Cuts into 10 slices

---

1 Preheat the oven to 180°C (160°C fan oven) mark 4. Grease two 18cm (7 inch) sandwich tins, or one deep 18cm (7 inch) round cake tin, and base-line with baking parchment.

2 Crush the cardamom seeds to a powder together with the saffron. Put the butter into a pan and heat gently until melted. Remove from the heat and leave to cool for a few minutes until beginning to thicken.

3 Put the eggs and caster sugar into a large heatproof bowl. Using a hand-held electric whisk, whisk until evenly blended. Put the bowl over a pan of hot water and whisk until pale and thick enough to leave a trail on the surface when the whisk is lifted. Remove the bowl from the pan and whisk until cool and thick.

4 Sift the spices and flour together. Using a large metal spoon or plastic spatula, fold half into the whisked mixture. Pour the cooled butter around the edge of the mixture, leaving the sediment behind. Gradually fold it in very lightly, until it is all incorporated. Carefully fold in the remaining flour as lightly as possible. Pour into the prepared tins.

5 Bake for 25–30 minutes until well risen and the cakes spring back when lightly pressed in the centre. Run a small knife around the cake's edge to loosen and leave in the tins for 5 minutes, then turn out on to a wire rack and leave to cool completely.

6 To make the filling, peel the mangoes, then cut one of them into slices. Whip the cream until it holds a shape. Stir in the yogurt with 2 tbsp icing sugar. Sandwich the cakes with the cream mixture and mango slices. Chill for 2–3 hours.

7 To make the mango sauce, put the remaining mango flesh, 1 tbsp icing sugar and the orange juice into a blender and whizz to a purée. Pass this through a nylon sieve to remove all the fibres. Cover and chill.

8 Just before serving, decorate the cake with orange segments and dust with icing sugar. Serve with the mango sauce.

Banana Cake

Preparation Time
20 minutes
Cooking Time
about 1 hour

- 125g (4oz) unsalted butter, softened, plus extra to grease
- 125g (4oz) light muscovado sugar
- 2 large eggs, lightly beaten
- 50g (2oz) smooth apple sauce
- 3 very ripe bananas, about 375g (13oz) peeled weight, mashed
- 1½ tsp mixed spice
- 150g (5oz) gluten-free plain flour blend
- 1 tsp gluten-free baking powder
- a pinch of salt

ICING
- 75g (3oz) unsalted butter, softened
- 100g (3½oz) icing sugar, sifted
- 50g (2oz) light muscovado sugar
- ½ tbsp milk (optional)
- dried banana chips to decorate (optional)

NUTRITIONAL INFORMATION
Per slice (for 10) 363 cals; 18g fat (of which 11g saturates); 50g carbohydrate; 0.4g salt

Cuts into 8–10 slices

1 Preheat the oven to 180°C (160°C fan oven) mark 4. Grease the base and sides of a 900g (2lb) loaf tin and line with baking parchment.

2 Using a hand-held electric whisk, beat the butter and muscovado sugar in a large bowl until pale and creamy. Gradually whisk in the eggs, then the apple sauce. Stir in the bananas.

3 Sift the spice, flour, baking powder and salt into the bowl, then use a large metal spoon to fold in (the mixture may look a little curdled). Spoon the mixture into the prepared tin and bake for 50 minutes–1 hour until risen and a skewer inserted into centre comes out clean. Cool in the tin for 10 minutes, then turn out on to a wire rack and leave to cool completely.

4 Peel off the lining paper and put the cake on a serving plate. To make the icing, whisk together the butter and both sugars until smooth. If needed, add a little milk to loosen. Spread over the top of the cooled cake. Decorate with banana chips, if you like. Slice the loaf to serve.

Creamy Coffee and Praline Gateau

Preparation Time
45 minutes
Cooking Time
25 minutes, plus cooling

- 50g (2oz) unsalted butter, melted, plus extra to grease
- 125g (4oz) plain flour, sifted, plus extra to dust
- 4 large eggs, separated
- 125g (4oz) caster sugar
- 1 tbsp coffee granules, dissolved in 2 tsp boiling water

PRALINE
- 50g (2oz) whole blanched hazelnuts
- 150g (5oz) caster sugar

FILLING
- 500g (1lb 2oz) mascarpone cheese
- 250g (9oz) icing sugar, sifted
- 2 tbsp coffee granules, dissolved in 1 tbsp boiling water

NUTRITIONAL INFORMATION
Per slice 548 cals; 21g fat (of which 10g saturates); 83g carbohydrate; 0.2g salt

Cuts into 8 slices

1 Preheat the oven to 190°C (170°C fan oven) mark 5. Grease two 18cm (7 inch) loose-based sandwich tins. Dust lightly with flour and tip out the excess.

2 Put the egg whites into a large, grease-free bowl and, using a hand-held electric whisk, whisk until soft peaks form. Whisk in 1 egg yolk, then repeat with the other three yolks. Add the sugar, 1 tbsp at a time, and continue to whisk. The mixture should be thick enough to leave a trail when the whisk is lifted. Using a large metal spoon, fold half the flour into the mixture.

3 Mix the coffee into the melted butter, then pour around the edge of the egg mixture. Add the remaining flour and gradually fold in. Divide the mixture between the prepared tins and bake for 25 minutes or until risen and firm to the touch. Turn out on to a wire rack and leave to cool completely.

4 To make the praline, line a baking sheet with non-stick baking parchment and scatter the nuts on it. Dissolve the sugar in a heavy-based pan over a low heat, shaking the pan once or twice to help it dissolve evenly. Cook until it forms a dark golden-brown caramel. Pour over the nuts and leave to cool.

5 To make the filling, put the mascarpone and icing sugar into a large bowl, add the coffee and mix with a hand-held electric whisk. Slice each cake in half horizontally. Put one cake layer on a plate and spread with a quarter of the filling. Continue layering in this way, finishing with a layer of mascarpone filling.

6 Break the praline into two or three pieces and put into a plastic bag. Using a rolling pin, smash it into smaller pieces. Use to decorate the top of the cake.

Gluten-free Chocolate Cake

Preparation Time
30 minutes
Cooking Time
45 minutes–1 hour, plus cooling

- 125g (4oz) unsalted butter, softened, plus extra to grease
- 200g (7oz) light muscovado sugar
- 2 large eggs, lightly beaten
- 125g (4oz) gluten-free plain chocolate, broken into pieces, melted (see page 46) and left to cool slightly
- 100g (3½oz) natural yogurt
- a few drops of vanilla extract
- 200g (7oz) brown rice flour
- ½ tsp wheat-free baking powder
- 1 tsp bicarbonate of soda

ICING
- 150g (5oz) gluten-free plain chocolate, broken into pieces
- 150ml (¼ pint) double cream
- large milk and plain or white chocolate buttons (gluten-free) to decorate

NUTRITIONAL INFORMATION
Per slice 476 cals; 28g fat (of which 16g saturates); 60g carbohydrate; 0.3g salt

Cuts into 10 slices

1 Preheat the oven to 180°C (160°C fan oven) mark 4. Grease a deep 18cm (7 inch) square cake tin and line with greaseproof paper.

2 Cream the butter and sugar together until light and fluffy. Gradually beat in the eggs, then the melted chocolate, yogurt and vanilla extract. Sift the rice flour, baking powder and bicarbonate of soda together, then beat into the mixture a little at a time. Pour into the prepared tin and bake for 45 minutes–1 hour until a skewer inserted into the centre comes out clean. Cool in the tin for 10 minutes, then turn out on to a wire rack and leave to cool completely.

3 To make the icing, put the chocolate into a heatproof bowl. Heat the cream to just below boiling point. Pour on to the chocolate and leave for 5 minutes, then beat until the chocolate has melted and the mixture is smooth. Cool until thickened, then, using a palette knife, spread all over the cake. Decorate the top and sides of the cake with alternate milk and plain or white chocolate buttons to create a polka-dot effect.

Cappuccino and Walnut Cake

Preparation Time
30 minutes
Cooking Time
about 45 minutes, plus cooling

- ◆ 65g (2½oz) unsalted butter, melted and cooled, plus extra to grease
- ◆ 100g (3½oz) plain flour
- ◆ 1 tsp baking powder
- ◆ 4 medium eggs
- ◆ 125g (4oz) caster sugar
- ◆ 1 tbsp chicory and coffee essence
- ◆ 75g (3oz) walnuts, toasted, cooled and finely chopped

DECORATION
- ◆ 50g (2oz) walnuts
- ◆ 1 tbsp granulated sugar
- ◆ ¼ tsp ground cinnamon

ICING
- ◆ 200g (7oz) good-quality white chocolate
- ◆ 4 tsp chicory and coffee essence
- ◆ 2 x 250g tubs mascarpone cheese
- ◆ fresh unsprayed violets to decorate (optional)

NUTRITIONAL INFORMATION
Per slice 449 cals; 30g fat (of which 13g saturates); 36g carbohydrate; 0.3g salt

1 Preheat the oven to 190°C (170°C fan oven) mark 5. Grease two 20.5 x 4cm (8 x 1½ inch) round cake tins and base-line each with a circle of greased greaseproof paper.

2 Sift the flour and baking powder together twice.

3 Using an electric mixer, whisk the eggs and caster sugar in a large heatproof bowl set over a pan of barely simmering water for 3–4 minutes until light, thick and fluffy. Remove the bowl from the heat and continue whisking until the mixture has cooled and the whisk leaves a ribbon trail for 8 seconds when lifted out of the bowl.

4 Fold in the butter, coffee essence and chopped walnuts. Sift half the flour into the mixture, then use a metal spoon to fold in carefully but quickly. Sift and fold in the rest, taking care not to knock out too much air. Pour into the prepared tins and tap them lightly on the worksurface. Bake for 20–25 minutes until the tops feel springy. Cool in the tins for 10 minutes, then turn out on to a wire rack and leave to cool completely.

5 To make the decoration, whizz the walnuts in a food processor or blender with the granulated sugar and cinnamon until finely chopped. Take care not to over-process the nuts or they'll become oily. Set aside.

6 To make the icing, break up the chocolate and put into a heatproof bowl set over a pan of gently simmering water, making sure the base of the bowl doesn't touch the water. Allow to melt slowly without stirring. In another bowl, add the coffee essence to the mascarpone and beat until smooth, then slowly beat in the melted chocolate.

7 Spread one-third of the icing on top of one cake, then sandwich with the other half. Smooth the remaining icing over the top and sides. Lift the cake on to a large piece of greaseproof paper and scatter the chopped nuts all around it. Then lift the greaseproof up to press nuts on to the sides. Transfer to a plate and decorate with the violets, if you like.

Cuts into 10 slices

Decadent Chocolate Cake

Preparation Time
30 minutes
Cooking Time
1½ hours, plus cooling and setting

- 225g (8oz) unsalted butter, softened, plus extra to grease
- 300g (11oz) plain chocolate, broken into pieces
- 225g (8oz) golden caster sugar
- 225g (8oz) ground almonds
- 8 large eggs, separated
- 125g (4oz) fresh brown breadcrumbs
- 4 tbsp apricot jam (optional)
- cream to serve (optional)

GANACHE

- 175g (6oz) plain chocolate, broken into pieces
- 75g (3oz) butter, softened
- 4 tbsp double cream

NUTRITIONAL INFORMATION
Per slice 687 cals; 49g fat (of which 23g saturates); 54g carbohydrate; 0.7g salt

Cuts into 12 slices

1 Preheat the oven to 180°C (160°C fan oven) mark 4. Grease a 23cm (9 inch) springform cake tin and line with greaseproof paper.

2 Melt the chocolate in a heatproof bowl set over a pan of gently simmering water, making sure the base of the bowl doesn't touch the water. Remove the bowl from the pan.

3 Put the butter and sugar into a large bowl and beat until light and creamy. Add the almonds, egg yolks and breadcrumbs and beat well until thoroughly mixed. Slowly add the chocolate and carefully stir it in. Do not over-mix, as the chocolate may seize up and become unworkable.

4 Put the egg whites into a large, grease-free bowl and, using a hand-held electric whisk, whisk until stiff peaks form. Add half the whites to the chocolate mixture and, using a large metal spoon, fold in lightly. Carefully fold in the remainder. Pour into the prepared tin and level the surface.

5 Bake for 1 hour 20 minutes or until the cake is firm to the touch and a skewer inserted into the centre comes out clean. Cool in the tin for 5 minutes, then transfer to a wire rack and leave for 2–3 hours to cool completely.

6 Put the jam, if using, into a pan and melt over a low heat. Brush the jam over the top and sides of the cake.

7 To make the ganache, melt the chocolate, butter and cream in a heatproof bowl set over a pan of gently simmering water, making sure the base of the bowl doesn't touch the water. Stir just once until smooth. Either raise the cake off the worksurface on the upturned tin or put it (still on the rack) on a tray to catch the drips. Pour the ganache into the centre and tip the cake to let it run down the sides evenly, or spread it with a palette knife. Leave to set, then serve with cream, if you like.

Chocolate and Berry Squares

Preparation Time
20 minutes
Cooking Time
about 50 minutes

- 225g (8oz) unsalted butter, roughly chopped, plus extra to grease
- 275g (10oz) dark chocolate, roughly chopped
- 75g (3oz) plain flour
- 1 tsp baking powder
- 50g (2oz) walnuts, roughly chopped
- 75g (3oz) milk chocolate, cut into chunks
- 3 large eggs
- 200g (7oz) light soft brown sugar
- 175g (6oz) frozen forest fruits, thawed on kitchen paper
- 40g (1½oz) white chocolate, finely chopped

NUTRITIONAL INFORMATION
Per slice 442 cals; 29g fat (of which 16g saturates); 43g carbohydrate; 0.5g salt

Makes 12

---

1 Preheat the oven to 190°C (170°C fan oven) mark 5. Grease a baking tin, about 19 x 23 x 4cm (7.5 x 9 x 1.5 inches), and line with greaseproof paper. Melt the butter and dark chocolate in a heatproof bowl set over a pan of barely simmering water, making sure the base of the bowl doesn't touch the water. Set aside to cool for 10 minutes. Meanwhile, sift the flour and baking powder into a large bowl. Stir in the walnuts and milk chocolate.

2 In a separate bowl, beat the eggs and sugar until combined. Stir in the cooled Bournville mixture, then pour into the flour bowl and stir well until combined. Carefully fold in the forest fruits and pour into the prepared tin. Bake for 40–45 minutes until just set. Leave to cool in the tin.

3 Melt the white chocolate as in step 1, then use a teaspoon to drizzle it over the top of the cake. Cut into squares and serve.

Note
For convenience, complete the recipe to the end of step 2 up to one day in advance. Wrap the cooled cake in its tin in clingfilm and store at room temperature. Complete the recipe to serve.

Cuts into 10 slices

Sticky Orange Cake

Preparation Time
20 minutes
Cooking Time
about 50 minutes

- 2 tbsp golden syrup
- 3 large oranges
- 225g (8oz) unsalted butter, softened
- 225g (8oz) caster sugar
- 3 medium eggs, lightly beaten
- 100g (3½oz) plain flour, sifted
- 75g (3oz) polenta or semolina
- 1½ tsp baking powder
- icing sugar to dust (optional)
- crème fraîche to serve

NUTRITIONAL INFORMATION
Per slice 374 cals; 21g fat (of which 12g saturates); 45g carbohydrate; 0.2g salt

1 Preheat the oven to 170°C (150°C fan oven) mark 3. Line a 20.5cm (8 inch) springform tin with one piece of baking parchment, pushing it down into the edges as much as possible. Measure the golden syrup into the bottom of the lined tin.

2 Using a small serrated knife, cut the peel and pith off two oranges. Cut the peeled oranges into slices 5mm (¼ inch) thick (cutting across the segments). Discard any pips. Arrange the slices in the bottom of the tin, over the syrup. Zest and juice the remaining orange and set aside.

3 Put the butter and caster sugar into a large bowl and, using a hand-held electric whisk, beat together until pale and fluffy (about 3 minutes). Gradually beat in the eggs, then use a large metal spoon to fold in the flour, polenta or semolina, baking powder and reserved zest and juice. Spoon the mixture into the prepared tin and gently level the surface. Bake for 40-45 minutes until golden and a skewer inserted into the centre comes out clean.

4 Leave the cake to cool in the tin for 10 minutes, then unclip the tin, put a large serving plate on top of the tin and invert it. Lift off the tin and peel off the lining paper. If you like, dust the top of the cake with icing sugar and caramelize with a blowtorch. Serve in slices with crème fraîche.

Banoffee Cake

Preparation Time
25 minutes
Cooking Time
about 55 minutes, plus cooling

- 200g (7oz) unsalted butter, softened, plus extra to grease
- 200g (7oz) light soft brown sugar
- 4 large eggs, beaten
- 2 ripe bananas, peeled and broken into chunks
- 75g (3oz) walnuts, chopped
- 200g (7oz) self-raising flour

ICING AND DECORATION
- 150g (5oz) butter, softened
- 250g (9oz) icing sugar, sifted
- 3 tbsp dulce de leche toffee sauce
- 40g (1½oz) fudge chunks

NUTRITIONAL INFORMATION
Per slice 653 cals; 39g fat (of which 20g saturates); 73g carbohydrate; 0.9g salt

1 Preheat the oven to 180°C (160°C fan oven) mark 4. Grease a deep 20.5cm (8 inch) cake tin and line with baking parchment.

2 Put the butter and brown sugar into a large bowl and beat together with a hand-held electric whisk until pale and fluffy (about 5 minutes). Gradually beat in the eggs, then whisk in the bananas until smooth (if you don't have an electric beater, mash the bananas with a fork and fold into the mixture). The mixture might look a little curdled, but don't worry.

3 Using a large metal spoon, fold in the walnuts and flour. Spoon into the prepared tin and bake for 50–55 minutes until a skewer inserted into the centre comes out clean. Cool in the tin for 5 minutes, then turn out on to a wire rack and leave to cool completely.

4 Meanwhile, make the icing. Put the butter, icing sugar and dulce de leche into a large bowl and beat together until smooth and creamy. Spread the icing over the top and sides of the cake, then scatter the fudge chunks over the top.

Cuts into 10 slices

Red Velvet Cake

Preparation Time
20 minutes
Cooking Time
1 hour 10 minutes, plus cooling

- 200g (7oz) unsalted butter, softened, plus extra to grease
- 250g (9oz) plain flour
- 40g (1½oz) cocoa powder
- 1½ tsp baking powder
- 225g (8oz) caster sugar
- 2 large eggs, beaten
- 250ml (9fl oz) soured cream
- 1 tbsp white wine vinegar
- 1 tsp bicarbonate of soda
- ¼ tsp red food colouring paste

FROSTING
- 400g (14oz) cream cheese
- 125g (4oz) unsalted butter, softened
- 125g (4oz) icing sugar
- red sugar sprinkles to decorate (optional)

NUTRITIONAL INFORMATION
Per slice 724 cals, 53g fat (of which 33g saturates); 58g carbohydrate; 1.4g salt

Cuts into 10 slices

1 Preheat the oven to 180°C (160°C fan oven) mark 4. Grease a deep 20.5cm (8 inch) cake tin and line with baking parchment.

2 Sift the flour, cocoa powder and baking powder into a medium bowl. In a separate large bowl, beat together the butter and caster sugar with a hand-held electric whisk until pale and fluffy (about 5 minutes). Gradually beat in the eggs, until combined.

3 Alternately beat the flour mixture and the soured cream into the butter bowl until completely combined. Beat in the vinegar, bicarbonate of soda and food colouring. Spoon the mixture into the

prepared tin, level the surface and bake for 1 hour–1 hour 10 minutes until a skewer inserted into the centre comes out clean. Cool in the tin for 10 minutes, then turn out on to a wire rack and leave to cool completely.

4 To make the frosting, put the cream cheese and butter into a large bowl and beat together until combined. Sift in the icing sugar and mix well. Halve the cooled cake horizontally, then sandwich back together using half the icing. Spread the remaining icing over the top of the cake, and decorate with sugar sprinkles, if you like.

Sticky Gingerbread

BREAD MACHINE RECIPE
Preparation Time
15 minutes
Cooking Time
1 hour 10 minutes, plus cooling

- 125g (4oz) unsalted butter, plus extra to grease
- 125g (4oz) light muscovado sugar
- 75g (3oz) black treacle
- 200g (7oz) golden syrup
- 250g (9oz) plain flour
- 2 tsp ground mixed spice
- 65g (2½oz) preserved stem ginger, finely chopped
- 2 large eggs
- 100ml (3½fl oz) milk
- 1 tsp bicarbonate of soda
- extra treacle or golden syrup to glaze (optional)

NUTRITIONAL INFORMATION
Per slice 341 cals; 12g fat (of which 7g saturates); 58g carbohydrate; 0.7g salt

Cuts into 10 slices

1 Put the butter, sugar, treacle and golden syrup into a pan and heat gently until the butter has melted. Leave to cool for 5 minutes. Grease the bread-maker's bucket and line with baking parchment, if specified in the manual.

2 Sift the flour and mixed spice together into a bowl. Add the syrup mixture, chopped ginger, eggs and milk and stir well until combined.

3 Mix the bicarbonate of soda with 2 tbsp hot water in a cup, then add to the bowl. Stir the mixture well and pour into the bread-maker's bucket. Fit the bucket into the bread-maker and set to the cake or bake only program. Select 1 hour 10 minutes on the timer and choose a light crust. Press Start.

4 To check whether the cake is done, pierce the centre with a skewer – it should come out fairly clean. If necessary, reset the timer for a little longer.

5 Remove the bucket from the machine, leave the cake in it for 5 minutes, then turn out on to a wire rack. Brush the top of the cake with the treacle or syrup to glaze, if you like, and leave to cool.

Cuts into 10 slices

Battenberg Delight

Preparation Time
35 minutes
Cooking Time
about 35 minutes

- 175g (6oz) butter, softened, plus extra to grease
- 175g (6oz) caster sugar
- 3 large eggs, lightly beaten
- 200g (7oz) self-raising flour
- 25g (1oz) ground almonds
- a few drops of almond extract
- pink and yellow food colouring
- 3–4 tbsp lemon curd
- 500g (1lb 2oz) marzipan
- icing sugar to dust

NUTRITIONAL INFORMATION
Per slice: 555 cals; 31g fat (of which 11g saturates); 63g carbohydrate; 0.5g salt

1 Preheat the oven to 180°C (160°C fan oven) mark 4. Grease a 20.5cm (8 inch) square, straight-sided roasting/brownie tin. Cut a rectangle of baking parchment that measures exactly 20.5 x 30.5cm (8 x 12 inches). Fold it in half (short end to short end), then make a fold 5cm (2 inches) wide down the length of the closed side, bending it both ways to mark a pleat. Open up the parchment, then pinch the pleat back together (so it stands perpendicular to the rest of the parchment). Position the parchment in the bottom of the tin – it should line the bottom exactly and provide a 5cm (2 inch) divider down the middle.

2 Using a hand-held electric whisk, beat the butter and caster sugar together in a large bowl until pale and fluffy. Gradually beat in the eggs, then use a large metal spoon to fold in the flour, ground almonds and almond extract.

3 Spoon half the mixture into a separate bowl. Use the food colouring to tint one half yellow and the other pink. Spoon one batter into each side of the lined tin (making sure the parchment doesn't shift) and level the surface. Bake for 30–35 minutes until a skewer inserted into the centre of each side comes out clean. Leave to cool in the tin.

4 Take the cake out of the tin and peel off the lining paper. Using a bread knife, level the top of each cake and remove any browned sponge. Stack the cakes and trim the sides and ends to reveal coloured sponge. With the sponges still stacked, halve the cakes lengthways to make four equal strips of sponge.

5 Spread a thin layer of lemon curd along one long side of a yellow strip, then stick to a long side of a pink strip. Repeat with the remaining two strips. Stick the pairs of sponges on top of one another with more curd to give a chequerboard effect, then trim to neaten. Spread the ends of the cake with more curd.

6 Lightly dust the worktop with icing sugar, then roll out one-eighth of the marzipan until 5mm (¼ inch) thick. Stick to one end of the cake and trim with scissors. Repeat with the other end.

7 Roll out the remaining marzipan into a long strip, 5mm (¼ inch) thick – it needs to be at least 22cm (8½ inches) wide and 35.5cm (14 inches) long. Brush with lemon curd. Place the cake on the marzipan at one of the short ends, then trim the width of the marzipan strip to match the cake. Roll the cake, sticking it to the marzipan as you go. Trim the end to neaten. Serve in slices.

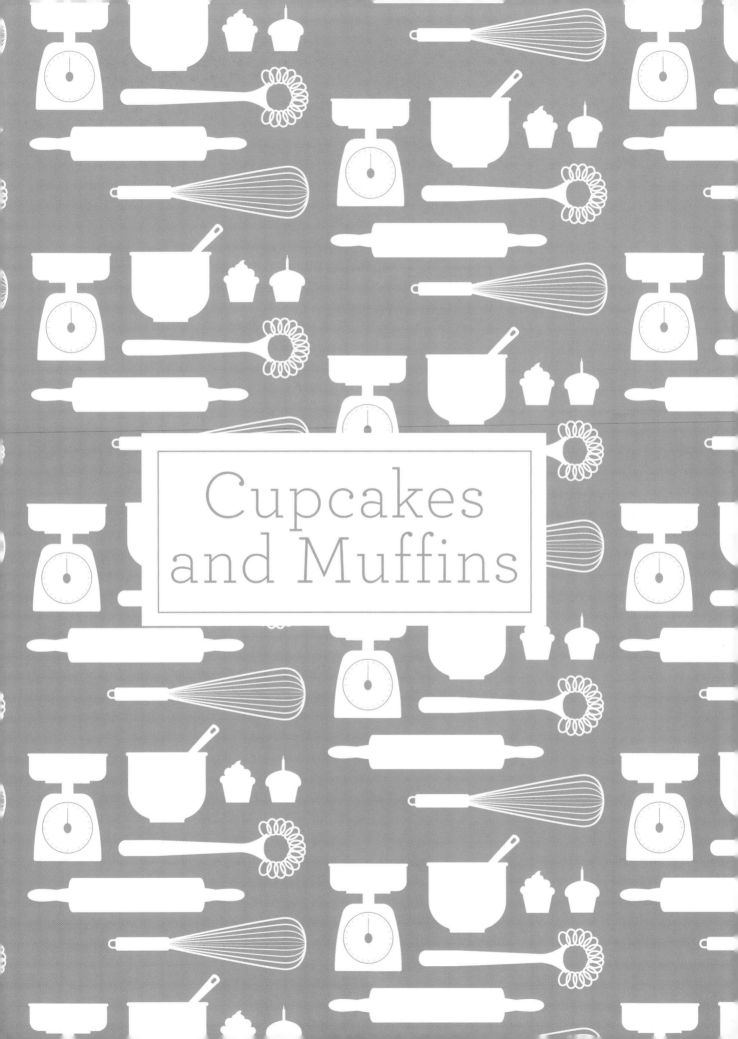

Cupcakes and Muffins

Peanut Butter Cupcakes

Preparation Time
30 minutes
Cooking Time
5 minutes, plus cooling and
setting

- 75g (3oz) unsalted peanuts or
  cashew nuts, toasted
- 100g (3½oz) unsalted butter,
  softened
- 50g (2oz) light soft brown
  sugar
- 50g (2oz) dark muscovado
  sugar
- 3 medium eggs
- 175g (6oz) self-raising flour,
  sifted
- ½ tsp baking powder

TOPPING AND DECORATION
- 100ml (3½fl oz) milk
- 50g (2oz) cocoa powder
- 300g (11oz) icing sugar
- 100g (3½oz) peanut butter
- chocolate sprinkles or
  vermicelli

NUTRITIONAL
INFORMATION
Per cupcake 363 cals, 17g fat (of
which 7g saturates); 49g
carbohydrate; 0.5g salt

Makes 12

1 Preheat the oven to 190°C (170°C fan oven) mark 5. Line a 12-hole muffin tin with paper muffin cases.

2 Whizz the peanuts or cashews in a food processor until finely ground. Set aside.

3 Using a hand-held electric whisk, whisk the butter with the light soft brown and muscovado sugars, or beat with a wooden spoon, until pale and creamy. Gradually whisk in the eggs until just combined. Using a metal spoon, fold in the flour, baking powder and finely ground nuts until combined. Spoon the mixture equally into the paper cases.

4 Bake for 20 minutes or until golden and risen. Leave to cool in the tin for 5 minutes, then transfer to a wire rack to cool completely.

5 To make the topping, warm the milk in a small pan. Sift the cocoa and icing sugar into a large bowl, then gradually stir in the warm milk until it forms a smooth icing.

6 Put a small spoonful of peanut butter on the top of each cake and then spoon on the chocolate icing to cover it and to coat the top of the cupcake. Decorate with sprinkles or vermicelli. Stand the cakes on the wire rack and leave for about 1 hour to set.

Sticky Gingerbread Cupcakes

Preparation Time
35 minutes
Cooking Time
20 minutes, plus cooling

- 175g (6oz) self-raising flour
- 75g (3oz) unsalted butter, chilled and cut into cubes
- ¼ tsp bicarbonate of soda
- 2 tsp ground ginger
- 25g (1oz) stem ginger in syrup, finely chopped, plus 3 tbsp syrup from the jar
- 50g (2oz) dark muscovado sugar
- 50g (2oz) golden syrup
- 50g (2oz) treacle
- juice of 1 orange
- 2 medium eggs, beaten

TOPPING AND DECORATION

- 100g (3½oz) unsalted butter, softened
- 200g (7oz) icing sugar, sifted
- 3 tbsp syrup from the stem ginger jar
- 1 tsp ground ginger
- ready-made sugar flowers (optional)

NUTRITIONAL
INFORMATION
Per cupcake 386 cals; 17g fat (of which 11g saturates); 58g carbohydrate; 0.5g salt

Makes 9

1 Preheat the oven to 190°C (170°C fan oven) mark 5. Line a 12-hole muffin tin with nine paper muffin cases.

2 Put the flour into a large bowl. Using your fingertips, rub in the butter until it resembles breadcrumbs. Stir in the bicarbonate of soda, ground ginger and stem ginger and set aside. Put the muscovado sugar, syrup, treacle and orange juice into a small pan and heat gently until the sugar dissolves. Cool for 5 minutes.

3 Mix the eggs and warm sugar mixture into the flour mixture and stir with a spatula until just combined. Spoon the mixture equally into the paper cases.

4 Bake for 20 minutes or until golden and risen. Remove from the oven. Drizzle each cake with 1 tsp ginger syrup. Leave to cool in the tin for 5 minutes, then transfer to a wire rack to cool completely.

5 To make the buttercream topping, put the butter into a bowl and whisk until fluffy. Add the icing sugar, ginger syrup and ground ginger. Whisk until light and fluffy. Using a small palette knife, spread a little buttercream over the top of each cake. Decorate with sugar flowers, if you like.

Tropical Burst Cupcakes

Preparation Time
35 minutes
Cooking Time
20 minutes, plus cooling and
setting

- 200g (7oz) self-raising flour, sifted
- ½ tsp bicarbonate of soda
- 100g (3½oz) caster sugar
- 50g (2oz) ready-to-eat dried tropical fruit, finely chopped
- 3 medium eggs
- 100ml (3½fl oz) sunflower oil
- 75ml (2½fl oz) buttermilk
- 1 x 227g tin pineapple pieces, drained and finely chopped

TOPPING AND DECORATION
- 225g (8oz) royal icing sugar, sifted
- zest and juice of 1 lime
- sugar decorations (optional)

NUTRITIONAL
INFORMATION
Per cupcake 256 cals; 8g fat (of
which 1g saturates); 45g
carbohydrate; 0.2g salt

Makes 12

1 Preheat the oven to 190°C (170°C fan oven) mark 5. Line a 12-hole muffin tin with paper muffin cases.

2 Put the flour, bicarbonate of soda, caster sugar and dried fruit into a large bowl. Put the eggs, oil and buttermilk into a jug and lightly beat together until combined. Pour the oil mixture and the pineapple pieces into the flour mixture and stir with a spatula until just combined. Spoon the mixture equally into the paper cases.

3 Bake for 20 minutes or until lightly golden and risen. Leave to cool in the tin for 5 minutes, then transfer to a wire rack to cool completely.

4 To make the topping, put the icing sugar, lime juice and zest and 1 tbsp cold water into a bowl and whisk for 5 minutes or until soft peaks form. Using a small palette knife, spread a little over the top of each cake. Stand the cakes on the wire rack, scatter with sugar decorations, if you like, and leave for 1 hour to set.

Coconut and Lime Cupcakes

Preparation Time
30 minutes
Cooking Time
18–20 minutes, plus cooling and setting

- 275g (10oz) plain flour, sifted
- 1 tbsp baking powder
- 100g (3½oz) caster sugar
- zest of 1 lime
- 50g (2oz) desiccated coconut
- 2 medium eggs
- 100ml (3½fl oz) sunflower oil
- 225ml (8fl oz) natural yogurt
- 50ml (2fl oz) milk

TOPPING

- 150g (5oz) icing sugar, sifted
- juice of 1 lime
- 50g (2oz) desiccated coconut

NUTRITIONAL INFORMATION

Per cupcake 291 cals; 13g fat (of which 6g saturates); 42g carbohydrate; 0.1g salt

Makes 12

1 Preheat the oven to 200°C (180°C fan oven) mark 6. Line a 12-hole muffin tin with paper muffin cases.

2 Put the flour, baking powder, caster sugar, lime zest and coconut into a large bowl. Put the eggs, oil, yogurt and milk into a jug and lightly beat together until combined.

3 Pour the yogurt mixture into the flour mixture and stir with a spatula until just combined. Spoon the mixture equally into the paper cases.

4 Bake for 18–20 minutes until lightly golden and risen. Leave to cool in the tin for 5 minutes, then transfer to a wire rack to cool completely.

5 To make the topping, mix the icing sugar with the lime juice and 1–2 tsp boiling water to make a thick, smooth icing. Put the coconut into a shallow bowl. Dip the top of each cake into the icing until coated, allowing the excess to drip off, then carefully dip into the coconut until coated. Stand the cakes on the wire rack and leave for about 1 hour to set.

Fairy Cakes

Preparation Time
20 minutes
Cooking Time
10–15 minutes, plus cooling and
setting

- 125g (4oz) self-raising flour,
  sifted
- 1 tsp baking powder
- 125g (4oz) caster sugar
- 125g (4oz) unsalted butter,
  very soft
- 2 medium eggs
- 1 tbsp milk

ICING AND DECORATION
- 225g (8oz) icing sugar, sifted
- assorted food colourings
  (optional)
- sweets, sprinkles or coloured
  sugar

NUTRITIONAL
INFORMATION
Per cake 160 cals; 6g fat (of which
4g saturates); 26g carbohydrate;
0.2g salt

Makes 18

1 Preheat the oven to 200°C (180°C fan oven) mark 6.
Put paper cases into 18 of the holes in two bun tins.

2 Put the flour, baking powder, sugar, butter, eggs and
milk into a mixing bowl and beat with a hand-held
electric whisk for 2 minutes or until the mixture is pale
and very soft. Half-fill each paper case with the
cake mixture.

3 Bake for 10–15 minutes until golden brown. Transfer
to a wire rack and leave to cool completely.

4 Put the icing sugar into a bowl and gradually blend
in 2–3 tbsp warm water until the icing is fairly stiff, but
spreadable. Add a couple of drops of food colouring, if
you like.

5 When the cakes are cold, spread the tops with the
icing and decorate. Leave to set.

Chocolate Cupcakes

Preparation Time
15 minutes
Cooking Time
20 minutes, plus cooling and
setting

- 125g (4oz) unsalted butter, softened
- 125g (4oz) light muscovado sugar
- 2 medium eggs, beaten
- 15g (½oz) cocoa powder
- 100g (3½oz) self-raising flour
- 100g (3½oz) plain chocolate (at least 70% cocoa solids), roughly chopped

TOPPING
- 150ml (¼ pint) double cream
- 100g (3½oz) plain chocolate (at least 70% cocoa solids), broken up

NUTRITIONAL INFORMATION
Per cupcake 203 cals; 14g fat (of which 8g saturates); 19g carbohydrate; 0.2g salt

Makes 18

1 Preheat the oven to 190°C (170°C fan oven) mark 5. Line a 12-hole and a 6-hole bun tin or muffin tin with paper muffin cases.

2 Beat the butter and sugar together until light and fluffy. Gradually beat in the eggs. Sift the cocoa powder into the flour and fold into the creamed mixture with the chopped chocolate. Spoon the mixture equally into the paper cases and lightly flatten the surface with the back of a spoon.

3 Bake for 20 minutes, then transfer to a wire rack and leave to cool completely.

4 To make the topping, put the cream and chocolate into a heavy-based pan over a low heat and heat until melted, then allow to cool and thicken slightly. Spoon on to the cooled cakes, then stand the cakes on the wire rack and leave for 30 minutes to set.

The Ultimate Carrot Cupcakes

Preparation Time
30 minutes
Cooking Time
20 minutes, plus cooling

- 150g (5oz) carrots, peeled
- 50g (2oz) raisins
- 175g (6oz) self-raising flour, sifted
- ½ tsp bicarbonate of soda
- 150g (5oz) light soft brown sugar
- zest of 1 orange
- ½ tsp ground mixed spice
- 3 medium eggs
- 100ml (3½fl oz) sunflower oil
- 75ml (2½fl oz) buttermilk

TOPPING AND DECORATION
- 50g (2oz) icing sugar, sifted
- 250g (9oz) mascarpone cheese
- 100g (3½oz) quark cheese
- juice of ½ orange
- red, yellow and green sugarpaste (optional)

NUTRITIONAL
INFORMATION
Per cupcake 255 cals; 12g fat (of which 4g saturates); 34g carbohydrate; 0.3g salt

Makes 12

1 Preheat the oven to 190°C (170°C fan oven) mark 5. Line a 12-hole muffin tin with paper muffin cases.

2 Coarsely grate the carrots and put into a large bowl. Add the raisins, flour, bicarbonate of soda, brown sugar, orange zest and mixed spice. Put the eggs, oil and buttermilk into a jug and lightly beat together until combined. Pour the egg mixture into the flour mixture and stir with a spatula until just combined. Spoon the mixture equally into the paper cases.

3 Bake for 20 minutes or until lightly golden and risen. Cool in the tin for 5 minutes, then transfer to a wire rack and leave to cool completely.

4 To make the topping, mix the icing sugar with the mascarpone, quark and orange juice to a smooth icing. Using a small palette knife, spread a little of the icing over each cake. Use the coloured sugarpaste to make small carrots, if you like, and decorate the cakes with them.

Honeycomb Cream Cupcakes

Preparation Time
30 minutes
Cooking Time
20 minutes, plus cooling

- 125g (4oz) unsalted butter, softened
- 50g (2oz) caster sugar
- 2 medium eggs
- 75g (3oz) clear honey
- 125g (4oz) self-raising flour, sifted
- 50g (2oz) rolled oats
- ½ tsp baking powder
- 1 tbsp milk

TOPPING AND DECORATION

- 125g (4oz) unsalted butter, softened
- 300g (11oz) golden icing sugar, sifted
- 2 tbsp milk
- 1 Crunchie bar, thinly sliced

NUTRITIONAL
INFORMATION
Per cupcake 480 cals; 25g fat (of which 15g saturates); 65g carbohydrate; 0.6g salt

Makes 9

1 Preheat the oven to 190°C (170°C fan oven) mark 5. Line a 12-hole muffin tin with nine paper muffin cases.

2 Using a hand-held electric whisk, whisk the butter and caster sugar in a bowl, or beat with a wooden spoon, until pale and creamy. Gradually whisk in the eggs and honey until just combined. Using a metal spoon, fold in the flour, oats, baking powder and milk. Spoon the mixture equally into the paper cases.

3 Bake for 20 minutes or until the cupcakes are golden and risen. Cool in the tin for 5 minutes, then transfer the cupcakes to a wire rack and leave them to cool completely.

4 To make the buttercream topping, put the butter into a bowl and whisk until fluffy. Gradually whisk in half the icing sugar, then add the milk and the remaining icing sugar and whisk until light and fluffy.

5 Insert a star nozzle into a piping bag, then fill the bag with the buttercream and pipe a swirl on the top of each cake. When ready to serve, decorate each with a few slices of Crunchie.

Lavender and Honey Cupcakes

Preparation Time
35 minutes
Cooking Time
15–20 minutes, plus cooling and
setting

- 125g (4oz) unsalted butter, softened
- 125g (4oz) clear honey
- 2 medium eggs
- 125g (4oz) self-raising flour, sifted
- 1 tsp baking powder

ICING AND DECORATION
- 3 honey and lavender tea bags
- 2 tsp unsalted butter
- 250g (9oz) icing sugar, sifted
- red and blue food colouring
- purple sugar stars
- edible silver dust (optional)

NUTRITIONAL
INFORMATION
Per cupcake 316 cals; 13g fat (of which 8g saturates); 50g carbohydrate; 0.3g salt

Makes 9

1 Preheat the oven to 190°C (170°C fan oven) mark 5. Line a 12-hole muffin tin with nine paper muffin cases.

2 Using a hand-held electric whisk, whisk the butter and honey in a bowl, or beat with a wooden spoon, until combined. Gradually whisk in the eggs until just combined. Using a metal spoon, fold in the flour and baking powder until combined. Spoon the mixture equally into the paper cases.

3 Bake for 15–20 minutes until golden and risen. Cool in the tin for 5 minutes, then transfer to a wire rack and leave to cool completely.

4 To make the icing, infuse the tea bags in 50ml (2fl oz) boiling water in a small bowl for 5 minutes. Remove the tea bags and squeeze out into the bowl. Stir in the butter until melted. Put the icing sugar into a large bowl, add the infused tea mixture and stir to make a smooth icing. Add a few drops of red and blue food colouring until it is lilac in colour.

5 Spoon a little icing on top of each cake, to flood the tops, then sprinkle with stars. Stand the cakes upright on the wire rack and leave for about 1 hour to set. Dust with edible silver dust, if you like, when set.

Cherry Bakewell Cupcakes

Preparation TIme
30 minutes, plus chilling
Cooking Time
25 minutes, plus cooling and setting

- 175g (6oz) unsalted butter, softened
- 175g (6oz) caster sugar
- 3 medium eggs
- 150g (5oz) self-raising flour, sifted
- 1 tsp baking powder
- 75g (3oz) ground almonds
- 1 tsp almond extract
- 75g (3oz) glacé cherries, finely chopped

TOPPING AND DECORATION

- 1 tbsp custard powder
- 100ml (3½fl oz) milk
- 50g (2oz) unsalted butter, softened
- 250g (9oz) icing sugar, sifted
- red sugar sprinkles

NUTRITIONAL
INFORMATION
Per cupcake 405 cals; 21g fat (of which 11g saturates); 53g carbohydrate; 0.4g salt

Makes 12

1 Preheat the oven to 190°C (170°C fan oven) mark 5. Line a 12-hole muffin tin with paper muffin cases.

2 Using a hand-held electric whisk, whisk the butter and caster sugar in a bowl, or beat with a wooden spoon, until pale and creamy. Gradually whisk in the eggs until just combined. Using a metal spoon, fold in the flour, baking powder, ground almonds, almond extract and cherries until combined. Spoon the mixture equally into the paper cases.

3 Bake for 20 minutes or until golden and risen. Cool in the tin for 5 minutes, then transfer to a wire rack and leave to cool completely.

4 To make the topping, put the custard powder into a jug and add a little of the milk to make a smooth

paste. Put the remaining milk into a pan and bring just to the boil. Pour the hot milk on to the custard paste and stir. Return to the milk pan and heat gently for 1–2 minutes until it thickens. Remove from the heat, cover with dampened greaseproof paper to prevent a skin forming and cool completely.

5 Put the custard into a bowl and, using a hand-held electric whisk, whisk in the butter. Chill for 30 minutes.

6 Gradually whisk the icing sugar into the chilled custard mixture until you have a smooth, thick icing. Using a small palette knife, spread a little custard cream over the top of each cake, then decorate with sugar sprinkles. Stand the cakes on the wire rack and leave for about 1 hour to set.

Mini Green Tea Cupcakes

Preparation Time
40 minutes, plus infusing
Cooking Time
25 minutes, plus cooling

- 100ml (3½fl oz) milk
- 2 tsp loose green tea leaves
- 100g (3½oz) unsalted butter, softened
- 125g (4oz) caster sugar
- 2 medium eggs
- 150g (5oz) self-raising flour, sifted
- ½ tsp baking powder

TOPPING AND DECORATION

- 3 tsp loose green tea leaves
- about 75ml (2½fl oz) boiling water
- 75g (3oz) unsalted butter, softened
- 250g (9oz) icing sugar, sifted
- ready-made sugar flowers

NUTRITIONAL INFORMATION
Per cupcake 282 cals; 13g fat (of which 8g saturates); 41g carbohydrate; 0.3g salt

Makes 12

1 Preheat the oven to 190°C (170°C fan oven) mark 5. Line a 12-hole muffin tin with paper fairy cake or bun cases.

2 Put the milk into a small pan and bring to the boil. Add the green tea leaves and leave to infuse for 30 minutes.

3 Using a hand-held electric whisk, whisk the butter and caster sugar in a bowl, or beat with a wooden spoon, until pale and creamy. Gradually whisk in the eggs until just combined. Pass the green tea milk through a sieve into the bowl, then discard the tea. Using a metal spoon, fold in the flour and baking powder until combined. Spoon the mixture equally into the paper cases.

4 Bake for 18–20 minutes until golden and risen. Cool in the tin for 5 minutes, then transfer to a wire rack and leave to cool completely.

5 To make the topping, put the green tea leaves into a jug, add about 75ml (2½fl oz) boiling water and leave to infuse for 5 minutes.

6 Put the butter into a bowl and whisk until fluffy. Gradually add the icing sugar and whisk until combined. Pass the green tea through a sieve into the bowl, then discard the tea. Continue to whisk until light and fluffy.

7 Insert a star nozzle into a piping bag, then fill the bag with the buttercream and pipe a swirl on the top of each cake. Decorate each with a sugar flower.

Raspberry Ripple Cupcakes

Preparation Time
30 minutes
Cooking Time
20 minutes, plus cooling

Makes 9

- ◆ 50g (2oz) seedless raspberry jam
- ◆ 50g (2oz) fresh raspberries
- ◆ 125g (4oz) unsalted butter, softened
- ◆ 100g (3½oz) caster sugar
- ◆ 2 medium eggs
- ◆ 1 tbsp milk
- ◆ 150g (5oz) self-raising flour, sifted

TOPPING AND DECORATION

- ◆ 150g (5oz) fresh raspberries
- ◆ 300ml (½ pint) whipping cream
- ◆ 50g (2oz) icing sugar, sifted

NUTRITIONAL
INFORMATION
Per cupcake 385 cals; 26g fat (of which 16g saturates); 36g carbohydrate; 0.5g salt

1 Preheat the oven to 190°C (170°C fan oven) mark 5. Line a 12-hole muffin tin with nine paper muffin cases.

2 Mix the raspberry jam with the 50g (2oz) raspberries, lightly crushing the raspberries. Set aside.

3 Using a hand-held electric whisk, whisk the butter and caster sugar in a bowl, or beat with a wooden spoon, until pale and creamy. Gradually whisk in the eggs and milk until just combined. Using a metal spoon, fold in the flour until just combined, then carefully fold in the raspberry jam mixture until just marbled, being careful not to over-mix. Spoon the mixture equally into the paper cases.

4 Bake for 20 minutes or until golden and risen. Cool in the tin for 5 minutes, then transfer to a wire rack and leave to cool completely.

5 To make the decoration, reserve nine raspberries. Mash the remaining raspberries in a bowl with a fork. Pass through a sieve into a bowl to remove the seeds. Using a hand-held electric whisk, whip the cream and icing sugar together until stiff peaks form. Mix the raspberry purée into the cream until combined.

6 Insert a star nozzle into a piping bag, then fill the bag with the cream and pipe a swirl on the top of each cake. Decorate each with a raspberry.

Pistachio and Polenta Cupcakes

Preparation Time
35 minutes
Cooking Time
25 minutes, plus cooling

- 150g (5oz) shelled pistachio nuts
- 175g (6oz) unsalted butter, softened
- 175g (6oz) caster sugar
- 3 medium eggs
- 200g (7oz) fine polenta
- ½ tsp baking powder
- 150g (5oz) ground almonds
- zest of 2 lemons
- 2 tbsp milk

ICING

- 75g (3oz) unsalted butter, softened
- 300g (11oz) icing sugar, sifted
- juice of 2 lemons

NUTRITIONAL INFORMATION
Per cupcake 542 cals; 33g fat (of which 13g saturates); 56g carbohydrate; 0.6g salt

Makes 12

1 Preheat the oven to 180°C (160°C fan oven) mark 4. Line a 12-hole muffin tin with paper muffin cases.

2 Whizz the pistachio nuts in a food processor until really finely chopped.

3 Using a hand-held electric whisk, whisk the butter and caster sugar in a bowl, or beat with a wooden spoon, until pale and creamy. Gradually whisk in the eggs until just combined. Using a metal spoon, fold in the polenta, baking powder, ground almonds, lemon zest, milk and 100g (3½oz) ground pistachio nuts until combined. Spoon the mixture equally into the paper cases.

4 Bake for 25 minutes or until golden and risen. Cool in the tin for 5 minutes, then transfer to a wire rack and leave to cool completely.

5 To make the icing, put the butter into a bowl and whisk until fluffy. Gradually whisk in half the icing sugar, then add the lemon juice and the remaining icing sugar, whisking until light and fluffy. Using a small palette knife, spread a little of the buttercream over the top of each cake, then sprinkle each with a little of the remaining chopped pistachio nuts.

Easter Cupcakes

Preparation Time
30 minutes
Cooking Time
30 minutes, plus cooling and setting

- 2 medium eggs
- 75g (3oz) caster sugar
- 150ml (¼ pint) sunflower oil
- 150g (5oz) plain flour, sifted
- ½ tsp baking powder
- 1 tsp vanilla extract
- 15g (½oz) Rice Krispies

TOPPING AND DECORATION
- 100g (3½oz) white chocolate, broken into pieces
- 15g (½oz) unsalted butter
- 25g (1oz) Rice Krispies
- 12 chocolate mini eggs

NUTRITIONAL INFORMATION
Per cupcake 378 cals; 27g fat (of which 8g saturates); 32g carbohydrate; 0.2g salt

Makes 6

1 Preheat the oven to 180°C (160°C fan oven) mark 4. Line a 6-hole muffin tin with paper muffin cases.

2 Separate the eggs, putting the whites in a clean, grease-free bowl and the egg yolks in another. Add the sugar to the yolks and whisk with a hand-held electric whisk until pale and creamy. Then whisk in the oil until combined.

3 Whisk the egg whites until soft peaks form. Using a metal spoon, quickly fold the flour, baking powder, vanilla extract and Rice Krispies into the egg yolk mixture until just combined. Add half the egg whites to the egg yolk mixture to loosen, then carefully fold in the remaining egg whites. Spoon the mixture equally into the paper cases.

4 Bake for 20–25 minutes until golden and risen. Leave to cool in the tin for 5 minutes, then transfer to a wire rack to cool completely.

5 To make the topping, put the chocolate and butter into a heatproof bowl and place over a pan of barely simmering water, making sure the base of the bowl doesn't touch the water. Heat gently until the chocolate has melted, stirring occasionally until smooth. Remove the bowl from the heat, add the Rice Krispies and fold in until coated. Spoon the mixture on top of each cake, pressing down lightly, then top each with two chocolate eggs. Stand the cakes on the wire rack and leave for about 1 hour to set.

Be Mine Cupcakes

Preparation Time
30 minutes
Cooking Time
15 minutes, plus cooling

- 125g (4oz) unsalted butter, softened
- 100g (3½oz) caster sugar
- 2 medium eggs
- 125g (4oz) self-raising flour, sifted
- ½ tsp baking powder
- 1 x 51g bar Turkish Delight, finely chopped
- 1 tbsp rosewater

TOPPING AND DECORATION
- 75g (3oz) unsalted butter, softened
- 250g (9oz) icing sugar, sifted
- 2 tbsp rosewater
- pink and white heart-shaped sugar sprinkles
- 12 Loveheart sweets (optional)

NUTRITIONAL
INFORMATION
Per cupcake 289 cals; 15g fat (of which 9g saturates); 40g carbohydrate; 0.3g salt

Makes 12

1 Preheat the oven to 190°C (170°C fan oven) mark 5. Line a 12-hole muffin tin with paper fairy cake cases.

2 Using a hand-held electric whisk, whisk the butter and caster sugar in a bowl, or beat with a wooden spoon, until pale and creamy. Gradually whisk in the eggs until just combined. Using a metal spoon, fold in the flour, baking powder, Turkish Delight and rosewater until combined. Spoon the mixture equally into the paper cases.

3 Bake for 15 minutes or until golden and risen. Leave to cool in the tin for 5 minutes, then transfer to a wire rack to cool completely.

4 To make the topping, put the butter into a bowl and whisk until fluffy. Add the icing sugar and rosewater and whisk until light and fluffy. Using a small palette knife, spread a little buttercream over the top of each cake. Decorate with sugar hearts, then top each with a Loveheart, if you like.

Lemon & Vanilla Cupcakes

Preparation Time
25 minutes
Cooking Time
15 minutes, plus cooling

- 200g (7oz) golden caster sugar
- 200g (7oz) unsalted butter, very soft
- finely grated zest and juice of 1 lemon
- 4 medium eggs, beaten
- 200g (7oz) self-raising flour

ICING AND DECORATION

- 75g (3oz) unsalted butter, softened
- 175g (6oz) icing sugar, sifted
- 1–2 tbsp milk
- 1 tsp vanilla extract
- selection of sugar sprinkles

NUTRITIONAL INFORMATION
Per cupcake 387 cals; 21g fat; (of which 13g saturates); 47g carbohydrate; 0.6 salt

Makes 12

1 Preheat the oven to 200°C (180°C fan oven) mark 6. Line a 12-hole muffin tin with paper muffin cases.

2 Put the sugar, butter and lemon zest into a large bowl and, using a hand-held electric whisk, whisk together until pale and creamy. Beat in the eggs a little at a time, folding in 1 tbsp flour if the mixture looks as if it's about to curdle.

3 Using a metal spoon, fold in the flour and lemon juice. Spoon the mixture equally into the paper cases. Bake for 12–15 minutes until golden. Leave to cool in the tin for 5 minutes, then transfer to a wire rack to cool completely.

4 To make the icing, put the butter into a large bowl and, using a hand-held electric whisk, beat in two-thirds of the icing sugar. Gradually beat in the rest of the icing sugar with the milk and vanilla until you have a soft but spreadable consistency that holds a shape.

5 When the cakes are completely cold, top each one with icing and swirl with a flat-bladed knife to form peaks. Decorate with sugar sprinkles.

St Clements Cupcakes

Preparation Time
40 minutes
Cooking Time
15–18 minutes, plus cooling and
setting

- 1 small orange (about 200g/7oz)
- 175g (6oz) self-raising flour, sifted
- 100g (3½oz) caster sugar
- 100ml (3½fl oz) milk
- 1 medium egg, beaten
- 50g (2oz) unsalted butter, melted
- 1 tsp baking powder
- zest of 1 large lemon

TOPPING AND DECORATION
- 400g (14oz) royal icing sugar, sifted
- juice and zest of 1 small orange
- sugar star sprinkles
- edible glitter (optional)

NUTRITIONAL
INFORMATION
Per cupcake 309 cals; 1g fat (of
which trace saturates); 76g
carbohydrate; 0g salt

Makes 9

1 Preheat the oven to 190°C (170°C fan oven) mark 5. Line a 12-hole muffin tin with nine paper muffin cases.

2 Grate the zest from the orange into a large bowl and set aside. Cut the top and bottom off the orange and stand it upright on a board. Using a serrated knife, cut away the pith in a downward motion. Roughly chop the flesh of the orange, discarding any pips. Put the chopped orange into a food processor and whizz until puréed.

3 Transfer the orange purée into the bowl with the zest. Add the flour, caster sugar, milk, egg, melted butter, baking powder and lemon zest. Stir with a spatula until just combined. Spoon the mixture equally into the paper cases.

4 Bake for 15–18 minutes until golden and risen. Leave to cool in the tin for 5 minutes, then transfer to a wire rack to cool completely.

5 To make the topping, put the icing sugar, orange juice and zest into a bowl and whisk for 5 minutes or until soft peaks form. Spoon a little over the top of each cake to flood the surface, then sprinkle with the stars. Stand the cakes on the wire rack and leave for about 1 hour to set. Dust with edible glitter, if you like, when set.

Sweetshop Cupcakes

Preparation Time
30 minutes
Cooking Time
20 minutes, plus cooling and
setting

- 175g (6oz) unsalted butter, softened
- 175g (6oz) caster sugar
- 3 medium eggs
- 175g (6oz) self-raising flour, sifted
- zest of 1 lemon
- ½ tsp baking powder
- 125g (4oz) lemon curd

TOPPING AND DECORATION

- 75g (3oz) unsalted butter, softened
- 350g (12oz) icing sugar, sifted
- 50ml (2fl oz) milk
- dolly mixtures, jelly beans or chocolate buttons

**NUTRITIONAL
INFORMATION**
Per cupcake 424 cals; 19g fat (of which 12g saturates); 64g carbohydrate; 0.6g salt

Makes 12

1 Preheat the oven to 190°C (170°C fan oven) mark 5. Line a 12-hole muffin tin with paper muffin cases.

2 Using a hand-held electric whisk, whisk the butter and caster sugar in a bowl, or beat with a wooden spoon, until pale and creamy. Gradually whisk in the eggs until just combined. Using a metal spoon, fold in the flour, lemon zest and baking powder until combined. Spoon the cake mixture equally into the paper cases.

3 Bake for 20 minutes or until golden and risen. Leave to cool in the tin for 5 minutes, then transfer to a wire rack to cool completely.

4 Cut a small cone shape from the top of each cake. Put a teaspoonful of lemon curd into the hole in each cake and then replace the cone, pressing down lightly.

5 To make the topping, put the butter into a bowl and whisk until fluffy. Gradually add half the icing sugar, whisking until combined. Add the milk and remaining icing sugar and whisk until light and fluffy, then, using a small palette knife, spread a little over each cake. Stand the cakes on the wire rack and leave for about 30 minutes to set. Decorate each cake with sweets when set.

Banoffee Cupcakes

Preparation Time
30 minutes
Cooking Time
20 minutes, plus cooling

- 175g (6oz) self-raising flour, sifted
- ½ tsp bicarbonate of soda
- 150g (5oz) light soft brown sugar
- 1 banana (about 150g/5oz), peeled
- 3 medium eggs
- 100g (3½oz) unsalted butter, melted
- 75ml (2½fl oz) buttermilk

TOPPING AND DECORATION
- 150g (5oz) dulce de leche toffee sauce
- 75g (3oz) unsalted butter, softened
- 250g (9oz) golden icing sugar, sifted
- mini fudge chunks (optional)

NUTRITIONAL INFORMATION
Per cupcake 404 cals: 16g fat (of which 10g saturates); 63g carbo-hydrate; 0.4g salt

Makes 12

1 Preheat the oven to 190°C (170°C fan oven) mark 5. Line a 12-hole muffin tin with paper muffin cases.

2 Put the flour, bicarbonate of soda and brown sugar into a large bowl. Mash the banana with a fork in a small bowl. Put the eggs, melted butter and buttermilk into a jug and lightly beat together until combined. Pour into the flour mixture along with the mashed banana and stir with a spatula until just combined. Spoon the mixture equally into the paper cases.

3 Bake for 18–20 minutes until lightly golden and risen. Leave to cool in the tin for 5 minutes, then transfer to a wire rack to cool completely.

4 To make the topping, whisk together the dulce de leche and butter in a bowl until combined. Gradually whisk in the icing sugar until light and fluffy. Use a palette knife to spread the buttercream on top of each cake. Decorate with the mini fudge chunks, if using.

Rocky Road Cupcakes

Preparation Time
30 minutes
Cooking Time
15–20 minutes, plus cooling and setting

◆ 100g (3½oz) unsalted butter, softened
◆ 125g (4oz) caster sugar
◆ 2 medium eggs
◆ 150g (5oz) self-raising flour, sifted
◆ 25g (1oz) glacé cherries, diced
◆ 25g (1oz) milk chocolate chips
◆ 25g (1oz) pinenuts

TOPPING AND DECORATION
◆ 100g (3½oz) milk chocolate
◆ 50ml (2fl oz) double cream
◆ 25g (1oz) mini marshmallows
◆ 25g (1oz) glacé cherries, finely chopped
◆ 1 x 37g bag Maltesers

NUTRITIONAL
INFORMATION
Per cupcake 360 cals; 20g fat (of which 11g saturates); 45g carbohydrate; 0.5g salt

Makes 9

1 Preheat the oven to 190°C (170°C fan oven) mark 5. Line a 12-hole muffin tin with nine paper muffin cases.

2 Using a hand-held electric whisk, whisk the butter and sugar in a bowl, or beat with a wooden spoon, until pale and creamy. Gradually whisk in the eggs until just combined. Using a metal spoon, fold in the flour, cherries, chocolate chips and pinenuts until combined. Spoon the mixture equally into the paper cases.

3 Bake for 15–20 minutes until golden and risen. Leave to cool in the tin for 5 minutes, then transfer to a wire rack.

4 To make the topping, break the chocolate into pieces, then put into a heatproof bowl with the cream. Set over a pan of gently simmering water, making sure the base of the bowl doesn't touch the water. Heat until melted, stirring occasionally until smooth.

5 Remove from the heat and, using a small palette knife, spread a little over the top of each cake (once the cakes have cooled completely). Decorate each with marshmallows, cherries and Maltesers. Stand the cupcakes on the wire rack and leave for about 1 hour to set.

Truffle Kisses Cupcakes

Preparation Time
40 minutes
Cooking Time
30 minutes, plus cooling and
setting

- 150g (5oz) unsalted butter,
  softened
- 200g (7oz) caster sugar
- 3 medium eggs
- 75g (3oz) self-raising flour, sifted
- 200g (7oz) plain flour, sifted
- ½ tsp bicarbonate of soda
- 75g (3oz) roasted chopped
  hazelnuts
- 200ml (7fl oz) buttermilk
- 15g (½oz) dark chocolate,
  finely grated

TOPPING AND DECORATION
- 200ml (7fl oz) double cream
- 150g (5oz) dark chocolate
- 100g (3½oz) milk chocolate,
  finely chopped
- 18 small chocolate truffles
  (optional)

NUTRITIONAL
INFORMATION
Per cupcake 317 cals; 20g fat (of
which 10g saturates); 34g
carbohydrate; 0.2g salt

Makes 18

1 Preheat the oven to 180°C (160°C fan oven) mark 4. Line a 12-hole and a 6-hole muffin tin with paper muffin cases.

2 Using a hand-held electric whisk, whisk the butter and sugar in a bowl, or beat with a wooden spoon, until pale and creamy. Gradually whisk in the eggs until just combined. Using a metal spoon, fold in both flours, the bicarbonate of soda, hazelnuts, buttermilk and grated chocolate until combined. Spoon the mixture equally into the paper cases.

3 Bake for 20–25 minutes until golden and risen. Leave to cool in the tin for 5 minutes, then transfer to a wire rack to cool completely.

4 To make the topping, heat the cream in a small pan until nearly boiling. Finely chop 100g (3½oz) dark chocolate and put into a bowl along with all the milk chocolate. Pour the hot cream over the chocolate and leave to stand for 5 minutes, then stir gently until smooth. Chill the mixture for 15–20 minutes until thickened slightly.

5 Using a palette knife, spread a little chocolate cream over the top of each cake. Finely grate the remaining dark chocolate over the top of each cake. Finish each with a chocolate truffle, if you like. Stand the cupcakes on the wire rack and leave for about 1 hour to set.

Sea Breeze Cupcakes

Preparation Time
40 minutes
Cooking Time
20 minutes, plus cooling and
setting

- 1 pink grapefruit (about 350g/12oz)
- 50g (2oz) ready-to-eat dried cranberries
- 250g (9oz) self-raising flour, sifted
- 125g (4oz) caster sugar
- 50ml (2fl oz) milk
- 1 medium egg, beaten
- 75g (3oz) unsalted butter, melted
- 1 tsp baking powder

ICING AND DECORATION

- 300g (11oz) fondant icing sugar, sifted
- red and yellow food colouring
- 50g (2oz) Apricot Glaze (see page 313)
- edible silver balls
- cocktail umbrellas (optional)

NUTRITIONAL
INFORMATION
Per cupcake 287 cals; 6g fat (of
which 4g saturates); 61g
carbohydrate; 0.1g salt

Makes 12

1 Preheat the oven to 190°C (170°C fan oven) mark 5. Line a 12-hole muffin tin with paper muffin cases.

2 Grate the zest from half the grapefruit into a bowl. Set aside. Cut the top and bottom off the grapefruit and stand it upright on a board. Using a serrated knife, cut away the pith in a downward motion. Cut in between the membranes to remove the segments. Whizz the segments in a food processor until puréed.

3 Transfer the purée into the bowl with the zest. Add the cranberries, flour, caster sugar, milk, egg, melted butter and baking powder and stir with a spatula until just combined. Spoon the mixture equally into the paper cases.

4 Bake for 20 minutes or until golden and risen. Leave to cool in the tin for 5 minutes, then transfer to a wire rack to cool completely.

5 To make the icing, put the icing sugar into a bowl and add enough water (2–4 tbsp) to make a smooth icing. Add a few drops of food colouring to make it pinky-orange in colour. Brush the tops of the cakes with the apricot glaze, then spoon a little icing on to each cake to flood the top. Decorate with the silver balls. Stand the cakes on the wire rack and leave for about 1 hour to set. Decorate with a cocktail umbrella once set, if you like.

Toast and Marmalade Cupcakes

Preparation Time
30 minutes
Cooking Time
20–25 minutes, plus cooling and
setting

- 150g (5oz) low-fat olive oil spread
- 200g (7oz) wholemeal self-raising flour, sifted
- 150g (5oz) light soft brown sugar
- 3 medium eggs
- 50g (2oz) marmalade
- 100ml (3½fl oz) milk
- zest of 1 orange
- 50g (2oz) fresh wholemeal breadcrumbs

ICING AND DECORATION
- 125g (4oz) marmalade
- 300g (11oz) icing sugar, sifted

NUTRITIONAL
INFORMATION
Per cupcake 336 cals; 10g fat (of
which 2g saturates); 57g
carbohydrate; 1.5g salt

Makes 12

1 Preheat the oven to 180°C (160°C fan oven) mark 4. Line a 12-hole muffin tin with paper muffin cases.

2 Put the low-fat spread, flour, brown sugar, eggs, marmalade, milk, orange zest and breadcrumbs into a large bowl. Using a hand-held electric whisk, whisk together until pale and creamy. Spoon the mixture equally into the paper cases.

3 Bake for 20–25 minutes until golden and risen. Cool in the tin for 5 minutes, then transfer to a wire rack and leave to cool completely.

4 To make the icing, pass the marmalade through a sieve into a bowl to remove the rind. Reserve the rind. Mix the icing sugar with the sieved marmalade in a bowl until it forms a smooth icing. Spoon a little icing on to each cake to flood the top, then scatter on the reserved rind. Stand the cakes on the wire rack and leave for about 1 hour to set.

Cookies and Cream Cupcakes

Preparation Time
30 minutes
Cooking Time
15–20 minutes, plus cooling

- 75g (3oz) mini Oreo cookies
- 175g (6oz) unsalted butter, softened
- 150g (5oz) caster sugar
- 3 medium eggs
- 175g (6oz) self-raising flour, sifted
- ½ tsp baking powder
- 3 tbsp milk
- ½ tsp vanilla extract

TOPPING

- 75g (3oz) unsalted butter, softened
- 150g (5oz) icing sugar, sifted
- 2 tsp vanilla extract
- 1 tsp cocoa powder

NUTRITIONAL
INFORMATION
Per cupcake 357 cals; 21g fat (of which 13g saturates); 41g carbohydrate; 0.5g salt

Makes 12

1 Preheat the oven to 200°C (180°C fan oven) mark 6. Line a 12-hole muffin tin with paper muffin cases. Reserve 12 mini Oreo cookies and roughly chop the remainder.

2 Using a hand-held electric whisk, whisk the butter and caster sugar in a bowl (or beat with a wooden spoon) until pale and creamy. Gradually whisk in the eggs until just combined. Using a metal spoon, fold in the flour, baking powder, milk, vanilla extract and chopped cookies until combined. Spoon the mixture equally into the paper cases.

3 Bake for 15–20 minutes until golden and risen. Leave to cool in the tin for 5 minutes, then transfer to a wire rack to cool completely.

4 To make the topping, put the butter into a bowl and whisk until fluffy. Gradually add the icing sugar and vanilla extract and whisk until light and fluffy. Using a small palette knife, spread the buttercream over the top of each cake. Sift a little cocoa powder on to the top of each cake and then decorate each with a reserved Oreo cookie.

Chocolate Fairy Cakes

Preparation Time
20 minutes
Cooking Time
10–15 minutes, plus cooling and
setting

- 100g (3½oz) self-raising flour
- 25g (1oz) cocoa powder
- 1 tsp baking powder
- 125g (4oz) caster sugar
- 125g (4oz) unsalted butter,
  very soft
- 2 medium eggs
- 1 tbsp milk
- 50g (2oz) chocolate drops

ICING AND DECORATION
- 225g (8oz) icing sugar, sifted
- assorted food colourings
  (optional)
- sweets, sprinkles or coloured
  sugar

NUTRITIONAL INFORMATION
Per cupcake 171 cals; 7g fat (of
which 4g saturates); 28g
carbohydrate; 0.3g salt

Makes 18

1 Preheat the oven to 200°C (180°C fan oven) mark 6. Put paper cases into 18 of the holes in two bun tins.

2 Sift the flour into a mixing bowl, then sift in the cocoa powder, baking powder and sugar. Add the butter, eggs and milk and beat with a hand-held electric whisk for 2 minutes or until the mixture is pale and very soft. Stir in the chocolate drops, and spoon the mixture equally into the paper cases.

3 Bake for 10–15 minutes until risen and springy to the touch. Transfer to a wire rack to cool completely.

4 To make the icing, put the icing sugar into a bowl and gradually blend in 2–3 tbsp warm water until the icing is fairly stiff, but spreadable. Add a couple of drops of food colouring, if you like.

5 Spread the tops of the cakes with the icing and decorate with sweets, sprinkles or coloured sugar.

Jewelled Cupcakes

Preparation Time
40 minutes
Cooking Time
30 minutes, plus cooling and
setting

- 75g (3oz) unsalted butter, softened
- 150g (5oz) caster sugar
- 3 medium eggs
- 175g (6oz) self-raising flour, sifted
- 175g (6oz) mincemeat

DECORATION
- 75g (3oz) Apricot Glaze (see page 313)
- 50g (2oz) toasted flaked almonds
- 50g (2oz) ready-to-eat apricots, chopped
- 12 glacé cherries
- 40g (1½oz) caster sugar
- 1 tbsp unsalted butter

NUTRITIONAL INFORMATION
Per cupcake 276 cals; 10g fat (of which 4g saturates); 46g carbohydrate; 0.4g salt

Makes 12

1 Preheat the oven to 190°C (170°C fan oven) mark 5. Line a 12-hole muffin tin with paper muffin cases.

2 Using a hand-held electric whisk, whisk the butter and sugar in a bowl, or beat with a wooden spoon, until pale and creamy. Gradually whisk in the eggs until just combined. Using a metal spoon, fold in the flour and mincemeat until combined. Spoon the mixture equally into the paper cases.

3 Bake for 20 minutes or until golden and risen. Leave to cool in the tin for 5 minutes, then transfer to a wire rack.

4 To make the decoration, brush each cake with a little glaze (once the cakes have cooled completely), then scatter on a few almonds and apricots and a cherry. Stand the cakes on the wire rack.

5 Put the sugar and 1 tbsp cold water into a small pan and heat gently until the sugar dissolves. Increase the heat and bubble for 3–4 minutes until the sugar caramelizes and turns golden in colour. Remove from the heat and quickly stir in the butter until combined. Being very careful, drizzle the hot caramel over the top of each cake. Leave for about 10 minutes to set.

Aniseed Cupcakes

Preparation Time
30 minutes
Cooking Time
20–25 minutes, plus cooling

- 125g (4oz) unsalted butter, softened
- 200g (7oz) caster sugar
- 2 medium eggs
- 200g (7oz) self-raising flour, sifted
- 25g (1oz) custard powder
- 2 tbsp caraway seeds
- 125ml (4fl oz) milk

TOPPING AND DECORATION
- 75g (3oz) unsalted butter, softened
- 300g (11oz) icing sugar, sifted
- 2 tbsp Pernod
- pale blue sugar sprinkles

NUTRITIONAL
INFORMATION
Per cupcake 291 cals; 15g fat (of which 9g saturates); 37g carbohydrate; 0.4g salt

Makes 12

1 Preheat the oven to 190°C (170°C fan oven) mark 5. Line a 12-hole muffin tin with paper muffin cases.

2 Using a hand-held electric whisk, whisk the butter and caster sugar in a bowl, or beat with a wooden spoon, until pale and creamy. Gradually whisk in the eggs until just combined.

3 Using a metal spoon, fold in the flour, custard powder, caraway seeds and milk until combined. Spoon the cake mixture equally into the paper cases.

4 Bake for 20–25 minutes until golden and risen. Leave to cool in the tin for 5 minutes, then transfer to a wire rack to cool completely.

5 To make the topping, put the butter into a bowl and whisk until fluffy. Gradually whisk in half the icing sugar, then add the Pernod, 1 tbsp boiling water and the remaining icing sugar and whisk until light and fluffy. Using a small palette knife, spread a little of the buttercream over the top of each cake, then sprinkle with the blue sugar sprinkles.

Nutty Cupcakes

Preparation Time
40 minutes
Cooking Time
25 minutes, plus cooling and
setting

- 150g (5oz) unsalted butter,
  softened
- 175g (6oz) self-raising flour,
  sifted
- 50g (2oz) caster sugar
- 100ml (3½fl oz) golden syrup
- 3 medium eggs
- 1 tsp baking powder
- 1 tsp ground mixed spice
- 50g (2oz) mixed chopped
  nuts

TOPPING
- 3 tbsp double cream
- 1 tbsp milk
- 50g (2oz) milk chocolate,
  finely chopped
- 25g (1oz) dark chocolate,
  finely chopped
- 75g (3oz) roasted chopped
  hazelnuts

NUTRITIONAL
INFORMATION
Per cupcake 338 cals; 23g fat (of
which 10g saturates); 31g
carbohydrate; 0.4g salt

Makes 12

1 Preheat the oven to 190°C (170°C fan oven) mark 5. Line a 12-hole muffin tin with paper muffin cases.

2 Put the butter, flour, sugar, syrup, eggs, baking powder, mixed spice and nuts into a large bowl. Using a hand-held electric whisk, whisk together until pale and creamy. Spoon the cake mixture equally into the paper cases.

3 Bake for 20 minutes or until golden and risen. Leave to cool in the tin for 5 minutes, then transfer to a wire rack to cool completely.

4 To make the topping, heat the cream and milk in a small pan until nearly boiling. Put both chocolates into a bowl and pour the hot cream over them. Leave to stand for 5 minutes, then stir gently until smooth.

5 Put the hazelnuts into a shallow bowl. Dip the top of each cake into the chocolate cream, allow the excess to drip off, then dip into the hazelnuts until coated all over. Stand the cakes on the wire rack and leave for about 1 hour to set.

Pavlova Cupcakes

Preparation Time
30 minutes
Cooking Time
25 minutes, plus cooling and
setting

- 125g (4oz) unsalted butter, softened
- 100g (3½oz) caster sugar
- 2 medium eggs
- 150g (5oz) self-raising flour, sifted
- 1 tbsp milk
- zest of 1 lemon
- 50g (2oz) small fresh blueberries
- 12 fresh raspberries

FROSTING
- 1 medium egg white
- 175g (6oz) caster sugar
- a pinch of cream of tartar

NUTRITIONAL INFORMATION
Per cupcake 226 cals; 10g fat (of which 6g saturates); 34g carbohydrate; 0.2g salt

Makes 12

1 Preheat the oven to 190°C (170°C fan oven) mark 5. Line a 12-hole muffin tin with paper fairy cake or bun cases.

2 Using a hand-held electric whisk, whisk the butter and sugar in a bowl, or beat with a wooden spoon, until pale and creamy. Gradually whisk in the eggs until just combined. Using a metal spoon, fold in the flour, milk, lemon zest and blueberries until combined.

3 Spoon the mixture equally into the paper cases and press one raspberry into the centre of each cake. Bake for 15 minutes or until golden and risen. Leave to cool in the tin for 5 minutes, then transfer to a wire rack to cool completely.

4 To make the frosting, put the egg white, caster sugar, 2 tbsp water and cream of tartar into a heatproof bowl and, using a hand-held electric whisk, whisk lightly. Put the bowl over a pan of simmering water and whisk continuously for about 7 minutes or until the mixture thickens sufficiently to stand in peaks.

5 Insert a star nozzle into a piping bag, then fill the bag with the frosting and pipe a swirl on the top of each cake. Stand the cakes on the wire rack and leave for about 1 hour to set.

Mango and Passion Fruit Cupcakes

Preparation Time
30 minutes
Cooking Time
25 minutes, plus cooling

- 4 ripe passion fruit
- about 75ml (2½fl oz) orange juice
- 150g (5oz) unsalted butter, softened
- 250g (9oz) plain flour, sifted
- 175g (6oz) caster sugar
- 3 medium eggs
- 1 tbsp baking powder
- 75g (3oz) ready-to-eat dried mango, finely chopped

TOPPING AND DECORATION
- 100g (3½oz) cream cheese
- 25g (1oz) unsalted butter, softened
- 200g (7oz) icing sugar, sifted
- 1 large, ripe passion fruit
- white sugar sprinkles

NUTRITIONAL INFORMATION
Per cupcake 374 cals; 18g fat (of which 11g saturates); 52g carbohydrate; 0.4g salt

Makes 12

1 Preheat the oven to 180°C (160°C fan oven) mark 4. Line a 12-hole muffin tin with paper muffin cases.

2 Cut the passion fruit in half and pass the seeds and juice through a sieve into a jug. Discard the seeds. Top up with orange juice to make 150ml (¼ pint) liquid.

3 Put the butter, flour, caster sugar, eggs, baking powder and juice into a large bowl. Using a hand-held electric whisk, whisk together, or beat with a wooden spoon, until pale and creamy. Add the chopped mango and fold in until combined. Spoon the mixture equally into the paper cases.

4 Bake for 25 minutes or until golden and risen. Leave to cool in the tin for 5 minutes, then transfer to a wire rack to cool completely.

5 To make the topping, whisk together the cream cheese and butter until fluffy. Gradually add the icing sugar until combined. Cut the passion fruit in half and pass the seeds and juice through a sieve into the icing. Discard the seeds. Stir to combine, then, using a small palette knife, spread a little over the top of each cake. Scatter with the sugar sprinkles.

Apple Crumble Cupcakes

Preparation Time
20 minutes
Cooking Time
25 minutes, plus cooling

- 320g (11½oz) eating apples, cored (about 2)
- juice of 1 lemon
- 200g (7oz) self-raising flour, sifted
- 1 tsp baking powder
- 1 tsp ground cinnamon
- 125g (4oz) light soft brown sugar
- 2 medium eggs
- 100g (3½oz) unsalted butter, melted

CRUMBLE TOPPING
- 50g (2oz) plain flour
- 25g (1oz) unsalted butter, chilled and cut into cubes
- 15g (½oz) light soft brown sugar

NUTRITIONAL
INFORMATION
Per cupcake 215 cals; 10g fat (of which 6g saturates); 31g carbohydrate; 0.2g salt

Makes 12

1 Preheat the oven to 180°C (160°C fan oven) mark 4. Line a 12-hole muffin tin with paper muffin cases.

2 Make the crumble. Put the flour into a large bowl and, using your fingertips, rub in the butter until it resembles coarse breadcrumbs. Stir in the sugar and set aside.

3 Coarsely grate the apples into a large bowl and mix in the lemon juice. Add the flour, baking powder, cinnamon and sugar. Put the eggs and melted butter into a jug and lightly beat together, then pour into the flour mixture. Stir with a spatula until just combined. Spoon the cake mixture equally into the paper cases, then sprinkle the crumble equally over the top of each cake.

4 Bake for 25 minutes or until lightly golden and risen. Leave to cool in the tin for 5 minutes, then transfer to a wire rack to cool completely.

Cherry and Almond Muffins

Preparation Time
10 minutes
Cooking Time
25 minutes, plus cooling

- 225g (8oz) plain flour
- 1 tsp baking powder
- a pinch of salt
- 75g (3oz) caster sugar
- 50g (2oz) ground almonds
- 350g (12oz) glacé cherries, roughly chopped
- 300ml (½ pint) milk
- 3 tbsp lemon juice
- 50ml (2fl oz) sunflower oil or melted butter
- 1 large egg
- 1 tsp almond extract
- roughly crushed sugar cubes to decorate

NUTRITIONAL INFORMATION
Per muffin 230 cals; 6g fat (of which 1g saturates); 42g carbohydrate; 0.1g salt

Makes 12

1 Preheat the oven to 190°C (170°C fan oven) mark 5. Line a bun tin with 12 paper muffin cases.

2 Sift together the flour, baking powder and salt. Add the caster sugar and ground almonds. Stir in the chopped cherries.

3 Whisk together the milk, lemon juice, oil or butter, the egg and almond extract. Pour into the dry ingredients and stir until all the ingredients are just combined – the mixture should be lumpy. Don't over-mix or the muffins will be tough.

4 Spoon the mixture equally into the muffin cases and sprinkle with the crushed sugar cubes.

5 Bake for about 25 minutes until well risen and golden. Leave the muffins to cool in the tin for 5 minutes, then transfer to a wire rack to cool completely. These muffins are best eaten on the day they are made.

Spiced Carrot Muffins

Preparation Time
30 minutes
Cooking Time
20–25 minutes, plus cooling

- ◆ 125g (4oz) unsalted butter, softened
- ◆ 125g (4oz) light muscovado sugar
- ◆ 3 pieces preserved stem ginger, drained and chopped
- ◆ 150g (5oz) self-raising flour, sifted
- ◆ 1½ tsp baking powder
- ◆ 1 tbsp ground mixed spice
- ◆ 25g (1oz) ground almonds
- ◆ 3 medium eggs
- ◆ finely grated zest of ½ orange
- ◆ 150g (5oz) carrots, peeled and grated
- ◆ 50g (2oz) pecan nuts, chopped
- ◆ 50g (2oz) sultanas
- ◆ 3 tbsp white rum or orange liqueur (optional)

TOPPING AND DECORATION
- ◆ 200g (7oz) cream cheese
- ◆ 75g (3oz) icing sugar
- ◆ 1 tsp lemon juice
- ◆ 12 unsprayed rose petals (optional)

NUTRITIONAL
INFORMATION
Per muffin 333 cals; 22g fat (of which 11g saturates); 31g carbohydrate; 0.5g salt

Makes 12

---

1 Preheat the oven to 180°C (160°C fan oven) mark 4. Line a 12-hole muffin tin with paper muffin cases.

2 Beat the butter, muscovado sugar and stem ginger together until pale and creamy. Add the flour, baking powder, spice, ground almonds, eggs and orange zest and beat well until combined. Stir in the carrots, pecan nuts and sultanas. Spoon the mixture equally into the paper cases.

3 Bake for 20–25 minutes until risen and just firm. A skewer inserted into the centre of a cupcake should come out clean. Transfer to a wire rack and leave to cool completely.

4 To make the topping, beat the cream cheese in a bowl until softened. Beat in the icing sugar and lemon juice to give a smooth icing that just holds its shape.

5 Drizzle each cake with a little liqueur, if you like. Using a small palette knife, spread a little icing over each cake. Decorate with a rose petal, if you like.

Blueberry Muffins

Preparation Time
10 minutes
Cooking Time
20–25 minutes, plus cooling

- 2 medium eggs
- 250ml (9fl oz) semi-skimmed milk
- 250g (9oz) golden granulated sugar
- 2 tsp vanilla extract
- 350g (12oz) plain flour
- 4 tsp baking powder
- 250g (9oz) blueberries, frozen
- finely grated zest of 2 lemons

NUTRITIONAL INFORMATION
Per muffin 218 cals; 2g fat (of which trace saturates); 49g carbohydrate; 0.5g salt

Makes 12

1 Preheat the oven to 200°C (180°C fan oven) mark 6. Line a 12-hole muffin tin with paper muffin cases.

2 Put the eggs, milk, sugar and vanilla extract into a bowl and mix well.

3 Sift the flour and baking powder together into another bowl, then add the blueberries and lemon zest. Toss together and make a well in the centre.

4 Pour the egg mixture into the flour and blueberries and mix in gently – over-beating will make the muffins tough. Spoon the mixture equally into the paper cases.

5 Bake for 20–25 minutes until risen and just firm. Transfer to a wire rack and leave to cool completely. These are best eaten on the day they are made.

Chocolate Banana Muffins

Preparation Time
15 minutes
Cooking Time
20 minutes, plus cooling

- 275g (10oz) self-raising flour
- 1 tsp bicarbonate of soda
- ½ tsp salt
- 3 large bananas, about 450g (1lb)
- 125g (4oz) golden caster sugar
- 1 large egg, beaten
- 50ml (2fl oz) semi-skimmed milk
- 75g (3oz) unsalted butter, melted and cooled
- 50g (2oz) plain chocolate, chopped

NUTRITIONAL INFORMATION
Per muffin 228 cals, 7g fat (of which 4g saturates), 40g carbohydrate, 0.5g salt

Makes 12

1 Preheat the oven to 180°C (160°C fan oven) mark 4. Line a bun tin or muffin tin with 12 paper muffin cases. Sift the flour, bicarbonate of soda and salt into a large mixing bowl and put to one side.

2 Peel the bananas and mash with a fork in a bowl. Add the caster sugar, egg, milk and melted butter, and mix until well combined.

3 Add this to the flour mixture, with the chopped chocolate. Stir gently, using only a few strokes, until the flour is only just incorporated – do not over-mix. The mixture should be lumpy.

4 Spoon the mixture into the muffin cases, half-filling them. Bake in the oven for 20 minutes or until the muffins are well risen and golden. Transfer to a wire rack to cool. Serve warm or cold.

Double Chocolate Muffins

Preparation Time
20 minutes
Cooking Time
about 25 minutes, plus cooling

- 125g (4oz) unsalted butter
- 100g (3½oz) plain chocolate
- 225g (8oz) plain flour
- 1 tsp bicarbonate of soda
- 40g (1½oz) cocoa powder, sifted
- 175g (6oz) golden caster sugar
- 200g (7oz) white chocolate, chopped
- a pinch of salt
- 1 medium egg
- 200ml (7fl oz) milk
- 150g carton natural yogurt
- 1 tsp vanilla extract

NUTRITIONAL INFORMATION
Per muffin 368 cals; 19g fat (of which 11g saturates); 47g carbohydrate; 0.8g salt

Makes 12

1 Preheat the oven to 190°C (170°C fan oven) mark 5. Line a 12-hole muffin tin with paper cases.

2 Melt the butter and plain chocolate in a heatproof bowl set over a pan of barely simmering water, making sure the base of the bowl doesn't touch the water. Mix together very gently and leave to cool a little.

3 Meanwhile, put the flour into a large bowl. Add the bicarbonate of soda, cocoa powder, caster sugar, white chocolate and salt and stir everything together. Put

the egg, milk, yogurt and vanilla extract in a jug and beat together.

4 Pour both the egg mixture and the chocolate mixture on to the dry ingredients, then roughly fold together. Be careful not to over-mix, or the muffins won't rise properly. Spoon the mixture equally into the paper cases.

5 Bake for 20–25 minutes until well risen and springy. Take the muffins out of the tin and cool on a wire rack before serving.

Brown Sugar Muffins

Preparation Time
10 minutes
Cooking Time
30–35 minutes, plus cooling

- ◆ 12 brown sugar cubes
- ◆ 150g (5oz) plain flour
- ◆ 1½ tsp baking powder
- ◆ ¼ tsp salt
- ◆ 1 medium egg, beaten
- ◆ 40g (1½oz) golden caster sugar
- ◆ 50g (2oz) unsalted butter, melted
- ◆ ½ tsp vanilla extract
- ◆ 100ml (3½fl oz) milk

NUTRITIONAL INFORMATION
Per muffin 233 cals; 8g fat (of which 5g saturates); 38g carbohydrate; , 0.4g salt

Makes 6

1 Preheat the oven to 200°C (180°C fan oven) mark 6. Line a 6-hole bun tin or muffin tin with paper muffin cases.

2 Roughly crush the sugar cubes and put to one side. Sift together the flour, baking powder and salt.

3 Put the beaten egg, caster sugar, melted butter, vanilla extract and milk into a large bowl and stir to combine.

4 Fold in the sifted flour and divide equally between the muffin cases. Sprinkle with the brown sugar.

5 Bake for 30–35 minutes until well risen and springy. Take the muffins out of the tin and cool on a wire rack before serving.

Bran and Apple Muffins

Preparation Time
20 minutes
Cooking Time
30 minutes, plus cooling

- 250ml (9fl oz) semi-skimmed milk
- 2 tbsp orange juice
- 50g (2oz) All Bran
- 9 ready-to-eat dried prunes
- 100g (3½oz) light muscovado sugar
- 2 medium egg whites
- 1 tbsp golden syrup
- 150g (5oz) plain flour, sifted
- 1 tsp baking powder
- 1 tsp ground cinnamon
- 1 eating apple, peeled and grated
- demerara sugar to sprinkle

NUTRITIONAL INFORMATION
Per muffin 137 cals; 1g fat (of which trace saturates); 31g carbohydrate; 0.3g salt

Makes 10

1 Preheat the oven to 190°C (170°C fan oven) mark 5. Line a 10-hole bun tin or muffin tin with paper muffin cases.

2 Put the milk, orange juice and All Bran into a bowl and stir to mix. Put to one side for 10 minutes.

3 Put the prunes into a food processor or blender with 100ml (3½fl oz) water and whizz for 2–3 minutes to make a purée, then add the muscovado sugar and whizz briefly to mix.

4 Put the egg whites into a large, grease-free bowl and, using a hand-held electric whisk, whisk until soft peaks form. Add the whites to the milk mixture with the syrup, flour, baking powder, cinnamon, grated apple and prune mixture. Fold all the ingredients together gently – don't over-mix. Spoon the mixture equally into the muffin cases.

5 Bake for 30 minutes or until well risen and golden brown. Transfer to a wire rack and leave to cool completely. Sprinkle with demerara sugar just before serving. These are best eaten on the day they are made.

Lamingtons

Preparation Time
40 minutes
Cooking Time
30 minutes, plus cooling and
setting

- 125g (4oz) unsalted butter, softened, plus extra to grease
- 125g (4oz) golden caster sugar
- 2 medium eggs
- 125g (4oz) self-raising flour, sifted
- 1 tsp baking powder
- 2 tsp vanilla extract

COATING
- 200g (7oz) icing sugar
- 50g (2oz) cocoa powder
- 25g (1oz) unsalted butter, cubed
- 5 tbsp milk
- 200g (7oz) desiccated coconut

**NUTRITIONAL
INFORMATION**
Per square 273 cals; 17g fat (of which 12g saturates); 29g carbohydrate; 0.4g salt

1 Preheat the oven to 180°C (160°C fan oven) mark 4. Grease a 15cm (6 inch) square cake tin and base-line with baking parchment.

2 Put the butter, caster sugar, eggs, flour, baking powder and vanilla extract into a bowl and, using a hand-held electric whisk, beat until creamy. Turn the mixture into the prepared tin and level the surface.

3 Bake for about 30 minutes or until just firm to the touch and a skewer inserted into the centre comes out clean. Transfer to a wire rack and leave to cool completely. Wrap and store, preferably overnight, so that the cake is easier to slice.

4 To make the topping, sift the icing sugar and cocoa powder into a bowl. Put the butter and milk into a small pan and heat until the butter has just melted. Pour over the icing sugar and stir until smooth, adding 2–3 tbsp water if necessary, so that the icing thickly coats the back of a spoon.

5 Trim off the side crusts from the cake and cut into 16 squares. Place a sheet of greaseproof paper under a wire rack to catch the drips. Scatter the coconut on a large plate. Pierce a piece of cake through the top crust and dip into the icing until coated, turning the cake gently. Transfer to the wire rack. Once you've coated half the pieces, roll them in the coconut and transfer to a plate. Repeat with the remainder and leave to set for a couple of hours before serving.

Note
If, towards the end of coating the cakes, the chocolate topping mixture has thickened, carefully stir in a drop of water to thin it out.

Makes 16

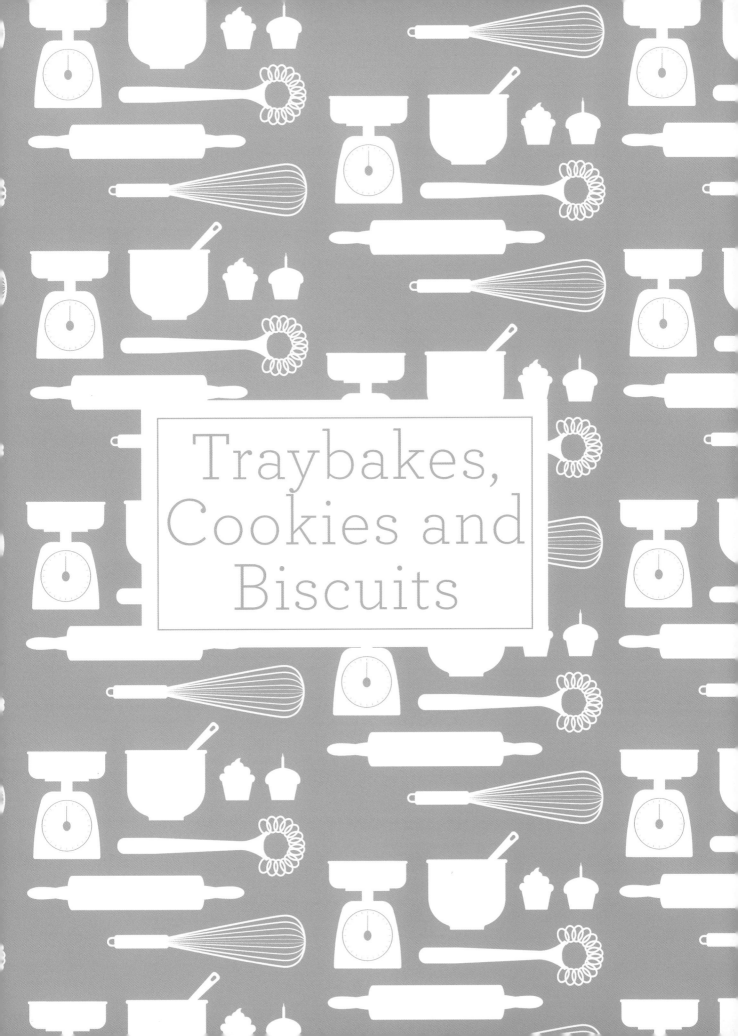

Traybakes, Cookies and Biscuits

Apricot and Almond Traybake

Preparation Time
20 minutes
Cooking Time
30–40 minutes, plus cooling

- 250g (9oz) unsalted butter, softened, plus extra to grease
- 225g (8oz) golden caster sugar
- 275g (10oz) self-raising flour, sifted
- 2 tsp baking powder
- finely grated zest of 1 orange and 2 tbsp orange juice
- 75g (3oz) ground almonds
- 5 medium eggs, lightly beaten
- 225g (8oz) ready-to-eat dried apricots, roughly chopped
- 25g (1oz) flaked almonds
- icing sugar to dust (optional)

NUTRITIONAL INFORMATION
Per bar 277 cals; 16g fat (of which 8g saturates); 30g carbohydrate; 0.4g salt

Cuts into 18 bars

1 Preheat the oven to 180°C (160°C fan oven) mark 4. Grease a 33 x 20.5cm (13 x 8 inch) baking tin and base-line with baking parchment.

2 Put the butter, caster sugar, flour, baking powder, orange zest, ground almonds and eggs into the bowl of a large freestanding mixer. Mix on a low setting for 30 seconds, then increase the speed and mix for 1 minute or until thoroughly combined. (Alternatively, mix well using a wooden spoon.)

3 Remove the bowl from the mixer. Using a large metal spoon, fold in the apricots. Spoon the mixture into the prepared tin, level the surface and sprinkle the flaked almonds over the top.

4 Bake for 30–40 minutes until risen and golden brown and a skewer inserted into the centre comes out clean. Leave to cool in the tin.

5 Cut into 18 bars. Dust with icing sugar, if you like.

Quick Chocolate Slices

Preparation Time
10 minutes
Cooking Time
2 minutes, plus chilling

- 225g (8oz) unsalted butter or olive oil spread, plus extra to grease
- 50g (2oz) cocoa powder, sifted
- 3 tbsp golden syrup
- 300g pack digestive biscuits, crushed
- 400g (14oz) plain chocolate (at least 70% cocoa solids), broken into pieces

NUTRITIONAL INFORMATION
Per slice 137 cals; 9g fat (of which 6g saturates); 13g carbohydrate; 0.3g salt

Makes 40

1 Grease a 25.5 x 16.5cm (10 x 6½ inch) tin. Put the butter or olive oil spread into a heatproof bowl, add the cocoa powder and syrup and melt over a pan of gently simmering water. Mix everything together.

2 Remove from the heat and stir in the biscuits. Mix well until thoroughly coated in chocolate, crushing any large pieces of biscuit. Turn into the prepared tin and leave to cool, then cover and chill for 20 minutes.

3 Put the chocolate in a microwaveable bowl and melt it in a 900W microwave oven on full power for 1 minute 40 seconds, stirring twice. (Alternatively, put into a heatproof bowl set over a pan of gently simmering water, making sure the base of the bowl doesn't touch the water.) Stir once more and pour over the chocolate biscuit base, then chill for 20 minutes.

4 Cut in half lengthways. Cut each half into 20 rectangular slices.

Blackberry Traybake

Preparation Time
20 minutes
Cooking Time
about 45 minutes, plus cooling
and setting

- 275g (10oz) unsalted butter, softened, plus extra to grease
- 275g (10oz) golden caster sugar
- 400g (14oz) self-raising flour
- 1½ tsp baking powder
- 5 medium eggs, beaten
- finely grated zest of 1 large orange
- 1 tbsp vanilla extract
- 4–5 tbsp milk
- 250g (9oz) blackberries
- 40g (1½oz) flaked almonds

ICING
- 150g (5oz) icing sugar
- 1 tsp vanilla extract
- about 2 tbsp orange juice

NUTRITIONAL
INFORMATION
Per square 239 cals; 12g fat (of which 7g saturates); 32g carbohydrate; 0.4g salt

1 Preheat the oven to 190°C (170°C fan oven) mark 5. Grease a shallow 30.5 x 20.5cm (12 x 8 inch) baking tin and line with greaseproof paper.

2 Put the butter and caster sugar into a large bowl. Sift in the flour and baking powder, then add the eggs, orange zest and juice, vanilla extract and milk and beat together until light and fluffy.

3 Using a metal spoon, fold in half the blackberries. Spoon into the prepared tin and dot with the remaining blackberries, then the almonds.

4 Bake for 40–45 minutes until springy to the touch. Cool in the tin for 5 minutes, then turn out on to a wire rack and leave to cool completely.

5 When the cake is cool, make the icing. Sift the icing sugar into a bowl, then add the vanilla extract and orange juice, mixing as you go, until smooth and runny. Drizzle over the cake and leave for 30 minutes to set. Cut into 24 squares to serve.

Cuts into 24 squares

Carrot Traybake

Preparation Time
30 minutes
Cooking Time
50 minutes–1 hour 5 minutes, plus cooling

- 100g (3½oz) unsalted butter, chopped, plus extra to grease
- 140g (4½oz) carrots, peeled and grated
- 100g (3½oz) sultanas
- 100g (3½oz) dried dates, chopped
- 50g (2oz) tenderized coconut
- 1 tsp ground cinnamon
- ½ tsp freshly grated nutmeg
- 330g bottle maple syrup
- 150ml (¼ pint) apple juice
- zest and juice of 2 oranges
- 225g (8oz) wholemeal self-raising flour, sifted
- 2 tsp bicarbonate of soda
- 125g (4oz) walnut pieces

TOPPING

- pared zest from ½–1 orange
- 200g (7oz) cream cheese
- 200g (7oz) crème fraîche
- 2 tbsp icing sugar
- 1 tsp vanilla extract

NUTRITIONAL INFORMATION
Per square 399 cals; 25g fat (of which 13g saturates); 41g carbohydrate; 0.4g salt

Cuts into 15 squares

1 Grease a 23cm (9 inch) square cake tin and line with greaseproof paper.

2 Put the butter, carrots, sultanas, dates, coconut, spices, syrup, apple juice and orange zest and juice into a large pan. Cover and bring to the boil, then cook for 5 minutes. Tip into a bowl and leave to cool.

3 Preheat the oven to 190°C (170°C fan oven) mark 5. Put the flour, bicarbonate of soda and walnuts into a large bowl and stir together. Add the cooled carrot mixture and stir well. Spoon the mixture into the prepared tin and level the surface.

4 Bake for 45 minutes–1 hour until firm. Cool in the tin for 10 minutes, then turn out on to a wire rack and leave to cool completely.

5 To make the topping, finely slice the orange zest and put to one side. Put the cream cheese, crème fraîche, icing sugar and vanilla extract into a bowl and stir with a spatula. Spread over the cake and top with the zest. Cut into 15 squares to serve.

Chocolate Pecan Bars

Preparation Time
15 minutes
Cooking Time
1¼ hours, plus cooling

- 200g (7oz) unsalted butter, softened, plus extra to grease
- 125g (4oz) plain flour, sifted
- 25g (1oz) icing sugar
- 1 large egg yolk and 2 large eggs
- 125g (4oz) self-raising flour
- 1 tsp baking powder
- 125g (4oz) caster sugar
- 3–4 drops of vanilla extract
- 150g (5oz) milk chocolate chips
- 75g (3oz) pecan nuts, chopped
- 6 tbsp chocolate and hazelnut spread

NUTRITIONAL INFORMATION
Per bar 189 cals; 13g fat (of which 6g saturates); 18g carbohydrate; 0.2g salt

Makes 25

1 Preheat the oven to 200°C (180°C fan oven) mark 6. Grease a shallow 25.5 x 15cm (10 x 6 inch) baking tin and base-line with baking parchment.

2 Put the plain flour and icing sugar into a food processor with 75g (3oz) roughly chopped butter and whizz until crumb-like in texture. (Alternatively, rub the butter into the dry ingredients in a large bowl by hand or using a pastry cutter.) Add the egg yolk and whizz for 10–15 seconds, or add to the bowl with the dry ingredients and stir until the mixture begins to come together. Turn into the prepared tin and press into a thin layer. Bake for 15 minutes or until golden.

3 Meanwhile, put the self-raising flour, baking powder, caster sugar, vanilla extract and the

remaining eggs into the food processor with the remaining softened butter and blend for 15 seconds or until smooth (or put the ingredients into a bowl and mix well with a wooden spoon). Remove the blade and fold in the chocolate chips and pecan nuts. Set aside.

4 Spread the chocolate and hazelnut spread over the cooked base and top with the cake mixture. Lower the oven setting to 180°C (160°C fan oven) mark 4 and bake for 45–50 minutes until golden – cover the top of the cake with foil if it appears to be browning too quickly. Cool in the tin for about 10 minutes, then turn out on to a wire rack and leave to cool completely. Cut into 25 bars.

Traditional Flapjacks

Preparation Time
10 minutes
Cooking Time
about 20 minutes, plus cooling

- 200g (7oz) butter, plus extra to grease
- 150g (5oz) demerara sugar
- 4 tbsp golden syrup
- 1 tsp ground cinnamon
- finely grated zest of ½–1 orange
- 400g (14oz) jumbo oats
- 100g (3½oz) raisins or sultanas

NUTRITIONAL INFORMATION
Per flapjack 354 cals; 17g fat (of which 9g saturates); 50g carbohydrate; 0.4g salt

Makes 12

1 Preheat the oven to 190°C (170°C fan oven) mark 5. Grease a 20.5cm (8 inch) square baking tin and line with baking parchment.

2 Melt the butter in a large pan. Add the sugar, syrup, cinnamon and orange zest and heat gently until the sugar dissolves.

3 Remove the pan from the heat and stir in the oats and raisins or sultanas. Press the mixture into the tin and bake for 17–20 minutes until lightly golden. Leave to cool before cutting into 12 squares.

Hazelnut and Chocolate Flapjacks

Preparation Time
10 minutes
Cooking Time
30 minutes, plus cooling

- 125g (4oz) unsalted butter, plus extra to grease
- 125g (4oz) light muscovado sugar
- 1 tbsp golden syrup
- 50g (2oz) hazelnuts, roughly chopped
- 175g (6oz) jumbo or porridge oats
- 50g (2oz) plain chocolate, roughly chopped

NUTRITIONAL INFORMATION
Per flapjack 229 cals; 14g fat (of which 6g saturates); 26g carbohydrate; 0.2g salt

Makes 12

1 Preheat the oven to 180°C (160°C fan oven) mark 4. Lightly grease a shallow 28 x 18cm (11 x 7 inch) baking tin.

2 Put the butter, sugar and golden syrup in a pan and melt over a gentle heat. Stir in the hazelnuts and oats. Leave the mixture to cool slightly, then stir in the chocolate.

3 Spoon the mixture into the prepared tin and bake for about 30 minutes or until golden and firm.

4 Leave to cool in the tin for a few minutes, then cut into 12 pieces. Turn out on to a wire rack and leave to cool completely.

Sticky Ginger Flapjacks

Preparation Time
10 minutes
Cooking Time
40 minutes, plus cooling

- 350g (12oz) unsalted butter, plus extra to grease
- 275g (10oz) caster sugar
- 225g (8oz) golden syrup
- 450g (1lb) rolled oats
- 1 tbsp ground ginger

NUTRITIONAL INFORMATION
Per flapjack 259 cals; 14g fat (of which 8g saturates); 33g carbohydrate; 0.3g salt

Makes 24

1 Preheat the oven to 180°C (160°C fan oven) mark 4. Grease a shallow 28 x 18cm (11 x 7 inch) cake tin and base-line with non-stick baking parchment. Put the butter, sugar and golden syrup in a large pan and heat gently until melted. Mix in the rolled oats and ground ginger until they are thoroughly combined.

2 Put the mixture into the tin; level the surface. Bake for 30–35 minutes until golden brown at the edges.

3 Leave to cool in the tin for 15 minutes. While still warm, score into 24 pieces with a sharp knife. Leave in the tin to cool completely, then turn out and cut out the pieces.

Note
Don't overcook the flapjacks or they will be hard and dry. When they are cooked, they should still be sticky and slightly soft when you press them in the middle.

Vanilla Crumble Bars

Preparation Time
15 minutes
Cooking Time
50–60 minutes, plus cooling

- ◆ 250g (9oz) unsalted butter, softened, plus extra to grease
- ◆ 250g (9oz) caster sugar
- ◆ 125g (4oz) plain flour, sifted
- ◆ 175g (6oz) self-raising flour
- ◆ grated zest of 1 lemon
- ◆ 3 large eggs
- ◆ 1½ tsp vanilla extract

NUTRITIONAL INFORMATION
Per bar 295 cals; 10g fat (of which 5g saturates); 50g carbohydrate; 0.6g salt

Makes 25

1 Preheat the oven to 180°C (160°C fan oven) mark 4. Grease and line a shallow 25.5 x 18cm (10 x 7 inch) baking tin.

2 To make the crumble topping, put 75g (3oz) of the butter and 75g (3oz) of the sugar in a food processor and blend until smooth. Add the plain flour and blend for 8–10 seconds until the mixture forms very rough breadcrumbs, then put to one side.

3 Put the remaining butter and sugar, the self-raising flour, lemon zest, eggs and vanilla extract into the food processor and whizz for about 15 seconds or until smooth. Pour the mixture into the prepared tin, sprinkle the crumble topping over the surface and press down to cover.

4 Bake for 50–60 minutes, covering loosely with foil for the last 10 minutes if the mixture is browning too much. Leave in the tin for 5 minutes, then turn out on to a wire rack. Cut into 25 bars.

Makes 10

Apple Crumble Bars

Preparation Time
20 minutes, plus chilling
Cooking Time
about 45 minutes, plus cooling

- 200g (7oz) butter
- 125g (4oz) caster sugar
- 200g (7oz) plain flour
- a pinch of salt
- 3 dessert apples, peeled, cored and diced into 5mm (¼ inch) cubes
- 1 tsp ground cinnamon
- 2 tbsp lemon juice
- 1 tbsp cornflour
- 4 tbsp raspberry jam

TOPPING
- 50g (2oz) pecan nuts, roughly chopped
- 40g (1½oz) gingernut biscuits, crushed
- icing sugar to dust

NUTRITIONAL
INFORMATION
Per bar 355 cals; 21g fat (of which 11g saturates); 42g carbohydrate; 0.5g salt

1 Whizz 175g (6oz) butter in a food processor with 75g (3oz) caster sugar for 1 minute. Add the flour and salt and whizz until the mixture just comes together. Wrap the dough in clingfilm and chill for 30 minutes.

2 Preheat the oven to 190°C (170°C fan oven) mark 5 and line an 18cm (7 inch) square baking tin with baking parchment. Push the dough evenly into the bottom of the tin, then prick all over with a fork. Bake for 20–25 minutes until lightly golden, then take out of the oven.

3 Meanwhile, put the remaining butter and caster sugar into a pan with the apples and cinnamon and cook over a gentle heat for 5 minutes or until the apples are softening. In a small bowl, mix the lemon juice with the cornflour, then add this mixture to the apples. Continue to cook, stirring constantly, for 2–3 minutes until the sauce has thickened. Set aside.

4 Warm the jam in a small saucepan, then spread over the shortbread. Top with the apple mixture, then sprinkle the pecan nuts and crushed biscuits over the apples. Bake for 10 minutes, then leave to cool completely in the tin. When cold, dust with icing sugar and cut into 10 bars.

Note
For convenience, complete the recipe to the end of step 3 up to one day ahead. Transfer the apple mixture to a bowl and store, covered, in the fridge. Store the shortbread in a tin, covered, at room temperature. Complete the recipe to serve.

Snowy Rocky Road

Preparation Time
10 minutes, plus freezing
Cooking Time
about 1–2 minutes

- 400g (14oz) white chocolate, chopped
- 25g (1oz) mini marshmallows
- 50g (2oz) desiccated coconut, plus extra to scatter
- 50g (2oz) dried cranberries
- 40g (1½oz) pistachios
- 50g (2oz) ginger nut biscuits, roughly chopped
- silver balls to decorate (optional)

NUTRITIONAL
INFORMATION
Per square 155 cals; 9g fat (of which 5g saturates); 17g carbohydrate; 0.1g salt

Makes 20

1 Line a rectangular tin, about 15 x 20.5cm (6 x 8 inches), with clingfilm. Put the chocolate into a heatproof bowl and microwave on full power for 1 minute. Stir, then return to the microwave for 10-second bursts until melted and smooth. (Don't be tempted to give it longer blasts – white chocolate burns easily.) Alternatively, put the chocolate into a heatproof bowl set over a pan of gently simmering water, making sure that the bottom of the bowl doesn't touch the water, to melt it.

2 Stir in the marshmallows, coconut, cranberries, pistachios and biscuits, then empty into the prepared tin and level the surface.

3 Scatter with the extra coconut and the silver balls, if using, then freeze for 15 minutes until solid. Cut into squares and serve.

White Chocolate and Nut Brownies

Preparation Time
20 minutes
Cooking Time
30–35 minutes, plus cooling

- 75g (3oz) unsalted butter, plus extra to grease
- 500g (1lb 2oz) white chocolate, roughly chopped
- 3 large eggs
- 175g (6oz) golden caster sugar
- 175g (6oz) self-raising flour
- a pinch of salt
- 175g (6oz) macadamia nuts, roughly chopped
- 1 tsp vanilla extract

NUTRITIONAL INFORMATION
Per brownie 502 cals; 31g fat (of which 13g saturates); 52g carbohydrate; 0.4g salt

Makes 12

1 Preheat the oven to 190°C (170°C fan oven) mark 5. Grease a 25.5 x 20.5cm (10 x 8 inch) baking tin and base-line with baking parchment.

2 Melt 125g (4oz) white chocolate with the butter in a heatproof bowl set over a pan of gently simmering water, making sure the base of the bowl doesn't touch the water, stirring occasionally. Remove the bowl from the pan and leave to cool slightly.

3 Whisk the eggs and sugar together in a large bowl until smooth, then gradually beat in the melted chocolate mixture – the consistency will become quite firm. Sift the flour and salt into the mixture, then fold in with the nuts, the remaining chopped chocolate and the vanilla extract. Turn the mixture into the prepared tin and level the surface.

4 Bake for 30–35 minutes until risen and golden and the centre is just firm to the touch – the mixture will still be soft under the crust; it firms up on cooling. Leave to cool in the tin.

5 Turn out and cut into 12 individual brownies.

Makes 16

Low-fat Brownies

Preparation Time
10 minutes
Cooking Time
20 minutes, plus cooling

- 50ml (2fl oz) sunflower oil, plus extra to grease
- 250g (9oz) plain chocolate (at least 50% cocoa solids)
- 4 medium eggs
- 150g (5oz) light muscovado sugar
- 1 tsp vanilla extract
- 75g (3oz) plain flour
- ¼ tsp baking powder
- 1 tbsp cocoa powder

NUTRITIONAL INFORMATION
Per brownie 172 cals; 8g fat (of which 3g saturates); 24g carbohydrate; 0.1g salt

1 Preheat the oven to 200°C (180°C fan oven) mark 6. Grease and line a shallow 20.5cm (8 inch) square tin.

2 Melt the chocolate in a heatproof bowl set over a pan of gently simmering water, making sure the base of the bowl doesn't touch the water. Remove the bowl from the pan and put to one side to cool slightly.

3 Put the eggs into a large bowl, add the sunflower oil, sugar and vanilla extract and whisk together until pale and thick. Sift the flour, baking powder and cocoa powder into the bowl, then carefully pour in the chocolate. Using a large metal spoon, gently fold in all the ingredients – if you fold too roughly, the chocolate will seize up and become unworkable.

4 Carefully pour the brownie mixture into the prepared tin and bake for 20 minutes – when cooked, each brownies should still be fudgy in the centre and the top should be cracked and crispy. Cut the slab into 16 squares immediately, then leave to cool in the tin.

Raspberry and Cream Cheese Chocolate Brownies

Preparation Time
20 minutes
Cooking Time
about 35 minutes, plus cooling

- 200g (7oz) unsalted butter, plus extra to grease
- 150g (5oz) each dark chocolate and plain chocolate (at least 70% cocoa solids), chopped
- 4 medium eggs
- 150g (5oz) light muscovado sugar
- 125g (4oz) plus 1 tbsp self-raising flour, sifted
- 125g (4oz) curd cheese or cream cheese
- 2 tbsp raspberry jam
- crème fraîche to serve

NUTRITIONAL INFORMATION
Per brownie 465 cals; 32g fat (of which 20g saturates); 41g carbohydrate; 0.7g salt

1 Preheat the oven to 200°C (180°C fan oven) mark 6. Grease a 23cm (9 inch) square tin and line with greaseproof paper. Put both chocolates and the butter into a heatproof bowl set over a pan of gently simmering water and stir to combine. When they have melted, take off the heat and set aside to cool.

2 Put 3 of the eggs and all but 1 tsp sugar into a bowl and, using a hand-held electric whisk, whisk together until thick and mousse-like. Fold in the cooled chocolate mixture and all but 1 tbsp flour, then pour into the prepared tin.

3 Put the cheese into a bowl with the remaining egg and the reserved 1 tsp sugar and 1 tbsp flour. Mix well to combine.

4 Place dollops of the cheese mixture randomly over the surface, then top each with a teaspoonful of the raspberry jam. Use a skewer to marble the cheese, jam and brownie mixture together.

5 Bake for 25–30 minutes. Remove from the oven and cool in the tin for 10 minutes, then turn out on to a wire rack and leave to cool completely. Cut the slab into nine individual brownies and serve with a dollop of crème fraîche.

Makes 9

Macaroons

Preparation Time
10 minutes
Cooking Time
12–15 minutes, plus cooling

- 2 medium egg whites
- 125g (4oz) caster sugar
- 125g (4oz) ground almonds
- ¼ tsp almond extract
- 22 blanched almonds

NUTRITIONAL INFORMATION
Per macaroon 73 cals; 3g fat (of which trace saturates); 10g carbohydrate; 0g salt

Makes 22

1 Preheat the oven to 180°C (160°C fan oven) mark 4 and line two baking sheets with baking parchment. Put the egg whites in a large, grease-free bowl and, using a hand-held electric whisk, whisk until they form stiff peaks. Gradually fold in the sugar, then gently stir in the almonds and almond extract.

2 Spoon teaspoonfuls of the mixture on to the baking sheets, spacing them slightly apart. Press an almond into each and bake for 12–15 minutes until just golden and firm to the touch.

3 Leave on the baking sheets for 10 minutes, then transfer to a wire rack to cool completely.

Variation
Coffee Macaroons: Replace 15g (½oz) of the ground almonds with espresso powder and mix together before stirring into the egg mixture.

Chilled Chocolate Biscuit Cake

Preparation Time
15 minutes, plus 2 hours' chilling
Cooking Time
5 minutes

- 125g (4oz) unsalted butter, chopped, plus extra to grease
- 150g (5oz) plain chocolate, broken into pieces
- 250g (9oz) panforte, chopped
- 100g (3½ oz) Rich Tea biscuits, chopped
- 2–3 tbsp Amaretto, rum or brandy
- ice cream to serve (optional)

NUTRITIONAL INFORMATION
Per wedge 157 cals; 9g fat (of which 5g saturates); 17g carbohydrate; 0.3g salt

Makes 21

1 Grease an 18cm (7 inch) square cake tin and base-line with baking parchment. Put the butter and chocolate in a heatproof bowl set over a pan of gently simmering water. Stir until melted, then set aside.

2 In a large bowl, mix the panforte, biscuits and liqueur, rum or brandy. Add the melted chocolate mixture and stir to coat.

3 Pour the mixture into the cake tin and chill for at least 2 hours. Cut into wedges and serve with ice cream, if you like.

Note
Panforte is a flat Italian cake, a mixture of dried fruit and nuts bound with honey and baked on rice paper. It is a Christmas speciality, so look for it in Italian delicatessens and large supermarkets from November to January.

Makes about 25

The Ultimate Chocolate Chip Cookie

Preparation Time
15 minutes
Cooking Time
about 12 minutes, plus cooling

◆ 225g (8oz) unsalted butter, very soft
◆ 125g (4oz) caster sugar
◆ 150g (5oz) light muscovado sugar
◆ 1½ tbsp golden syrup
◆ 1 tsp vanilla extract
◆ 2 large eggs, beaten
◆ 375g (13oz) plain flour
◆ 1 tsp bicarbonate of soda
◆ ¼ tsp salt
◆ 350g (12oz) milk chocolate, cut into large chunks

NUTRITIONAL INFORMATION
Per cookie 223 cals; 11g fat (of which 7g saturates); 28g carbohydrate;0.9g salt

1 Preheat the oven to 200°C (180°C fan oven) mark 6. Line three baking sheets with baking parchment.

2 Put the butter, caster and muscovado sugars, golden syrup and vanilla extract into a bowl and, using a hand-held electric whisk or freestanding mixer, beat until pale and fluffy – this should take about 5 minutes.

3 Gradually beat in the eggs, adding 2 tbsp flour if the mixture looks as if it's about to curdle. Sift in the remaining flour, the bicarbonate of soda and salt all at once and beat quickly for a few seconds. Using a large metal spoon, mix in the milk chocolate chunks.

4 Spoon heaped teaspoonfuls of the mixture on to the prepared baking sheets, spacing them well apart. Don't press the mixture down – the mounds will spread during baking. For a chewy biscuit, bake for 10 minutes until pale and golden; for a crisper version, bake for 12 minutes. Transfer the cookies to wire racks and leave to cool.

Ginger Biscuits

Preparation Time
15 minutes
Cooking Time
about 12 minutes, plus cooling

- 50g (2oz) butter, plus extra to grease
- 125g (4oz) golden syrup
- 50g (2oz) dark muscovado sugar
- finely grated zest of 1 orange
- 2 tbsp orange juice
- 175g (6oz) self-raising flour
- 1 tsp ground ginger

NUTRITIONAL
INFORMATION
Per biscuit 55 cals; 2g fat (of which 1g saturates); 10g

1 Preheat the oven to 180°C (160°C fan oven) mark 4. Lightly grease two large baking sheets.

2 Put the butter, golden syrup, sugar, orange zest and juice into a heavy-based pan and heat very gently until melted and evenly blended.

3 Leave the mixture to cool slightly, then sift in the flour with the ginger. Mix thoroughly until smooth. Put small spoonfuls of the mixture on the prepared baking sheets, spacing them well apart to allow room for spreading.

4 Bake for 12 minutes or until the biscuits are golden brown. Leave on the baking sheets for 1 minute, then carefully transfer to a wire rack and leave to cool.

Makes 24

Sultana and Pecan Cookies

Preparation Time
15 minutes
Cooking Time
12–15 minutes, plus cooling

- 225g (8oz) unsalted butter, at room temperature, plus extra to grease
- 175g (6oz) light muscovado sugar
- 2 medium eggs, lightly beaten
- 225g (8oz) pecan nut halves
- 300g (11oz) self-raising flour, sifted
- ¼ tsp baking powder
- 125g (4oz) sultanas
- 2 tbsp maple syrup

NUTRITIONAL INFORMATION
Per cookie 276 cals; 18g fat (of which 7g saturates); 27g carbohydrate; 0.2g salt

Makes 20

1 Preheat the oven to 190°C (170°C fan oven) mark 5. Lightly grease four baking sheets.

2 Cream the butter and sugar together until the mixture is pale and fluffy. Gradually beat in the eggs until thoroughly combined.

3 Put 20 pecan nut halves to one side, then roughly chop the rest and fold into the mixture with the flour, baking powder, sultanas and syrup.

4 Roll the mixture into 20 balls and place them, spaced well apart, on the prepared baking sheets. Using a dampened palette knife, flatten the cookies and top each with a piece of pecan nut.

5 Bake for 12–15 minutes until pale golden. Leave on the baking sheets for 5 minutes, then transfer to a wire rack and leave to cool completely.

Almond Cookies

Preparation Time
15 minutes
Cooking Time
15–20 minutes, plus cooling

- rice paper to line
- 2 medium egg whites
- 200g (7oz) caster sugar
- 200g (7oz) ground almonds
- finely grated zest of 1 orange
- ½ tsp ground ginger
- 40g (1½oz) stem ginger in syrup, drained and roughly chopped
- 2 tbsp plain flour, sifted, to dust
- 12 natural glacé cherries

NUTRITIONAL INFORMATION
Per cookie 204 cals; 10g fat (of which 1g saturates); 27g carbohydrate; 0g salt

Makes 12

1 Preheat the oven to 180°C (160°C fan oven) mark 4. Line two baking sheets with rice paper. Put the egg whites into a large, grease-free bowl and, using a hand-held electric whisk, whisk until they form stiff peaks. In another large bowl, stir together the sugar, ground almonds, orange zest, ¼ tsp ground ginger and the stem ginger. With a wooden spoon, mix in the egg whites to form a sticky dough.

2 Roll the dough into 12 equal-sized balls. Mix together the flour and the remaining ground ginger in a bowl. Lightly coat each ball in the flour and shake off the excess. Put the balls, spaced well apart, on the prepared baking sheets. Flatten each one into a round and push a glacé cherry into the middle.

3 Bake for 15–20 minutes until lightly golden. Cool on a wire rack, then trim away the excess rice paper.

Makes 18

Florentines

Preparation Time
15 minutes
Cooking Time
16–20 minutes, plus cooling and
setting

- 65g (2½oz) unsalted butter,
  plus extra to grease
- 50g (2oz) golden caster sugar
- 2 tbsp double cream
- 25g (1oz) sunflower seeds
- 20g (¾oz) chopped mixed
  candied peel
- 20g (¾oz) sultanas
- 25g (1oz) natural glacé
  cherries, roughly chopped
- 40g (1½oz) flaked almonds,
  lightly crushed
- 15g (½oz) plain flour
- 125g (4oz) plain chocolate (at
  least 70% cocoa solids),
  broken into pieces

**NUTRITIONAL
INFORMATION**
Per florentine 115 cals; 8g fat (of
which 4g saturates); 11g
carbohydrate; 0.1g salt

1 Preheat the oven to 180°C (160°C fan oven) mark 4. Lightly grease two large baking sheets.

2 Melt the butter in a small, heavy-based pan. Add the sugar and heat gently until dissolved, then bring to the boil. Take off the heat and stir in the cream, seeds, peel, sultanas, cherries, almonds and flour. Mix until evenly combined. Put heaped teaspoonfuls on the prepared baking sheets, spaced well apart to allow for spreading.

3 Bake one sheet at a time, for 6–8 minutes, until the biscuits have spread considerably and the edges are golden brown. Using a large, plain, metal biscuit cutter, push the edges into the centre to create neat rounds. Bake for a further 2 minutes or until deep golden. Leave on the baking sheet for 2 minutes, then transfer to a wire rack and leave to cool completely.

4 Melt the chocolate in a heatproof bowl set over a pan of gently simmering water, making sure the base of the bowl doesn't touch the water, stirring occasionally. Spread on the underside of each florentine and mark wavy lines with a fork. Put, chocolate-side up, on a sheet of baking parchment and leave to set.

Christmas Cookies

Preparation Time
25 minutes, plus chilling
Cooking Time
about 15 minutes, plus cooling

- 75g (3oz) unsalted butter, softened
- 100g (3½oz) caster sugar
- 1 medium egg
- ½ tsp vanilla extract
- 250g (9oz) plain flour, plus extra to dust
- ½ tsp baking powder
- a selection of coloured ready-to-roll fondant icings, royal icing, food colourings and edible decorations

NUTRITIONAL
INFORMATION
Per cookie 94 cals; 3g fat (of which 2g saturates); 16.5g carbohydrate; 0.1g salt

1 Using a wooden spoon, cream the butter and sugar together in a large bowl until smooth. Beat in the egg and vanilla extract. Sift the flour and baking powder into the bowl and stir until combined. Turn out on to a lightly floured surface and knead gently to make a soft dough. Shape into a disc and wrap in clingfilm, then chill for 1 hour until firm.

2 Preheat the oven to 180°C (160°C fan oven) mark 4. Roll out the dough on a lightly floured surface until 5mm (¼ inch) thick. Using Christmas cookie cutters, stamp out shapes, re-rolling the trimmings if necessary. If the cookies are to be hung as decorations, use a skewer to make a 5mm (¼ inch) hole in each one. Place on two non-stick baking trays and bake for 10–15 minutes until pale golden and risen. Leave to cool on the sheets for 3 minutes to harden, then transfer to a wire rack to cool completely.

3 When the cookies are completely cool, decorate with different coloured fondant icings or royal icing and edible decorations.

Makes about 22

White and Dark Chocolate Cookies

Preparation Time
15 minutes, plus 30 minutes'
chilling
Cooking Time
10–12 minutes, plus cooling

- 125g (4oz) unsalted butter, softened, plus extra to grease
- 125g (4oz) golden caster sugar
- 2 medium eggs, beaten
- 2 tsp vanilla extract
- 250g (9oz) self-raising flour, sifted
- finely grated zest of 1 orange
- 100g (3½oz) white chocolate, roughly chopped
- 100g (3½oz) plain chocolate (at least 70% cocoa solids), roughly chopped

NUTRITIONAL INFORMATION
Per cookie 133 cals; 7g fat (of which 4g saturates); 17g carbohydrate; 0.1g salt

Makes 26

1 Preheat the oven to 180°C (160°C fan oven) mark 4 and grease three baking sheets.

2 Cream together the butter and sugar until the mixture is pale and fluffy. Gradually beat in the eggs and vanilla extract. Sift in the flour and add the orange zest, then sprinkle in the white and dark chocolate. Mix the dough together with your hands, then knead lightly. Wrap in clingfilm and chill the cookie mixture for at least 30 minutes.

3 Divide the mixture into 26 pieces and roll each into a ball. Flatten each ball slightly to make a disc, then put on the prepared baking sheets, spaced well apart. Bake for about 10–12 minutes until golden.

4 Leave on the baking sheet for 5 minutes, then transfer to a wire rack to cool completely.

Peanut and Raisin Cookies

Preparation Time
10 minutes
Cooking Time
15 minutes, plus cooling

- 125g (4oz) unsalted butter, softened, plus extra to grease
- 150g (5oz) caster sugar
- 1 medium egg
- 150g (5oz) plain flour, sifted
- ½ tsp baking powder
- ½ tsp salt
- 125g (4oz) crunchy peanut butter
- 175g (6oz) raisins

NUTRITIONAL INFORMATION
Per cookie 111 cals; 6g fat (of which 3g saturates); 14g carbohydrate; 0.2g salt

Makes 30

1 Preheat the oven to 190°C (170°C fan oven) mark 5 and grease two baking sheets.

2 Beat together all the ingredients except the raisins, until well blended. Stir in the raisins. Spoon large teaspoonfuls of the mixture on to the prepared baking sheets, leaving room for the mixture to spread. Bake for about 15 minutes or until golden brown around the edges.

3 Leave to cool slightly, then transfer to a wire rack to cool completely.

Cherry Chip Cookies

Preparation Time
20 minutes
Cooking Time
10–12 minutes, plus cooling

- 75g (3oz) unsalted butter, softened, plus extra to grease
- 25g (1oz) caster sugar
- 50g (2oz) light soft brown sugar
- a few drops of vanilla extract
- 1 large egg, lightly beaten
- 175g (6oz) self-raising flour, sifted
- finely grated zest of 1 orange
- 125g (4oz) white chocolate, roughly broken
- 125g (4oz) glacé cherries, roughly chopped
- icing sugar to dust

NUTRITIONAL INFORMATION
Per cookie 179 cals; 8g fat (of which 5g saturates); 27g carbohydrate; 0.1g salt

Makes 14

1 Preheat the oven to 180°C (160°C fan oven) mark 4 and grease two baking sheets.

2 Using a hand-held electric whisk, beat together the butter, caster sugar, light soft brown sugar and vanilla extract until well combined. Gradually beat in the egg until the mixture is light and fluffy.

3 Using a metal spoon, lightly fold in the flour, orange zest, white chocolate pieces and glacé cherries. Put tablespoonfuls of the cookie mixture on the prepared baking sheets and bake for 10–12 minutes. The cherry chip cookies should have a crisp crust but remain soft underneath this.

4 Leave the cookies on the baking sheet for 1 minute, then transfer to a wire rack to cool completely. Dust with icing sugar just before serving.

Orange Tuile Biscuits

Preparation Time
10 minutes, plus chilling
Cooking Time
12 minutes per batch, plus
cooling

- 3 large egg whites
- 100g (3½oz) icing sugar, sifted
- 100g (3½oz) plain flour
- finely grated zest of 1 orange
- 75g (3oz) unsalted butter, melted

NUTRITIONAL INFORMATION
Per biscuit 55 cals; 3g fat (of which 2g saturates); 8g carbohydrate; 0.1g salt

Makes 24

1 Put the egg whites into a large, grease-free bowl, add the sugar and whisk lightly. Stir in the flour, orange zest and melted butter, then cover and chill for 30 minutes.

2 Preheat the oven to 200°C (180°C fan oven) mark 6. Line a baking sheet with baking parchment.

3 Put 3 teaspoonfuls of the mixture, spaced well apart, on the prepared baking sheet and spread out into 9cm (3½ inch) circles.

4 Bake for 12 minutes or until just brown around the edges. Remove from the oven and, while still warm, shape each biscuit over a rolling pin to curl. Repeat with the remaining mixture. Leave on a wire rack to cool completely.

Amaretti Biscuits

Preparation Time
5 minutes
Cooking Time
20 minutes, plus cooling

- 125g (4oz) ground almonds
- 15g (½oz) ground rice
- 225g (8oz) caster sugar
- 2 medium egg whites
- ½ tsp almond flavouring
- about 24 split almonds

**NUTRITIONAL
INFORMATION**
per biscuit 79 calories; 4g fat (of
which 0.3g saturates); 11g
carbohydrate; 0.1g salt

Makes about 24

1 Preheat the oven to 180°C (160°C fan oven) mark 4. Line two baking sheets with rice paper.

2 Mix together the ground almonds, ground rice and sugar. Add the egg whites and almond flavouring and beat together until smooth.

3 Insert a 1cm (½ inch) plain nozzle into a piping bag, then fill the bag with the mixture. Pipe small rounds about 2.5cm (1 inch) in diameter on the paper, leaving plenty of room for spreading. Top each biscuit with a split almond.

4 Bake in the oven for about 20 minutes until pale golden brown. Transfer to a wire rack and leave to cool. Remove the rice paper from around each amaretti before serving.

Cranberry Biscuits

Preparation Time
15 minutes, plus 30 minutes'
chilling
Cooking Time
8–10 minutes, plus cooling

- 125g (4oz) unsalted butter,
  chilled
- 50g (2oz) caster sugar
- 25g (1oz) dried cranberries
- 125g (4oz) plain flour, sifted,
  plus extra to dust
- 75g (3oz) ground rice

**NUTRITIONAL
INFORMATION**
Per biscuit 79 cals; 4g fat (of
which 3g saturates); 10g
carbohydrate; 0.1g salt

Makes 24

1 Whizz the butter and sugar in a food processor, or use a hand-held electric mixer. Add the cranberries, flour and ground rice and pulse or beat until the mixture comes together. Turn out on to a lightly floured surface and shape into a rectangle about 12.5 x 7.5 x 2cm (5 x 3 x ¾ inches). Wrap and chill for 30 minutes.

2 Preheat the oven to 200°C (180°C fan oven) mark 6. Cut the dough into 3mm (⅛ inch) slices and put on a non-stick baking sheet. Bake for 8–10 minutes until the biscuits are golden.

3 Leave to cool on the baking sheet.

Variations
Use dried cherries or dried blueberries instead of the cranberries.
Lemon and Poppy Seed Biscuits: Omit the cranberries and add 1 tbsp poppy seeds and the finely grated zest of 1 lemon.

Double-chocolate Brownies

Preparation Time
15 minutes
Cooking Time
20–25 minutes, plus cooling

- 250g (9oz) unsalted butter, plus extra to grease
- 250g (9oz) plain chocolate (at least 50% cocoa solids), broken into pieces
- 100g (3½oz) white chocolate, broken into pieces
- 4 medium eggs
- 175g (6oz) light muscovado sugar
- 1 tsp vanilla extract
- 75g (3oz) plain flour, sifted
- ¼ tsp baking powder
- 1 tbsp cocoa powder, sifted, plus extra to dust
- 100g (3½oz) pecan nuts, chopped
- a pinch of salt
- a little icing sugar to dust

NUTRITIONAL
INFORMATION
Per brownie 352 cals; 25g fat (of which 13g saturates); 29g carbohydrate; 0.3g salt

Makes 16

1 Preheat the oven to 200°C (180°C fan oven) mark 6. Grease a shallow 20.5cm (8 inch) square tin and base-line with baking parchment. Melt the butter and plain chocolate in a heatproof bowl set over a pan of gently simmering water, making sure the base of the bowl doesn't touch the water. Remove the bowl from the pan and put to one side.

2 In a separate bowl, melt the white chocolate in the same way. Remove the bowl from the pan and put to one side.

3 Put the eggs into a separate large bowl. Add the muscovado sugar and vanilla extract and whisk until the mixture is pale and thick. Add the flour, baking powder, cocoa powder, nuts and salt to the bowl, then pour in the dark chocolate mixture. Using a large

metal spoon, gently fold the ingredients together to make a smooth batter – if you fold too roughly, the chocolate will seize up and become unworkable.

4 Pour the brownie mixture into the prepared tin. Spoon dollops of the white chocolate over the top, then swirl a skewer through it several times to create a marbled effect. Bake for 20–25 minutes: when cooked, each brownie should be fudgy inside and the top should be cracked and crispy. Leave to cool in the tin.

5 Transfer the slab to a board and cut into 16 individual brownies. To serve, dust with a little icing sugar and cocoa powder, if you like.

Spiced Star Biscuits

Preparation Time
5 minutes, plus 4 hours' chilling
Cooking Time
15–20 minutes, plus cooling

- 2 tbsp runny honey
- 25g (1oz) unsalted butter
- 50g (2oz) light muscovado sugar
- finely grated zest of ½ lemon
- finely grated zest of ½ orange
- 225g (8oz) self-raising flour,
  plus extra to dust
- 1 tsp ground cinnamon
- 1 tsp ground ginger
- ½ tsp freshly grated nutmeg
- a pinch of ground cloves
- a pinch of salt
- 1 tbsp finely chopped candied peel
- 50g (2oz) ground almonds
- 1 large egg, beaten
- 1½ tbsp milk

DECORATION
- 150g (5oz) icing sugar
- silver sugar balls

**NUTRITIONAL
INFORMATION**
Per biscuit 51 cals; 2g fat (of
which 1g saturates); 8g
carbohydrate; 0g salt

Makes 35

1 Put the honey, butter, muscovado sugar and citrus zests into a small pan and stir over a low heat until the butter has melted and the ingredients are well combined.

2 Sift the flour, spices and salt into a bowl, then add the chopped candied peel and ground almonds. Add the melted mixture, beaten egg and milk and mix until the dough comes together. Knead the dough briefly until smooth, then wrap in clingfilm and chill for at least 4 hours, or overnight.

3 Preheat the oven to 180°C (160°C fan oven) mark 4. Roll out the dough on a lightly floured surface to 5mm (¼ inch) thick. Using a 5cm (2 inch) cutter, stamp out stars and put on to baking sheets.

4 Bake for 15–20 minutes or until just beginning to brown at the edges. Transfer the biscuits to a wire rack to cool.

5 To decorate, mix the icing sugar with 1½ tbsp warm water to make a smooth icing. Coat some of the biscuits with icing and finish with a piped edging if you like, then decorate with silver balls. Pipe dots of icing on the plain biscuits and attach silver balls. Allow the icing to set.

Choc and Nut Biscotti

Preparation Time
20 minutes
Cooking Time
about 40 minutes

- 225g (8oz) plain flour, plus extra to dust
- 1 tsp baking powder
- 175g (6oz) caster sugar
- 2 medium eggs, beaten
- 75g (3oz) each whole hazelnuts and pistachios
- 75g (3oz) milk chocolate, chopped into small chunks

NUTRITIONAL INFORMATION
Per biscuit 74 cals; 3g fat (of which 1g saturates); 10g carbohydrate; 0.1g salt

Makes about 40

1 Preheat the oven to 180°C (160°C fan oven) mark 4. Line a large baking sheet with baking parchment. Mix the flour, baking powder and sugar in a large bowl. Add the eggs and stir until clumps form, then bring together with your hands, kneading until smooth. Add the nuts and chocolate and knead until evenly distributed (the dough will be stiff and a bit sticky). Divide the dough in half.

2 Roll out each half of the dough on a lightly floured surface into a rough 33cm (13 inch) sausage shape. Place on the prepared baking sheet, spacing them apart. Bake for 20–25 minutes until the dough is lightly golden and has spread, then transfer to a wire rack and leave to cool for 10 minutes. Lower the oven setting to 140°C (120°C fan oven) mark 1.

3 Using a bread knife, cut the rolls diagonally into slices 1cm (½ inch) thick. Lay them flat on a baking sheet and bake for 15 minutes or until dry and lightly golden – they'll harden on cooling.

4 Cool completely on a wire rack.

Chocolate and Pistachio Biscotti

Preparation Time
15 minutes
Cooking Time
about 1 hour, plus cooling

- 300g (11oz) plain flour, sifted
- 75g (3oz) cocoa powder, sifted
- 1 tsp baking powder
- 150g (5oz) plain chocolate chips
- 150g (5oz) shelled pistachio nuts
- a pinch of salt
- 75g (3oz) unsalted butter, softened
- 225g (8oz) granulated sugar
- 2 large eggs, beaten
- 1 tbsp icing sugar

NUTRITIONAL INFORMATION
Per biscuit 152 cals; 7g fat (of which 3g saturates); 20g carbohydrate; 0.2g salt

Makes 30

1 Preheat the oven to 180°C (160°C fan oven) mark 4 and line a large baking sheet with baking parchment.

2 Mix together the flour, cocoa powder, baking powder, chocolate chips, pistachio nuts and salt.

3 Using a hand-held electric whisk, beat together the butter and granulated sugar until light and fluffy. Gradually whisk in the beaten eggs.

4 Stir the dry ingredients into the mixture until it forms a stiff dough. With floured hands, shape the dough into two slightly flattened logs, each about 30.5 x 5cm (12 x 2 inches). Sprinkle with icing sugar. Put the logs on the prepared baking sheet and bake for 40–45 minutes until they are slightly firm to the touch.

5 Leave the logs on the baking sheet for 10 minutes, then cut diagonally into slices 2cm (¾ inch) thick. Arrange the slices, cut-side down, on the baking sheet and bake again for 15 minutes or until crisp. Cool the biscotti on a wire rack.

Makes about 25

Iced Easter Biscuits

Preparation Time
25 minutes, plus chilling, cooling and setting
Cooking Time
about 12 minutes

- 75g (3oz) unsalted butter, softened, plus extra to grease
- 100g (3½oz) caster sugar
- 40g (1½oz) condensed milk
- 1 medium egg
- finely grated zest of ½ orange or ½ lemon
- ½ tsp baking powder
- 200g (7oz) plain flour, plus extra to dust
- a pinch of salt

ICING
- icing sugar
- food colouring pastes

NUTRITIONAL INFORMATION
Per biscuit 94 cals; 3g fat (of which 2g saturates); 17g carbohydrate; 0.1g salt

1 Put the butter, caster sugar and condensed milk into a large bowl and mix with a wooden spoon until pale and fluffy. Next, beat in the egg and zest, followed by the baking powder, flour and salt, then bring together with your hands. Wrap in clingfilm and chill for 30 minutes.

2 Lightly grease two large baking sheets with butter. Roll out the dough on a lightly floured surface to 5mm (¼ inch) thick. Stamp out Easter shapes, re-rolling the trimmings as you go.

3 Arrange the biscuits on the prepared baking sheets. If you later want to thread a ribbon through the top of each biscuit, make a 5mm (¼ inch) hole in each with a skewer. Chill for 15 minutes.

4 Preheat the oven to 180°C (160°C fan oven) mark 4. Bake the biscuits for 10–12 minutes until lightly golden. Loosen with a palette knife, then transfer to a wire rack to cool completely.

5 To make the icing, sift the icing sugar into a bowl and add just enough water to make a thick, spreadable icing. Divide the icing and colour as needed. Pipe or spread over the biscuits and leave to set. If you like, thread ribbons through the biscuits and hang up.

Chocolate Fudge Shortbread

Preparation Time
30 minutes
Cooking Time
20 minutes, plus cooling and
setting

- 175g (6oz) unsalted butter, at room temperature, diced, plus extra to grease
- 250g (9oz) plain flour, plus extra to dust
- 75g (3oz) golden caster sugar

TOPPING

- 2 x 397g cans sweetened condensed milk
- 100g (3½oz) light muscovado sugar
- 100g (3½oz) butter
- 250g (9oz) plain chocolate (at least 70% cocoa solids), broken into pieces

NUTRITIONAL
INFORMATION
Per shortbread 369 cals; 19g fat
(of which 12g saturates); 48g
carbohydrate; 0.4g salt

Makes 20

1 Preheat the oven to 180°C (160°C fan oven) mark 4. Grease a 33 x 23cm (13 x 9 inch) Swiss roll tin and line with baking parchment.

2 Put the flour, caster sugar and butter into a food processor and blend until the mixture forms crumbs, then pulse a little more until it forms a ball. Lightly dust the worktop with flour, then turn out the dough and knead lightly to combine. Press the mixture into the prepared tin.

3 Bake for 20 minutes or until firm to the touch and a very pale brown.

4 To make the topping, put the condensed milk, muscovado sugar and butter into a non-stick pan and cook over a medium heat, stirring continuously until a fudge-like consistency. (Alternatively, melt in a heatproof bowl in a 900W microwave oven on full power for 12 minutes or until the mixture is thick and fudgy, beating with a whisk every 2–3 minutes.) Spoon the caramel on to the shortbread, smooth over and leave to cool.

5 To finish, melt the chocolate in a heatproof bowl set over a pan of gently simmering water, making sure the base of the bowl doesn't touch the water, then pour over the caramel layer. Leave to set at room temperature, then cut into 20 squares to serve.

Nutty Fudge Shortbread

Preparation Time
40 minutes, plus 3 hours' chilling
Cooking Time
40 minutes, plus cooling

- 225g (8oz) unsalted butter, softened, plus extra to grease
- 300g (11oz) plain flour, sifted
- a pinch of salt
- 125g (4oz) caster sugar
- 125g (4oz) light muscovado sugar, sifted
- 2 tbsp golden syrup
- 170g can condensed milk
- 300g (11oz) plain chocolate
- 100g (3½oz) walnut halves
- 100g (3½oz) hazelnuts, lightly toasted

NUTRITIONAL INFORMATION
Per shortbread 450 cals; 26g fat (of which 12g saturates); 51g carbohydrate; 0.3g salt

Makes 16

1 Preheat the oven to 180°C (160°C fan oven) mark 4. Grease a 20.5 x 30.5cm (8 x 12 inch) Swiss roll tin.

2 Whizz the flour, salt, caster sugar and 150g (5oz) butter in a food processor until it begins to come together. (Alternatively, use a food mixer.) Press the mixture into the prepared tin and smooth over with the back of a spoon. Bake for 20–30 minutes until golden. Leave to cool in the tin.

3 Put the remaining butter, the muscovado sugar, golden syrup and condensed milk into a pan and heat gently but don't boil. Whisk together until combined. Pour over the shortbread, smooth the surface, cool, then chill for 3 hours.

4 Melt the chocolate in a heatproof bowl set over a pan of gently simmering water, making sure the base of the bowl doesn't touch the water. Stir in the nuts, then pour over the fudge mixture. Smooth the top and leave to set. Cut into 16 pieces to serve.

Variation
Vanilla Shortbread Fingers: Complete step 1, adding the seeds from 1 vanilla pod to the processor or mixer. Once baked, while warm from the oven, mark the shortbread into 24 fingers, sprinkle with caster sugar and cut when cool.

Shortbread

Preparation Time
20 minutes, plus chilling
Cooking Time
15–20 minutes, plus cooling

- 225g (8oz) butter, at room temperature
- 125g (4oz) golden caster sugar
- 225g (8oz) plain flour
- 125g (4oz) rice flour
- a pinch of salt
- golden or coloured granulated sugar to coat
- caster sugar to sprinkle

NUTRITIONAL
INFORMATION
Per shortbread 190–170 cals;
10–9g fat (of which 7–6g
saturates); 23–21g carbohydrate;
0.3–0.2g salt

1 Cream the butter and sugar together in a bowl until pale and fluffy. Sift the flours and salt into the creamed mixture then, using a wooden spoon, stir in until the mixture resembles breadcrumbs.

2 Gather the dough together with your hand and turn on to a clean surface. Knead very lightly until it forms a ball, then lightly roll into a sausage, about 5cm (2 inches) thick. Wrap in clingfilm and chill in the fridge until firm.

3 Preheat the oven to 190°C (170°C fan oven) mark 5. Line two baking sheets with greaseproof paper. Remove the clingfilm and slice the dough into discs, 7–10mm (¼–½ inch) thick. Pour some granulated sugar on to a plate and roll the edge of each disc in the sugar. Put the shortbread, cut-side up, on the baking sheets.

4 Bake the shortbread for 15–20 minutes, depending on thickness, until a very pale golden colour. Remove from the oven and sprinkle with caster sugar. Leave on the baking sheets for 10 minutes, then transfer to a wire rack and leave to cool.

Cheesecakes, Tortes and no-bake Cakes

Classic Baked Cheesecake

Preparation Time
30 minutes, plus chilling
Cooking Time
55 minutes, plus cooling and
overnight chilling

- 125g (4oz) unsalted butter,
  melted, plus extra to grease
- 250g pack digestive biscuits,
  finely crushed (see page 307)

FILLING
- 2 large lemons
- 2 x 250g cartons curd cheese
- 142ml carton soured cream
- 2 medium eggs
- 175g (6oz) golden caster
  sugar
- 1½ tsp vanilla extract
- 1 tbsp cornflour
- 50g (2oz) sultanas

NUTRITIONAL
INFORMATION
Per slice 340 cals; 19g fat (of
which 11g saturates); 36g
carbohydrate; 1g salt

1 Grease a 20.5cm (8 inch) springform cake tin. Put the biscuits in a bowl, add the melted butter and mix until well combined. Tip the crumb mixture into the prepared tin and press down evenly, using the back of a metal spoon to level the surface. Chill for 1 hour or until firm.

2 Preheat the oven to 180°C (160°C fan oven) mark 4. To make the filling, grate the zest from one of the lemons and set aside. Halve the same lemon and squeeze out the juice from both halves. Halve the other lemon and cut into very thin slices.

3 Put the lemon zest, lemon juice, curd cheese, soured cream, eggs, sugar, vanilla extract and cornflour into a large bowl. Using a hand-held electric whisk, beat together until thick and smooth, then fold in the sultanas. Pour the mixture into the tin and shake gently to level the surface.

4 Bake for 30 minutes. Put the lemon slices, overlapping, on top. Bake for a further 20–25 minutes until the cheesecake is just set and golden brown. Turn off the oven and leave the cheesecake inside, with the door ajar, until it is cool, then chill for at least 2 hours or overnight.

5 Remove the cheesecake from the fridge about 30 minutes before serving. Run a knife around the edge, release the clasp on the tin and remove the cake. Cut the cheesecake into slices to serve.

Cuts into 12 slices

Raspberry Cheesecake

Preparation Time
25 minutes, plus chilling
Cooking Time
5 minutes, plus cooling and
4 hours' chilling

◆ 100g (3½oz) unsalted butter,
 melted, plus extra to grease
◆ 25g (1oz) blanched almonds,
 lightly toasted, then finely
 chopped
◆ 225g (8oz) almond butter
 biscuits, finely crushed (see
 page 307)
◆ a few drops of almond extract

FILLING AND TOPPING
◆ 450g (1lb) raspberries
◆ 300g (11oz) Greek-style
 yogurt
◆ 150g (5oz) low-fat cream
 cheese
◆ 1 tbsp powdered gelatine
◆ 2 medium egg whites
◆ 50g (2oz) icing sugar

**NUTRITIONAL
INFORMATION**
Per slice 270 cals; 19g fat (of
which 10g saturates); 20g
carbohydrate; 0.5g salt

Cuts into 10 slices

1 Grease a 20.5cm (8 inch) round springform cake tin. Mix the almonds with the crushed biscuits and melted butter and add the almond extract. Tip the crumb mixture into the prepared tin and press down evenly, using the back of a metal spoon to level the surface. Chill for 1 hour or until firm.

2 To make the filling, purée 225g (8oz) raspberries in a blender, then press through a sieve. Put three-quarters of the purée to one side and return the rest to the blender. Add the yogurt and cheese, then whizz to blend. Transfer to a bowl. Sprinkle the gelatine over

2 tbsp cold water in a heatproof bowl and leave to soak for 2–3 minutes. Put the bowl over a pan of simmering water until the gelatine has dissolved. Leave to cool.

3 Whisk the egg whites with the sugar until thick and shiny. Fold into the cheese mixture and add the cooled gelatine. Arrange half the remaining berries on the biscuit base, then pour the cheese mixture over the berries. Add the reserved purée and swirl with a knife to marble. Top with the remaining berries and chill for 3–4 hours.

Blueberry Cheesecake

Preparation Time
15 minutes
Cooking Time
45 minutes, plus cooling and
2¼ hours' chilling

- 1 large sponge flan case, 23–25.5cm (9–10 inches) in diameter
- butter to grease
- 300g (11oz) cream cheese
- 1 tsp vanilla extract
- 100g (3½oz) golden caster sugar
- 150ml (¼ pint) soured cream
- 2 medium eggs
- 2 tbsp cornflour

TOPPING
- 150g (5oz) blueberries
- 2 tbsp redcurrant jelly

NUTRITIONAL INFORMATION
Per slice 376 cals; 24g fat (of which 14g saturates); 36g carbohydrate; 0.4g salt

Cuts into 8 slices

1 Preheat the oven to 180°C (160°C fan oven) mark 4. Use the base of a 20.5cm (8 inch) springform cake tin to cut out a circle from the flan case, discarding the edges. Grease the tin and base-line with greaseproof paper, then put the flan base into it. Press down with your fingers.

2 Put the cream cheese, vanilla extract, sugar, soured cream, eggs and cornflour into a food processor and whizz until evenly combined. Pour the mixture over the flan base and shake gently to level the surface. Bake for 45 minutes or until just set and a pale golden colour. Turn off the oven and leave the cheesecake inside, with the door ajar, for about 30 minutes. Leave to cool, then chill for at least 2 hours.

3 To serve, put the blueberries into a pan with the redcurrant jelly and heat through until the jelly has melted and the blueberries have softened slightly (or place in a heatproof bowl and cook in a 900W microwave oven on full power for 1 minute). Spoon them over the top of the cheesecake. Cool and chill for 15 minutes before serving.

Cuts into 8 slices

Rhubarb and Ginger Cheesecake

Preparation Time
30 minutes, plus chilling
Cooking Time
about 2 hours, plus cooling and
overnight chilling

- 2 balls preserved stem ginger,
  syrup reserved
- 175g (6oz) ginger nut biscuits,
  finely crushed (see page 307)
- 60g (2½oz) unsalted butter,
  melted

FILLING AND TOPPING
- 450g (1lb) rhubarb, cut into
  chunks
- 4 tbsp caster sugar
- 450g (1lb) cream cheese
- 3 medium eggs
- 1 tsp vanilla extract
- 4 tbsp icing sugar
- ½ tsp arrowroot

**NUTRITIONAL
INFORMATION**
Per slice 530 cals; 39g fat (of
which 23g saturates); 40g
carbohydrate; 0.9g salt

1 Put 225g (8oz) rhubarb chunks into a pan with the caster sugar, 3 tbsp
ginger syrup and 2 tbsp cold water. Simmer for 5-10 minutes until tender.
Transfer to a food processor and whizz until smooth, then set aside to cool.

2 Finely chop the stem ginger and combine with the ginger nuts and
butter. Press into the bottom of an 18cm (7 inch) round springform cake
tin and chill until firm.

3 Preheat the oven to 150°C (130°C fan oven) mark 2. Whisk together the
cream cheese, eggs, vanilla extract and 3 tbsp icing sugar. Fold in two-
thirds of the rhubarb purée. Pour into the cake tin. Stir the remainder of
the purée through the filling, making swirls and ripples. Bake for 1½ hours
or until just set, then leave in the oven with the door ajar until cool. Chill,
preferably overnight.

4 Put the remaining rhubarb into a pan with 150ml (¼ pint) cold water,
the remaining icing sugar and 2 tbsp ginger syrup. Poach gently for
5-10 minutes until just tender. Remove the rhubarb and put to one side,
then strain the liquid into a bowl and return it to the rinsed-out pan. Mix
1 tbsp of the liquid with the arrowroot until smooth, then add to the rest.
Bring to the boil, then remove from the heat as soon as it is slightly
thickened. Leave to cool.

5 To serve, remove the cheesecake from its tin and top with the poached
rhubarb. Slice and drizzle with sauce.

Coconut and Blackberry Cheesecake

Preparation Time
15 minutes, plus chilling
Cooking Time
about 1¼ hours, plus overnight
chilling

- 15g (½oz) unsalted butter, melted, plus extra to grease
- 75g (3oz) bran flakes, crushed
- 125g (4oz) caster sugar
- 1kg (2¼lb) ricotta cheese
- 200g (7oz) Greek-style coconut yogurt
- 1 tbsp cornflour, sifted
- 3 large eggs, beaten
- 400g (14oz) blackberries
- icing sugar to dust

NUTRITIONAL INFORMATION
Per slice 304 cals; 17g fat (of which 10g saturates); 25g carbohydrate; 0.5g salt

1 Preheat the oven to 150°C (130°C fan oven) mark 2. Grease the sides of a 20.5cm (8 inch) springform cake tin and line with baking parchment.

2 Pour the melted butter into a bowl, then mix with the bran flakes and 15g (½oz) caster sugar. Tip into the prepared tin and spread over the bottom. Set aside.

3 Put the remaining caster sugar, the ricotta, yogurt, cornflour and eggs into a large bowl and whisk until smooth. Carefully fold in 175g (6oz) of the blackberries, then turn the mixture into the tin and level the surface. Bake for 1¼ hours or until just set. Cool in the tin, then chill in the tin for at least 2 hours or preferably overnight. Don't worry if cracks appear – they'll be covered later.

4 Remove the cake from the tin and peel off the lining paper, then put on a serving plate. Decorate the cake with the remaining berries, dust with icing sugar and serve in slices.

Notes
- For convenience, complete the recipe to the end of step 2 up to one day in advance. Complete the recipe to serve.
- For extra flavour, add 25ml (1fl oz) Malibu to the ricotta mix before stirring in the fruit.

Cuts into 10 slices

Cuts into 12 slices

Orange and Chocolate Cheesecake

Preparation Time
45 minutes
Cooking Time
2–2¼ hours, plus cooling and
chilling

- 225g (8oz) chilled unsalted
  butter, plus extra to grease
- 250g (9oz) plain flour, sifted
- 150g (5oz) light muscovado
  sugar
- 3 tbsp cocoa powder

FILLING AND DECORATION
- 2 oranges
- 800g (1lb 12oz) cream cheese
- 250g (9oz) mascarpone
  cheese
- 4 large eggs
- 225g (8oz) golden caster
  sugar
- 2 tbsp cornflour
- ½ tsp vanilla extract
- 1 vanilla pod
- Chocolate Curls to decorate
  (optional)

NUTRITIONAL
INFORMATION
Per slice 767 cals; 60g fat (of
which 37g saturates); 53g
carbohydrate; 1.2g salt

1 Preheat the oven to 180°C (160°C fan oven) mark 4. Grease a 23cm (9 inch) springform cake tin and base-line with baking parchment.

2 Cut 175g (6oz) butter into cubes. Melt the remaining butter and set aside. Put the flour and cubed butter into a food processor with the sugar and cocoa powder. Whizz until the texture of fine breadcrumbs. (Alternatively, rub the butter into the flour in a large bowl by hand or using a pastry cutter. Stir in the sugar and cocoa powder.) Pour in the melted butter and pulse, or stir with a fork, until the mixture comes together.

3 Tip the crumb mixture into the prepared tin and press down evenly, using the back of a metal spoon to level the surface. Bake for 35–40 minutes until lightly puffed; avoid over-browning or the biscuit base will have a bitter flavour. Remove from the oven and leave to cool. Lower the oven setting to 150°C (130°C fan oven) mark 2.

4 Meanwhile, make the topping. Grate the zest from the oranges, then squeeze the juice – you will need 150ml (¼ pint). Put the cream cheese, mascarpone, eggs, sugar, cornflour, grated orange zest and vanilla extract into a large bowl. Using a hand-held electric whisk, whisk the ingredients together thoroughly until well combined.

5 Split the vanilla pod in half lengthways and, using the tip of a sharp knife, scrape out the seeds and add them to the cheese mixture. Beat in the orange juice and continue whisking until the mixture is smooth.

6 Pour the cheese mixture over the cooled biscuit base. Bake for about 1½ hours or until pale golden on top, slightly risen and just set around the edge. The cheesecake should still be slightly wobbly in the middle – it will set as it cools. Turn off the oven and leave the cheesecake inside, with the door ajar, to cool for 1 hour. Remove and allow to cool completely (about 3 hours), then chill.

7 Just before serving, unclip the tin and transfer the cheesecake to a plate. Scatter chocolate curls on top to decorate, if you like.

Peanut Caramel Cheesecake

Preparation Time
20 minutes, plus overnight
chilling

- 150g (5oz) Bourbon biscuits, finely crushed
- 2½ tbsp golden syrup

FILLING AND DECORATION
- 3 medium egg whites
- 175g (6oz) caster sugar
- 500g (1lb 2oz) full-fat cream cheese
- seeds of 1 vanilla pod
- 50g (2oz) plain chocolate, finely chopped
- 75g (3oz) salted peanuts
- 50g (2oz) caramel sauce
- chocolate, coarsely grated, to decorate
- 25g (1oz) fudge chunks (optional)

**NUTRITIONAL
INFORMATION**
Per slice 595 cals; 41g fat (of
which 23g saturates); 52g
carbohydrate; 0.8g salt

1 Line a 20.5cm (8 inch) round cake tin with baking parchment (use a little golden syrup to stick the parchment to the sides). Mix the crushed biscuits and golden syrup in a bowl – making sure the syrup is distributed as evenly as possible (use your fingers). Empty the mixture into the bottom of the prepared tin and press down to make an even layer.

2 Put the egg whites into a large, grease-free bowl and, using a hand-held electric whisk, whisk until they hold stiff peaks. Gradually add the caster sugar, whisking constantly, until the mixture turns glossy and thick. Put the cream cheese into a separate large bowl and add the vanilla seeds, then whisk to break up the cheese.

3 Using a large metal spoon, fold the egg mixture into the cream cheese bowl. Next, fold in the chopped chocolate. In another small bowl, mix the peanuts with the caramel sauce, then swirl through the cream cheese mixture. Spoon into the cake tin, then cover and chill until set – at least 6 hours or ideally overnight.

4 Carefully remove the cheesecake from the tin and use spatulas to lift off the lining paper on the base. Transfer to a serving plate and peel off the paper from around the edges. Decorate with grated chocolate and the fudge chunks, if you like. Serve in slices.

Note
For convenience, complete the recipe to the end of step 3 up to one day in advance. Complete the recipe to serve.

Cuts into 8 slices

Cuts into 12 slices

Refrigerator Cake

Preparation Time
10 minutes, plus chilling
Cooking Time
4 minutes

- ◆ 175g (6oz) unsalted butter, cut into 8 pieces, plus extra to grease
- ◆ 200g (7oz) natural glacé cherries, halved
- ◆ 2 tbsp kirsch
- ◆ 150g (5oz) dark chocolate with fruit, broken into pieces
- ◆ 200g (7oz) plain chocolate, broken into pieces
- ◆ 100g (3½oz) golden syrup
- ◆ 200g (7oz) digestive biscuits, roughly crushed (see page 307)

NUTRITIONAL INFORMATION
Per slice 411 cals; 24g fat (of which 14g saturates); 48g carbohydrate; 0.6g salt

1 Grease a 20.5cm (8 inch) round tin and base-line with greaseproof paper. Put the cherries into a bowl, add the kirsch and leave to soak.

2 Put all the chocolate, the butter and syrup into a large heatproof bowl and melt in a 900W microwave oven on medium for 2 minutes. Stir and cook for a further 2 minutes or until the chocolate has melted. (Alternatively, put into a heatproof bowl set over a pan of gently simmering water, making sure the base of the bowl doesn't touch the water, and leave until melted.)

3 Add half the soaked cherries and all the biscuits to the chocolate, then stir together. Spoon into the prepared tin and level the surface. Arrange the remaining cherries around the edge of the cake and chill for at least 15 minutes.

4 Cut into slices to serve.

Chocolate Iced Mille Feuilles

Preparation Time
45 minutes, plus chilling and
freezing
Cooking Time
about 10 minutes, plus cooling
and overnight freezing

- 200g (7oz) plain chocolate,
  broken into pieces
- 300g (11oz) white chocolate,
  broken into pieces
- 450ml (¾ pint) double cream
- 2 tsp vanilla extract
- 2 medium egg whites
- 25g (1oz) icing sugar
- sifted cocoa powder to dust

**NUTRITIONAL
INFORMATION**
Per slice 430 cals; 32g fat (of
which 20g saturates); 28g
carbohydrate; 0.1g salt

1 Use a little water to dampen a 900g (2lb) loaf tin. Line with a double layer of clingfilm. Melt the plain chocolate in a bowl set over a pan of gently simmering water, making sure the base of the bowl doesn't touch the water. Cut out two sheets of baking parchment, each 45.5 x 33cm (18 x 13 inches). Spoon half the chocolate on to one sheet and spread it to the edges in a thin layer. Repeat with the remaining chocolate and baking parchment. Lift on to baking sheets and chill for 30 minutes to set.

2 Put the white chocolate into another bowl with 150ml (¼ pint) cream, then melt slowly over a pan of simmering water, as above. Leave to cool. In a separate bowl, whip the remaining cream with the vanilla extract until just holding its shape. Fold into the melted white chocolate.

3 Whisk the egg whites in a clean, grease-free bowl and gradually whisk in the icing sugar. Fold the egg whites into the white chocolate mixture.

4 Peel the plain chocolate from the paper and break into large pieces. Put a quarter into a freezerproof container for decoration and freeze overnight.

5 Spoon a quarter of the cream mixture into the lined tin and layer with a third of the remaining plain chocolate pieces. Repeat, finishing with the cream mixture. Cover with clingfilm and freeze overnight.

6 Transfer the torte and reserved chocolate to the fridge for 1 hour before serving. Turn out on to a serving plate and peel away the clingfilm. Break the reserved chocolate into small jagged pieces and arrange on top. Dust with cocoa powder and serve.

Freezing tip
To freeze, complete the recipe to the end of step 5 up to one month ahead. To use, complete the recipe.

Cuts into 12 slices

Cuts into 20 slices

Chocolate and Raspberry Torte

Preparation Time
30 minutes
Cooking Time
5 minutes, plus 1½–4 hours' chilling

◆ 5 x 100g bars good-quality dark chocolate
◆ 50g (2oz) golden syrup or liquid glucose
◆ 50ml (2fl oz) amaretto liqueur (optional)
◆ 100g (3½oz) brandy snaps, crushed
◆ 600ml (1 pint) double cream
◆ 75g (3oz) icing sugar, sifted
◆ 200g (7oz) raspberries

NUTRITIONAL INFORMATION
Per slice 427 cals; 37g fat (of which 21g saturates); 24g carbohydrate; 0.1g salt

1 Put the chocolate and golden syrup or glucose into a heatproof bowl with the amaretto, if you like. Set the bowl over a pan of gently simmering water, making sure the base of the bowl doesn't touch the water. Allow the chocolate to melt without stirring – otherwise it might seize up and become unworkable. Remove the bowl from the pan and cool until the chocolate is just warm.

2 Line the base and sides of a 20.5cm (8 inch) round tin with baking parchment. Sprinkle the brandy snap pieces over the bottom of the tin.

3 Put the cream and icing sugar into a large bowl and whip until the mixture just holds its shape. Using a metal spoon, gently fold the chocolate into the cream – do this in two stages.

4 Spoon half the mixture into the tin and level the surface. Sprinkle the raspberries over it, cover with the remaining chocolate and cream mixture and smooth the top. Chill for 4 hours (see Note).

5 Half an hour before serving, take the torte out of the fridge. Remove from the tin, peel off the lining paper and put on a cake stand to serve.

Note
The texture of the torte becomes firmer the further ahead you make it. If you prefer a soft, mousse-like texture, make and chill no more than 1½ hours before serving.

Chocolate Torte

Preparation Time
15 minutes, plus chilling
Cooking Time
5 minutes, plus cooling

- ◆ 200g (7oz) plain chocolate, broken into pieces
- ◆ 25g (1oz) butter, melted, plus extra to grease
- ◆ 1½ tbsp golden syrup
- ◆ 125g (4oz) butter biscuits, finely crushed (see page 307)
- ◆ 40g (1½oz) icing sugar
- ◆ 300ml (½ pint) double cream, at room temperature
- ◆ 2–3 tbsp amaretto liqueur (optional)
- ◆ crème fraîche to serve

DECORATION
- ◆ plain chocolate, grated
- ◆ raspberries
- ◆ icing sugar to dust

NUTRITIONAL INFORMATION
Per slice 383 cals; 27g fat (of which 16g saturates); 31g carbohydrate; 0.2g salt

1 Melt the chocolate pieces in a heatproof bowl set over a pan of gently simmering water, making sure the base of the bowl doesn't touch the water. Put to one side to cool for 10 minutes. Grease a 20.5cm (8 inch) loose-bottomed cake tin and line the sides with greaseproof paper.

2 Put the butter, golden syrup and crushed biscuits into a medium bowl and mix together. Press the mixture into the bottom of the prepared tin.

3 Sift the icing sugar into a separate bowl. Pour in the cream and amaretto, if you like, and whip until the cream just holds a shape. Using a metal spoon, fold the cooled chocolate into the cream mixture. Spoon the chocolate mixture into the cake tin, level the surface, cover and chill until ready to serve.

4 Transfer the torte to a serving plate and peel off the lining paper. Scatter grated chocolate over the top, dot with a few raspberries and lightly dust with icing sugar. Serve in slices with crème fraîche.

Note
For convenience, prepare ahead. Complete the recipe to the end of step 3 up to one day ahead. Complete the recipe to serve.

Cuts into 10 slices

Luxury Chocolate Orange Torte

Preparation Time
30 minutes
Cooking Time
5 minutes–1 hour 5 minutes, plus cooling

- 75g (3oz) unsalted butter, diced, plus extra to grease
- 100g (3½oz) plain chocolate (at least 70% cocoa solids), broken into pieces
- 6 medium eggs
- 225g (8oz) golden caster sugar
- 150g (5oz) ground almonds, sifted
- grated zest and juice of 1 orange
- strawberries and raspberries to serve

NUTRITIONAL INFORMATION
Per slice 231 cals; 12g fat (of which 3g saturates); 25g carbohydrate; 0.1g salt

Cuts into 12 slices

1 Preheat the oven to 190°C (170°C fan oven) mark 5. Grease a 20.5cm (8 inch) springform cake tin and line with greaseproof paper.

2 Melt the butter and chocolate in a heatproof bowl set over a pan of gently simmering water, making sure the base of the bowl doesn't touch the water. Remove the bowl from the pan and set aside to cool a little.

3 Put the eggs and sugar into a large bowl and, using a hand-held electric whisk, whisk until the volume has tripled and the mixture is thick and foamy (5–10 minutes). Add the ground almonds, orange zest and juice to the egg mixture, then gently fold in with a metal spoon.

4 Pour about two-thirds of the mixture into the prepared tin. Add the melted chocolate and butter to the remaining mixture and fold in. Add to the tin and swirl around just once or twice to create a marbled effect. Bake for 50 minutes–1 hour. Leave to cool in the tin.

5 Carefully remove the cake from the tin and slice. Serve with strawberries and raspberries.

White Chocolate and Ginger Cheesecake with Cranberry Sauce

Preparation Time
25 minutes plus chilling
Cooking Time
Time 1 hour 40 minutes, plus cooling

- 175g (6oz) gingernut biscuits, finely crushed
- 50g (2oz) unsalted butter, melted
- 150g (5oz) white chocolate
- 250g (9oz) mascarpone cheese
- 400g (14oz) cream cheese
- 4 medium eggs, beaten
- 100g (3½oz) golden caster sugar
- 75g (3oz) preserved stem ginger, finely chopped
- icing sugar to dust

FOR THE SAUCE

- 175g (6oz) fresh cranberries
- 60g (2½oz) golden caster sugar
- 1 tsp ground ginger

NUTRITIONAL INFORMATION
Per slice 494 cals; 36g fat (of which 22g saturates); 36g carbohydrate; 0.7g salt

Cuts into 10 slices

1 Line the base and sides of a 23cm (9in) loose-bottomed cake tin with greaseproof paper. Pour the biscuits into a bowl and stir in the melted butter. Tip the crumb mixture into the prepared tin and press evenly on to the base, using the back of a spoon to smooth the surface. Chill for about 1 hour or until firm.

2 Preheat the oven to 150°C (130°C fan oven) mark 2. Put 100g (3½oz) chocolate into a heatproof bowl over a pan of gently simmering water, making sure the base of the bowl doesn't touch the water, and leave to melt. Leave to cool slightly. Put the mascarpone and cream cheese into a large bowl and beat together until smooth. Stir in the eggs, caster sugar, ginger and melted white chocolate.

3 Pour into the prepared tin and bake in the centre of the oven for 1½ hours or until the cheesecake just wobbles slightly when the tin is tapped. Leave in the tin, place on a wire rack and leave to cool. When cold, chill for at least 4 hours.

4 To make the sauce, heat the cranberries, sugar and ground ginger in a pan with 100ml (3½fl oz) water. Simmer for 5 minutes or until the cranberries burst. Blend until smooth, then push through a sieve into a bowl and leave to chill.

5 Remove the cake from the tin and transfer to a plate. Dust with icing sugar, grate the remaining chocolate over the top and serve with the cranberry sauce.

Almond and Orange Torte

Preparation Time
30 minutes
Cooking Time
1 hour 50 minutes, plus cooling

- oil to grease
- plain flour to dust
- 1 medium orange
- 3 medium eggs
- 225g (8oz) golden caster sugar
- 250g (9oz) ground almonds
- ½ tsp baking powder
- icing sugar to dust
- crème fraîche to serve

NUTRITIONAL INFORMATION
Per wedge 223 cals; 13g fat (of which 1g saturates); 22g carbohydrate; 0.1g salt

1 Oil and line, then oil and flour a 20.5cm (8 inch) springform cake tin. Put the whole orange into a small pan and cover with water. Bring to the boil, then cover and simmer for at least 1 hour or until tender (see Note). Remove from the water and leave to cool.

2 Cut the orange in half and remove the pips. Whizz in a food processor or blender to make a smooth purée.

3 Preheat the oven to 180°C (160°C fan oven) mark 4. Put the eggs and caster sugar into a bowl and whisk together until thick and pale. Fold in the almonds, baking powder and orange purée. Pour the mixture into the prepared tin.

4 Bake for 40–50 minutes until a skewer inserted into the centre comes out clean. Leave to cool in the tin.

5 Release the clasp on the tin and remove the cake. Carefully peel off the lining paper and put the cake on a serving plate. Dust with icing sugar, then cut into 12 wedges. Serve with crème fraîche.

Note
To save time, you can microwave the orange. Put it into a small heatproof bowl, cover with 100ml (3½fl oz) water and cook in a 900W microwave oven on full power for 10–12 minutes until soft.

Cuts into 12 wedges

Cuts into 8 slices

Sachertorte

Preparation Time
25 minutes, plus cooling and setting
Cooking Time
about 40 minutes

- ◆ 125g (4oz) unsalted butter, softened, plus extra to grease
- ◆ 150g (5oz) plain chocolate (at least 70% cocoa solids), chopped
- ◆ 125g (4oz) caster sugar
- ◆ a large pinch of salt
- ◆ 4 large eggs, separated
- ◆ 125g (4oz) plain flour

FILLING AND ICING
- ◆ 6 tbsp apricot jam
- ◆ 150g (5oz) plain chocolate (at least 70% cocoa solids), chopped
- ◆ 40ml (1½fl oz) strong black coffee
- ◆ 2 tbsp golden syrup
- ◆ 150g (5oz) icing sugar, sifted
- ◆ edible star decorations (optional)

NUTRITIONAL INFORMATION
Per slice 624 cals; 27g fat (of which 15g saturates); 94g carbohydrate; 0.5g salt

1 Preheat the oven to 180°C (160°C fan oven) mark 4. Grease a 20.5cm (8 inch) round cake tin and line with baking parchment. Melt the chocolate in a heatproof bowl set over a pan of simmering water, making sure the base of the bowl doesn't touch the water. Set aside to cool.

2 Put the butter, 100g (3½oz) of the caster sugar and the salt into a large bowl and, using a hand-held electric whisk, beat together until pale and fluffy (about 3 minutes). Gradually add the egg yolks, beating well after each addition. Next, beat in the cooled chocolate, then use a large metal spoon to fold in the flour (the mixture will be stiff).

3 In a separate bowl and using clean, dry beaters, whisk the egg whites until they hold stiff peaks. Add the remaining sugar and beat again. Stir a spoonful of the egg whites into the chocolate mixture to loosen it, then fold in the remaining whites. Scrape the mixture into the prepared tin, then bake for 30 minutes or until a skewer inserted into the centre comes out clean. Leave to cool in the tin for 10 minutes, then turn out on to a wire rack and leave to cool completely.

4 Peel off the lining paper, then cut the cake in half horizontally. Melt the jam in a small pan, then spread some on top of the bottom half of the cake. Top with the other cake half and brush the remaining jam over the top and sides. Leave to set for 10 minutes.

5 To make the icing, put the chocolate, coffee and golden syrup into a large pan and heat gently until melted. Mix in the icing sugar to make a smooth icing. Immediately spread over the cake. Scatter on the star decorations, if using, and allow to set for 2 hours before serving.

Note
For convenience, complete the recipe up to one day in advance and store at a cool room temperature (not in the fridge).

White Chocolate Torte

Preparation Time
about 50 minutes, plus chilling
and freezing
Cooking Time
about 2 minutes, plus cooling

- 125g (4oz) unsalted butter
- 225g (8oz) ginger snaps or
  digestive biscuits, roughly
  broken
- 750g (1lb 11oz) white
  chocolate
- 600ml (1 pint) double cream
- white Maltesers to decorate

**NUTRITIONAL
INFORMATION**
Per slice 563 cals; 44g fat (of
which 26g saturates); 40g
carbohydrate; 0.5g salt

1 Line the base and sides of a 20.5 x 6.5cm (8 x 2½ inch) springform tin with non-stick baking parchment or greaseproof paper. Melt the butter in a pan. Whizz the biscuits in a food processor until finely crushed. Tip the crumbs into a bowl and stir in the melted butter. Spread evenly over the base of the prepared tin and press down. Chill for 15 minutes to set.

2 Chop 700g (1½lb) chocolate and combine with half the cream in a bowl set over a pan of gently simmering water, making sure the base of the bowl doesn't touch the water. Leave the chocolate to melt, but don't stir it – this might take as long as 30 minutes. Once melted, remove from the heat and stir until smooth, then leave to cool for 15 minutes or until just beginning to thicken, stirring occasionally. Don't allow it to cool completely or the cream won't fold in evenly.

3 In a separate bowl, whip the remaining cream until soft peaks form, then fold into the chocolate mixture. Pour over the biscuit base and chill for 3 hours.

4 Pull a vegetable peeler across the remaining white chocolate to make rough curls and scatter them over the torte, then arrange the Maltesers on top. Freeze for 15 minutes, then remove from the tin and serve.

Freezing tip
To freeze, complete the recipe up to one month ahead, then freeze the torte in its tin. When frozen, remove the torte from the tin and carefully wrap in clingfilm before returning to the freezer. To use, thaw overnight in the fridge, then put back in the freezer for 15 minutes before serving to make sure it's chilled.

Cuts into 16 slices

Tarts and
Pastries

Tarte Tatin

Preparation Time
30 minutes, plus chilling
Cooking Time
about 1 hour, plus cooling

- Sweet Shortcrust Pastry (see page 330), made with 225g (8oz) plain flour, ¼ tsp salt, 150g (5oz) unsalted butter, 50g (2oz) golden icing sugar, 1 medium egg in place of the egg yolks and 2–3 drops of vanilla extract
- plain flour to dust

FILLING
- 200g (7oz) golden caster sugar
- 125g (4oz) chilled unsalted butter
- 1.4–1.6kg (3–3½lb) crisp dessert apples, peeled and cored
- juice of ½ lemon

NUTRITIONAL
INFORMATION
Per slice 727 cals; 39g fat (of which 24g saturates); 94g carbohydrate; 0.7g salt

Cuts into 6 slices

1 To make the filling, sprinkle the sugar over the bottom of a 20.5cm (8 inch) tarte tatin tin or ovenproof frying pan. Cut the butter into slivers and arrange on the sugar. Halve the apples and pack them tightly, cut-side up, on top of the butter.

2 Put the tin or pan on the hob and cook over a medium heat for 30 minutes (making sure it doesn't bubble over or catch on the bottom) or until the butter and sugar turn a dark golden brown (see Note). Sprinkle with the lemon juice, then leave to cool for 15 minutes. Meanwhile, preheat the oven to 220°C (200°C fan oven) mark 7.

3 Put the pastry on a large sheet of lightly floured baking parchment. Roll out to make a round 2.5cm (1 inch) larger than the tin or pan. Prick several times with a fork. Lay the pastry over the apples, tucking the edges down the side of the tin. Bake for 25–30 minutes until golden brown. Leave the tart tatin in the tin for 10 minutes, then carefully upturn on to a serving plate. Serve warm.

Note
When caramelizing the apples in step 2, be patient. Allow the sauce to turn a dark golden brown – any paler and it will be too sickly. Don't let it burn, though, as this will make the caramel taste bitter.

Plum and Almond Tart

Preparation Time
30 minutes, plus chilling
Cooking Time
40 minutes, plus cooling and setting

- 150g (5oz) unsalted butter, chilled and diced
- 175g (6oz) plain flour, plus extra to dust
- 7 tbsp soured cream

FILLING
- 50g (2oz) unsalted butter
- 50g (2oz) caster sugar, plus extra to dust
- 2 medium eggs, lightly beaten
- 100g (3½oz) ground almonds
- 1 tbsp kirsch or 3-4 drops of almond essence
- 900g (2lb) plums, stoned and quartered
- 50g (2oz) blanched almonds to decorate
- 175g (6oz) redcurrant jelly

NUTRITIONAL
INFORMATION
Per slice 535 cals; 35g fat (of which 16g saturates); 50g carbohydrate; 0.5g salt

Cuts into 8 slices

1 To make the pastry, put the butter and flour into a food processor and whizz for 1–2 seconds. Add the soured cream and process for a further 1–2 seconds until the dough just begins to come together. (Alternatively, rub the butter into the flour in a large bowl by hand or using a pastry cutter, then mix in the soured cream.) Turn out on to a lightly floured surface and knead lightly for about 30 seconds or until the pastry just comes together. Wrap in clingfilm and chill for 30 minutes.

2 To make the filling, put the butter into a bowl and beat until soft, then add the sugar and beat until light and fluffy. Beat in the eggs, alternating with the ground almonds. Add the kirsch or almond essence, cover and set aside.

3 Roll out the pastry on a lightly floured surface to a 30.5cm (12 inch) circle, then transfer to a baking sheet

and prick all over with a fork. Spread the almond mixture over the pastry, leaving a 3cm (1¼ inch) border all round. Scatter the plums over the filling and fold the edges of the pastry up over the fruit. Dust with caster sugar, then chill for 20 minutes.

4 Preheat the oven to 220°C (200°C fan oven) mark 7 and put a baking tray in the oven to heat for 10 minutes. Put the tart, on its baking sheet, on top of the hot baking tray. Cook for 35-40 minutes until a deep golden brown.

5 Leave the tart to cool for 10 minutes, then slide it on to a wire rack. Arrange the almonds among the fruit. Heat the redcurrant jelly gently in a pan, stirring until smooth, then brush generously over the tart. Leave to set.

Pinenut and Honey Tart

Preparation Time
50 minutes, plus chilling
Cooking Time
1 hour, plus cooling

- 250g (9oz) plain flour, plus extra to dust
- 200g (7oz) unsalted butter, softened
- 40g (1½oz) icing sugar
- 4 large eggs
- 100g (3½oz) pinenuts
- 200g (7oz) muscovado sugar
- 100ml (3½fl oz) clear honey
- 150ml (¼ pint) double cream
- ice cream to serve

NUTRITIONAL INFORMATION
Per slice 863 cals; 54g fat (of which 26g saturates); 88g carbohydrate; 0.6g salt

Cuts into 6 slices

1 Put 225g (8oz) flour, 150g (5oz) butter and the icing sugar into a food processor and pulse until the mixture resembles fine crumbs. (Alternatively, rub the butter into the flour in a large bowl, by hand or using a pastry cutter, until it resembles fine crumbs. Stir in the icing sugar.) Add 1 egg. Pulse, or stir with a fork, until the mixture forms a ball. Wrap in clingfilm and chill for 30 minutes.

2 Preheat the oven to 200°C (180°C fan oven) mark 6. Roll out the pastry on a lightly floured surface and use to line a 23cm (9 inch) loose-based tart tin. Prick the base all over with a fork and bake blind (see page 325), using a little of the remaining eggs to seal the pastry case. Remove from the oven. Increase the oven setting to 190°C (170°C fan oven) mark 5.

3 Sprinkle 75g (3oz) pinenuts over the pastry base. Melt 25g (1oz) butter and whisk with 175g (6oz)

muscovado sugar, the honey, remaining eggs and the cream. Pour into the pastry case and bake for 25–30 minutes.

4 Pulse the remaining pinenuts, flour, butter and sugar until the mixture forms a crumbly texture. (Alternatively, rub the butter into the flour in a large bowl and stir in the pinenuts and sugar.) When the tart is cooked, remove it from the oven, sprinkle with the crumble mixture and return to the oven for 8–10 minutes.

5 Remove from the oven and leave to cool slightly. Serve warm, with ice cream.

Bramley Apple and Custard Tart

Preparation Time
30 minutes, plus chilling
Cooking Time
about 2 hours, plus cooling and chilling

- 750g (1lb 11oz) Bramley apples, peeled, cored and roughly chopped
- 200g (7oz) golden caster sugar
- 500g (1lb 2oz) shortcrust pastry, chilled (see page 330)
- plain flour to dust
- a little beaten egg to seal the pastry case
- 400ml (14fl oz) double cream
- 1 cinnamon stick
- 3 large egg yolks, plus 1 large egg, beaten together
- 2 dessert apples to decorate
- Apple Sauce (see below) to serve

NUTRITIONAL INFORMATION
Per slice 472 cals; 32g fat (of which 15g saturates); 46g carbohydrate; 0.5g salt

Cuts into 12 slices

1 Cook the Bramley apples with 2 tbsp water over a low heat until soft. Add 50g (2oz) sugar and beat to make a purée. Leave to cool.

2 Roll out the pastry on a lightly floured surface and use to line a 20.5 x 4cm (8 x 1½ inch) loose-based fluted flan tin. Cover and chill for 1 hour.

3 Preheat the oven to 180°C (160°C fan oven) mark 4. Bake the pastry case blind (see page 325). Brush the inside with beaten egg and put back in the oven for 1 minute to seal. Remove from the oven.

4 Put the cream into a pan with 50g (2oz) sugar and the cinnamon stick. Bring slowly to the boil, then take off the heat and remove the cinnamon. Cool for 2–3 minutes, then beat in the egg yolks and egg.

5 Lower the oven setting to 170°C (150°C fan oven) mark 3. Put the tart on a baking sheet, then spoon the apple purée over the pastry. Pour the cream mixture on top and bake for 1–1½ hours until the custard is set. Remove from the oven, cool in the tin, then chill.

6 To decorate, preheat the grill. Cut the dessert apples into slices 5mm (¼ inch) thick and lay them on a lipped baking sheet. Sprinkle with 50g (2oz) sugar and grill for 4–5 minutes until caramelized. Turn them over and repeat on the other side, then cool. Remove the tart from the tin and decorate with the apple slices. Serve with Apple Sauce.

Apple Sauce
Pour 300ml (½ pint) apple juice into a measuring jug. Mix 2 tbsp of the apple juice with 1 tbsp arrowroot to make a smooth paste. Pour the remaining apple juice into a small pan and bring to a gentle simmer. Add the arrowroot paste and continue to heat, stirring constantly, for 2–3 minutes until the sauce has thickened slightly.

Mincemeat Bakewell Tart

Preparation Time
30 minutes, plus chilling
Cooking Time
about 40 minutes

- 175g (6oz) plain flour, plus extra to dust
- 80g (3¼oz) icing sugar, sifted
- finely grated zest of 1 large orange
- 100g (3½oz) chilled butter, cut into small pieces
- 1 large egg yolk

FILLING
- 100g (3½oz) butter, softened
- 100g (3½oz) caster sugar
- 2 large eggs
- 100g (3½oz) ground almonds
- 50g (2oz) plain flour
- a few drops of almond extract
- 250g (9oz) mincemeat
- 25g (1oz) flaked almonds
- 50g (2oz) icing sugar

NUTRITIONAL INFORMATION
Per slice (without ice cream or custard): 606 cals; 33g fat (of which 14g saturates); 73g carbohydrate; 0.5g salt

Cuts into 8 slices

1 To make the pastry, put the flour, icing sugar and orange zest into a food processor and pulse briefly to mix. Add the butter and whizz until the mixture resembles fine breadcrumbs (alternatively, rub the butter into the mixture using your fingers). Add the egg yolk and mix again until the pastry just comes together (add a few drops of water if the mixture still looks dry). Tip on to a lightly floured surface and press gently together to form a disc, then wrap in clingfilm. Chill for 45 minutes or until firm but pliable.

2 Roll out the dough on a lightly floured surface and use to line a 20.5 x 2.5cm (8 x 1 inch) round, deep-fluted flan tin. Chill until needed.

3 Meanwhile, make the filling: cream the butter and caster sugar together, then beat in the eggs until

smooth. Stir in the ground almonds, flour and almond extract to make a soft mixture. Spread the mincemeat over the bottom of the tart case, then cover with the almond mixture and smooth until level. Sprinkle the flaked almonds over the surface and chill for 10 minutes.

4 Preheat the oven to 180°C (160°C fan oven) mark 4 and put a baking sheet in to heat up. Put the tart on the preheated baking sheet and bake for 35 minutes or until golden and risen (cover with foil if it's browning too quickly).

5 Leave to cool in the tin for 10 minutes, then carefully transfer to a serving plate. In a small bowl, mix the icing sugar with just enough water to make a thick glacé icing. Drizzle over the tart, then serve warm or at room temperature with ice cream or custard.

Chocolate Orange Tart

Preparation Time
30 minutes, plus chilling
Cooking Time
about 1 hour, plus cooling

◆ Sweet Shortcrust Pastry (see
  page 330), made with 150g
  (5oz) plain flour, a pinch of
  salt, 75g (3oz) unsalted butter,
  50g (2oz) caster sugar, 25g
  (1oz) golden icing sugar,
  grated zest of 1 orange and
  2 large egg yolks
◆ plain flour to dust
◆ a little beaten egg to seal the
  pastry case
◆ icing sugar to dust

FILLING

◆ 175g (6oz) plain chocolate (at
  least 50% cocoa solids),
  chopped
◆ 175ml (6fl oz) double cream
◆ 75g (3oz) light muscovado
  sugar
◆ 2 medium eggs
◆ 1 tbsp Grand Marnier or
  Cointreau

NUTRITIONAL
INFORMATION
Per slice 441 cals; 28g fat (of
which 17g saturates); 42g
carbohydrate; 0.2g salt

Cuts into 8 slices

1 Roll out the pastry on a lightly floured surface and use to line a 20.5cm (8 inch) loose-based tart tin. Prick the base all over with a fork, put the tin on a baking sheet and chill for 30 minutes.

2 Preheat the oven to 190°C (170°C fan oven) mark 5. Bake the pastry case blind (see page 325). Brush the inside with egg and put back in the oven for 1 minute to seal. Remove from the oven. Lower the oven setting to 170°C (150°C fan oven) mark 3.

3 To make the filling, melt the chocolate in a heatproof bowl set over a pan of gently simmering water, making sure the base of the bowl doesn't touch the water. Remove the bowl from the pan and cool for 10 minutes.

4 Put the cream, muscovado sugar, eggs and liqueur into a bowl and, using a wooden spoon, stir to mix thoroughly. Gradually stir in the chocolate, then pour into the pastry case and bake for 20 minutes or until just set. Serve warm or cold, dusted liberally with icing sugar.

Chocolate Espresso Tart

Preparation Time
30 minutes, plus chilling
Cooking Time
25 minutes, plus cooling and
chilling

- 175g (6oz) plain flour, plus
  extra to dust
- a pinch of salt
- 100g (3½oz) cold unsalted
  butter, diced
- 25g (1oz) caster sugar
- 1 medium egg, separated, plus
  a little beaten egg to seal the
  pastry case

FILLING
- 200g bar dark chocolate (at
  least 64% cocoa solids),
  broken into squares
- 1 tbsp powdered espresso
  coffee
- 284ml carton double cream
- cocoa powder and Chocolate
  Curls to decorate

**NUTRITIONAL
INFORMATION**
Per slice 383 cals; 30g fat (of
which 18g saturates); 30g
carbohydrate; 0.2g salt

1 Sift the flour and salt into a bowl. Rub in the butter until it resembles fine breadcrumbs. Stir in the sugar.

2 Lightly beat the egg yolk with 2 tbsp ice-cold water. Using a flat-bladed knife, stir enough of this liquid into the flour mixture to make it clump together without being sticky or too dry. Bring together with your hands and knead lightly until smooth. Shape into a disc, wrap in clingfilm and chill for 30 minutes.

3 Roll out the pastry on a lightly floured surface to 3mm (⅛ inch) thick. Use to line a 20.5 x 2.5cm (8 x 1 inch) round tin. Prick the base all over, then chill for 30 minutes. Meanwhile, preheat the oven to 200°C (180°C fan oven) mark 6 and put a baking sheet in the oven to heat up.

4 Bake the pastry case blind (see page 325) for 12–15 minutes at the first stage and then 5–10 minutes. Brush the inside with egg and put back in the oven for 1 minute. Transfer to a wire rack and leave to cool.

5 Melt the chocolate and coffee in a heatproof bowl set over a pan of gently simmering water, making sure the base of the bowl doesn't touch the water. Stir once or twice. Set aside to cool.

6 Put the egg white into a large, grease-free bowl and whisk until stiff. Using a metal spoon, fold into the chocolate. Whip the cream until it just holds a shape, then fold into the chocolate mixture. Pour into the pastry case and chill until set.

7 Dust with cocoa powder and decorate with chocolate curls to serve.

Cuts into 10 slices

Cuts into 10 slices

Chocolate, Amaretti and Ginger Tart

Preparation Time
30 minutes, plus chilling
Cooking Time
about 55 minutes, plus cooling

- 225g (8oz) plain flour, sifted, plus extra to dust
- 125g (4oz) cold unsalted butter, diced
- 25g (1oz) caster sugar
- 1 large egg, beaten, plus a little beaten egg to seal the pastry case

FILLING
- 125g (4oz) dark chocolate, broken into pieces
- 100g (3½oz) milk chocolate, broken into pieces
- 125g (4oz) unsalted butter, cubed
- 75g (3oz) amaretti biscuits, crushed into small pieces
- 40g (1½oz) preserved stem ginger, finely chopped
- 75g (3oz) caster sugar
- 2 large eggs
- cocoa powder to dust (optional)

NUTRITIONAL INFORMATION
Per slice 485 cals; 31g fat (of which 18g saturates); 48g carbohydrate; 0.5g salt

1 Put the flour and butter into a food processor and pulse until the mixture resembles fine breadcrumbs (alternatively, rub the butter into the flour using your fingers). Add caster sugar and pulse to combine. Tip the mixture into a bowl, then add the egg and stir quickly with a blunt-ended knife. Bring the pastry together using your hands, then wrap it in clingfilm and chill for 30 minutes.

2 Roll out the pastry on a lightly floured surface to a 3mm (⅛ inch) thickness. Use to line a 20.5 x 4cm (8 x 1 inch) straight-sided, loose-based tart tin. Prick the pastry base all over and chill for 15 minutes.

3 Preheat the oven to 190°C (170°C fan oven) mark 5. Bake the pastry case blind (see page 325) for 15–18 minutes at the first stage and then 10–12 minutes. Brush with egg and bake for 1 minute. Remove from the oven. Lower the oven setting to 150°C (130°C fan oven) mark 2.

4 Meanwhile, make the filling. Melt both chocolates and the butter in a heatproof bowl set over a pan of gently simmering water, making sure the base of the bowl doesn't touch the water. Stir in the amaretti biscuits and ginger and set aside.

5 Put the sugar and eggs into a separate large bowl and, using a hand-held electric whisk, beat together until pale and mousse-like. Fold in the chocolate mixture, then pour the filling into the cooked pastry case. Bake for 25 minutes or until just set. Leave to cool completely in the tin, then remove from the tin, dust with cocoa powder, if you like, and slice the tart to serve.

Lemon Tart

Preparation Time
30 minutes, plus chilling
Cooking Time
about 50 minutes

- ◆ butter to grease
- ◆ plain flour to dust
- ◆ Sweet Shortcrust Pastry (see page 330), made with 150g (5oz) plain flour, 75g (3oz) unsalted butter, 50g (2oz) icing sugar and 2 large egg yolks

FILLING AND DECORATION

- ◆ 1 large egg, plus 4 large yolks
- ◆ 150g (5oz) caster sugar
- ◆ grated zest of 4 lemons
- ◆ 150ml (¼ pint) freshly squeezed lemon juice (about 4 medium lemons)
- ◆ 150ml (¼ pint) double cream
- ◆ peach slices and fresh or frozen raspberries, thawed, to decorate
- ◆ icing sugar to dust

NUTRITIONAL
INFORMATION
Per slice 385 cals; 23g fat (of which 13g saturates); 42g carbohydrate; 0.2g salt

Cuts into 8 slices

1 Grease and flour a 23 x 2.5cm (9 x 1 inch) loose-based flan tin. Roll out the pastry on a lightly floured surface to make a circle – if the pastry sticks to the surface, gently ease a palette knife under it to loosen. Line the tin with the pastry and trim the excess. Prick the base all over with a fork. Chill for 30 minutes.

2 Preheat the oven to 190°C (170°C fan oven) mark 5. Put the tin on a baking sheet and bake the pastry case blind (see page 325). Remove from the oven, leaving the flan tin on the baking sheet. Lower the oven setting to 170°C (150°C fan oven) mark 3.

3 Meanwhile, to make the filling, put the whole egg, egg yolks and caster sugar into a bowl and beat together with a wooden spoon or balloon whisk until

smooth. Carefully stir in the lemon zest, lemon juice and cream. Leave to stand for 5 minutes.

4 Ladle three-quarters of the filling into the pastry case, position the baking sheet on the oven shelf and ladle in the remainder. Bake for 25–30 minutes until the filling bounces back when touched lightly in the centre. Cool for 15 minutes to serve warm, or cool completely and chill. Decorate with peaches and raspberries and dust with icing sugar.

Caramelized Orange Tart

Preparation Time
15 minutes, plus chilling
Cooking Time
45 minutes, plus cooling

- 225g (8oz) plain flour, plus extra to dust
- a pinch of salt
- 125g (4oz) unsalted butter, diced
- 2 tbsp golden icing sugar
- 1 medium egg yolk, beaten

FILLING
- juice of 1 lemon
- juice of 1 orange
- zest of 2 oranges
- 75g (3oz) unsalted butter
- 225g (8oz) golden granulated sugar
- 3 medium eggs, beaten
- 75g (3oz) ground almonds
- 2 tbsp orange liqueur
- a few drops of orange food colouring (optional)

DECORATION
- 100g (3½oz) golden caster sugar
- pared zest of 1 orange, cut into slivers

NUTRITIONAL INFORMATION
Per slice 556 cals; 29g fat (of which 14g saturates); 70g carbohydrate; 0.5g salt

Cuts into 8 slices

1 To make the pastry, put the flour, salt, butter and icing sugar into a food processor and pulse until the mixture forms fine crumbs. (Alternatively, rub the fat into the flour, by hand or using a pastry cutter, then stir in the icing sugar.) Beat the egg yolk with 2 tbsp cold water and add to the flour mixture. Process (or stir) until the crumbs make a dough. Knead lightly, wrap and chill for 30 minutes.

2 To make the filling, put the juices, orange zest, butter, sugar and eggs into a heavy-based pan and heat gently, stirring until thickened. Stir in the almonds, liqueur and food colouring, if you like, then set aside.

3 Preheat the oven to 200°C (180°C fan oven) mark 6. Roll out the dough on a lightly floured surface and use

to line a 23cm (9 inch) tin. Prick the base all over with a fork. Cover and chill for 10 minutes.

4 Bake the pastry case blind (see page 325). Remove from the oven. Lower the oven setting to 180°C (160°C fan oven) mark 4. Pour the filling into the pastry case and bake for 20 minutes or until just firm. Cool in the tin.

5 To decorate, preheat the grill. Dissolve 50g (2oz) sugar in a pan with 300ml (½ pint) water. Add the orange zest and simmer for 10–15 minutes until the liquid has reduced and the zest is tender. Drain. Sprinkle the rest of the sugar over the tart. Caramelize under the hot grill, then leave to cool. Spoon the orange zest around the edge to serve.

Cherry and Almond Tart

Preparation Time
35 minutes, plus chilling
Cooking Time
30 minutes

- 200g (7oz) plain flour, sifted, plus extra to dust
- 100g (3½oz) unsalted butter, chilled and cut into cubes
- 50g (2oz) ground almonds
- 25g (1oz) caster sugar
- 2–3 drops of almond extract
- 1 large egg, beaten

FILLING

- 650g (1lb 7oz) fresh whole cherries (see Notes)
- 3 tbsp morello cherry conserve
- 250g (9oz) mascarpone cheese
- 4 tbsp elderflower cordial (see Notes)
- 75g (3oz) icing sugar, sifted
- seeds scraped from 1 vanilla pod
- 250ml (9fl oz) double cream

NUTRITIONAL INFORMATION

Per slice 425 cals; 30g fat (of which 18g saturates); 35g carbohydrate; 0.2g salt

1 To make the pastry, put the flour, butter and almonds into a food processor and pulse until the mixture resembles fine breadcrumbs. Add the caster sugar and almond extract and pulse again to combine. Tip into a bowl. Add just enough egg to bind the mixture, stirring with a blunt-ended knife, then use your hands to bring the pastry together. Wrap in clingfilm and chill for 30 minutes.

2 Roll out the pastry on a lightly floured surface to a thickness of 3mm (⅛ inch). Use to line a 23cm (9 inch) straight-sided, loose-based tart tin. Prick the base all over and chill for 30 minutes.

3 Preheat the oven to 190°C (170°C fan oven) mark 5. Bake the pastry case blind (see page 325) for 12–15 minutes, then remove the beans and paper and bake for a further 10–12 minutes until the base feels sandy. Cool in the tin on a wire rack.

4 Meanwhile, pit the cherries and put into a pan with the conserve and 125ml (4fl oz) water. Bring to a gentle simmer, then poach for 3 minutes or until the cherries are just starting to soften. Using a slotted spoon, strain off the cherries into a bowl and set aside to cool, leaving the syrup in the pan. Return the pan to the hob and simmer the liquid until syrupy and reduced by half. Strain and leave to cool.

5 Beat together the mascarpone, cordial, icing sugar and vanilla seeds until smooth. In a separate bowl, lightly whip the cream until soft peaks form. Fold the cream into the mascarpone mixture, then spoon into the cooked pastry case and level the surface. Up to 3 hours ahead, remove the filled pastry case from the tin and arrange the cooled cherries on top, then brush with syrup to glaze. Serve.

Notes

If you don't have fresh cherries, use tinned. Drain them well – no need to poach. Simmer the conserve and water in a pan, without the cherries, until syrupy, then complete the recipe.
Elderflower Cordial: Pick 20 large young elderflower heads (shake to release any insects). Bring 1.2 litres (2 pints) water to the boil, add 2kg (4½lb) golden granulated sugar and stir until dissolved. Then add 80g (3¼oz) citric acid and 2 medium lemons, sliced. Stir in the flower heads. Cover and leave overnight. In the morning, strain the liquid. If you want it to be clearer, strain again through muslin or a coffee filter. Bottle and store in the fridge – it will last for months.

Cuts into 12 slices

Cuts into 8 slices

Express Apple Tart

Preparation Time
10 minutes
Cooking Time
20 minutes

◆ 375g ready-rolled puff pastry
◆ 500g (1lb 2oz) dessert apples, such as Cox's Orange Pippins, cored and thinly sliced, then tossed in the juice of 1 lemon
◆ golden icing sugar to dust

NUTRITIONAL INFORMATION
per slice 197 cals; 12g fat (of which 0g saturates); 24g carbohydrate; 0.4g salt

1 Preheat the oven to 200°C (180°C fan oven) mark 6. Unroll the pastry on to a 28 x 38cm (11 x 15 inch) baking sheet and lightly roll a rolling pin over it to smooth down the pastry. Score lightly around the edge, leaving a 3cm (1¼ inch) border.

2 Put the apple slices on top of the pastry, within the border. Turn the edge of the pastry inwards to reach the edge of the apples, pressing it down and using your fingers to crimp the edge. Dust heavily with icing sugar.

3 Bake for 20 minutes or until the pastry is cooked and the sugar has caramelized. Serve warm, dusted with more icing sugar.

Note
The pastry will be easier to unroll if you remove it from the fridge 10–15 minutes beforehand.

Glazed Cranberry and Orange Tart

Preparation Time
15 minutes
Cooking Time
6 minutes

- ◆ 350g (12oz) fresh or frozen cranberries, thawed
- ◆ grated zest and juice of 1 orange
- ◆ 125g (4oz) golden caster sugar
- ◆ ½ tbsp arrowroot
- ◆ 250g tub mascarpone cheese
- ◆ 200ml (7fl oz) ready-made fresh custard with real vanilla
- ◆ 20.5cm (8 inch) cooked shortcrust pastry case

NUTRITIONAL INFORMATION
Per slice 234 cals; 11g fat (of which 3g saturates); 29g carbohydrate; 0.2g salt

1 Tip the cranberries into a pan, add the orange zest, juice and sugar and bring to the boil. Reduce the heat and simmer for 5 minutes or until the cranberries are just softened and the syrup has reduced slightly. Using a slotted spoon, strain off the cranberries into a bowl and set aside, leaving the syrup in the pan.

2 Mix the arrowroot with 1 tbsp cold water, add to the pan and cook for 1 minute, stirring until the syrup has thickened. Pour over the cranberries and leave to cool.

3 Tip the mascarpone and custard into a bowl and, using a hand-held electric whisk, mix until smooth. Spoon into the pastry case, top with the cranberry mixture and serve.

Note

A shop-bought pastry case helps to cut corners but, if you prefer, you can make a pie crust using Sweet Shortcrust Pastry (see page 330).

Cuts into 8 slices

Cuts into 8 slices

Treacle Tart

Preparation Time
35 minutes, plus chilling and
cooling
Cooking Time
about 45 minutes

- 175g (6oz) plain flour, plus
  extra to dust
- 125g (4oz) butter, cold and
  cubed
- 40g (1½oz) caster sugar
- 1 medium egg yolk

FILLING
- 600g (1lb 5oz) golden syrup
- ½–1 tsp ground ginger to
  taste
- finely grated zest and juice of
  1 lemon
- 175g (6oz) fine fresh white
  breadcrumbs
- double cream or crème
  fraîche to serve

NUTRITIONAL INFORMATION
Per slice (without cream or
crème fraîche) 490 cals; 14g fat
(of which 8g saturates); 91g
carbohydrate; 0.7g salt

1 To make the pastry, put the flour and butter into a food processor and pulse until the mixture resembles fine breadcrumbs (alternatively, rub the butter into the flour using your fingers). Add the caster sugar and whizz (or stir) briefly to combine. Next, add the egg yolk and 2 tsp water and pulse (or stir with a blunt-ended cutlery knife) until the pastry comes together. Bring the pastry together into a disc with your hands, then wrap in clingfilm and chill for 30 minutes.

2 Roll out the pastry on a lightly floured surface and use to line a 20.5 x 4cm (8 x 1½ inch) round, loose-based tart tin. Prick the base all over with a fork and chill for 20 minutes.

3 Preheat the oven to 200°C (180°C fan oven) mark 6. Line the pastry case with a large square of baking parchment, then fill with ceramic baking beans or uncooked rice. Put the tin on a baking sheet and bake for 15 minutes. Carefully remove the baking parchment and baking beans or rice, return the tin to the oven and bake for 8 minutes or until the pastry is cooked through and feels sandy to the touch. Remove from the oven, but keep in the tin.

4 Gently heat the golden syrup, ground ginger and lemon zest and juice in a pan. When the mixture is loose and runny, take off the heat and stir in the breadcrumbs. Pour into the pastry case.

5 Return the tart to the oven and cook for 15–20 minutes until the filling looks lightly firm (give the tin a tap). Lift out of the tin and serve just warm or at room temperature with cream or crème fraîche.

Note
For convenience, complete the recipe to the end of step 3 up to one day in advance. Once cool, wrap the pastry case (in the tin) in clingfilm and store at a cool room temperature. You can then finish the tart up to 6 hours ahead and store at room temperature. To serve warm, reheat in an oven preheated to 200°C (180°C fan oven) mark 6 for 10 minutes. Serve with cream or crème fraîche.

Classic Custard Tart

Preparation Time
25 minutes, plus chilling
Cooking Time
1¼ hours, plus cooling

- Sweet Shortcrust Pastry (see page 330), made with 225g (8oz) plain flour, 175g (6oz) unsalted butter, 50g (2oz) golden caster sugar, finely grated zest of 1 lemon, 1 medium egg yolk
- plain flour to dust

FILLING
- 8 large egg yolks
- 75g (3oz) golden caster sugar
- 450ml (¾ pint) single cream
- nutmeg to grate

NUTRITIONAL
INFORMATION
Per slice 399 cals; 28g fat (of which 16g saturates); 32g carbohydrate; 0.4g salt

Cuts into 10 slices

1 Roll out the pastry on a lightly floured surface to a 3mm (⅛ inch) thickness. Use to line a 23 x 4cm (9 x 1½ inch) round flan tin. Prick the base all over with a fork and chill for 30 minutes.

2 Preheat the oven to 200°C (180°C fan oven) mark 6. Put the flan tin on a baking sheet and bake blind (see page 325). Remove from the oven. Lower the oven setting to 130°C (110°C fan oven) mark ½.

3 Using a wooden spoon, mix the egg yolks with the sugar. Gradually stir in the cream, then strain into a

jug to remove any eggy strands. Pour the mixture into the pastry case and bake for 40–50 minutes until just set with a little wobble. Grate plenty of nutmeg over the top and cool in the tin on a wire rack. Serve at room temperature.

Sweet Ricotta Tart

Preparation Time
25 minutes, plus chilling
Cooking Time
1 hour, plus cooling

- Sweet Shortcrust Pastry (see page 330), made with 200g (7oz) plain flour, 75g (3oz) unsalted butter, 50g (2oz) golden caster sugar and 1 medium egg in place of the egg yolks
- plain flour to dust
- a little beaten egg to seal the pastry case
- icing sugar to dust

FILLING

- 100g (3½oz) cracked wheat or bulgur wheat
- 200ml (7fl oz) milk
- 250g (9oz) ricotta cheese
- 150g (5oz) golden caster sugar
- 2 medium eggs
- 1 tbsp orange flower water
- 1 tsp vanilla extract
- ½ tsp ground cinnamon
- 1 piece – about 40g (1½oz) – candied peel, finely chopped

NUTRITIONAL INFORMATION
Per slice 404 cals; 15g fat (of which 9g saturates); 60g carbohydrate; 0.3g salt

Cuts into 8 slices

1 To make the filling, put the bulgur wheat into a pan and add the milk, then cover and bring to the boil. Reduce the heat and simmer for 5–8 minutes until all the liquid has been absorbed and the wheat still has a slight bite. Leave to cool.

2 Preheat the oven to 190°C (170°C fan oven) mark 5. Roll out the pastry on a lightly floured surface and use to line a 20.5cm (8 inch) loose-based sandwich tin. Prick the base all over with a fork. Cover and chill for 10 minutes. Knead together the trimmings, then wrap and chill. Bake the pastry case blind (see page 325).

Brush with beaten egg and put back in the oven for 1 minute to seal. Remove from the oven.

3 Put the ricotta into a bowl and add the sugar, eggs, orange flower water, vanilla extract and cinnamon. Beat well. Add the peel and wheat and mix.

4 Roll out the trimmings. Cut out six strips of 1 x 20.5cm (½ x 8 inches). Pour the filling into the pastry case, then lay the strips on top. Bake for 45 minutes. Leave in the tin for 10 minutes, then turn out on to a wire rack and cool completely. Dust with icing sugar.

Strawberry Tart

Preparation Time
40 minutes, plus chilling
Cooking Time
35–40 minutes, plus cooling

- Sweet Shortcrust Pastry (see page 330), made with 125g (4oz) plain flour, a pinch of salt, 50g (2oz) caster sugar, 50g (2oz) unsalted butter and 2 medium egg yolks
- plain flour to dust
- a little beaten egg to seal the pastry case

CRÈME PÂTISSIÈRE
- 300ml (½ pint) milk
- 1 vanilla pod, split, seeds separated
- 2 medium egg yolks
- 50g (2oz) golden caster sugar
- 2 tbsp plain flour
- 2 tbsp cornflour
- 50ml (2fl oz) crème fraîche

TOPPING
- 450g (1lb) medium strawberries, hulled and halved
- 6 tbsp redcurrant jelly

NUTRITIONAL INFORMATION
Per slice 384 cals; 15g fat (of which 8g saturates); 57g carbohydrate; 0.2g salt

1 To make the crème pâtissière, pour the milk into a pan and add the vanilla pod and seeds. Heat gently to just below boiling, then remove from the heat. Put the egg yolks and sugar into a bowl and beat until pale, then stir in the flours. Discard the vanilla pod, then gradually mix the hot milk into the yolk mixture. Return to the pan and slowly bring to the boil, stirring for 3–4 minutes until thick and smooth. Scrape into a bowl, cover with a circle of damp greaseproof paper and leave to cool.

2 Put the pastry between two sheets of lightly floured greaseproof paper and roll out thinly. Use to line a 23cm (9 inch) loose-based flan tin. Prick with a fork, line with greaseproof paper and chill for 30 minutes.

3 Preheat the oven to 190°C (170°C fan oven) mark 5. Bake the pastry case blind (see page 325). Brush the inside with beaten egg and put back in the oven for
1 minute to seal. Cool for 5 minutes, then remove from the tin and leave to cool completely.

4 Add the crème fraîche to the crème pâtissière and beat until smooth. Spread evenly in the pastry case. Arrange the strawberry halves on top, working from the outside edge into the centre.

5 Heat the redcurrant jelly in a pan until syrupy, whisking lightly. Using a pastry brush, cover the strawberries with jelly. Serve within 2 hours.

Cuts into 6 slices

Makes 8

Raspberry and White Chocolate Tarts

Preparation Time
40 minutes, plus chilling
Cooking Time
40 minutes, plus cooling,
overnight chilling and thawing

- 225g (8oz) plain flour, plus extra to dust
- 150g (5oz) butter, cut into cubes
- 50g (2oz) icing sugar, plus extra to dust
- 2–3 drops of vanilla extract
- 1 large egg, lightly beaten
- 350–450g (12oz–1lb) raspberries
- pouring cream to serve

FILLING
- 275g (10oz) good-quality white chocolate, broken into small pieces
- 300ml (½ pint) double cream
- 1 vanilla pod, split
- 2 large eggs, separated
- 2 tbsp kirsch

NUTRITIONAL INFORMATION
Per tart 648 cals; 49g fat (of which 28g saturates); 52g carbohydrate; 0.6g salt

1 Put the flour, butter and icing sugar into a food processor and pulse until the mixture resembles fine crumbs. (Alternatively, rub the butter into the dry ingredients in a large bowl by hand or using a pastry cutter.) Add the vanilla extract and the beaten egg. Pulse, or stir with a fork, until the dough comes together to form a ball. Wrap in clingfilm and chill for at least 30 minutes.

2 Roll out the pastry thinly on a lightly floured surface. Cut out rounds and use to line eight 9 x 3cm (3½ x 1¼ inch) loose-based tart tins. If the pastry cracks as you line the tins, just patch it together. Prick the base all over with a fork, then chill for 30 minutes.

3 Preheat the oven to 200°C (180°C fan oven) mark 6. Bake the pastry cases blind (see page 325). Remove from the oven and leave in the tins to cool slightly. Lower the oven setting to 190°C (170°C fan oven) mark 5.

4 To make the filling, put the chocolate into a bowl. Pour the cream into a small, heavy-based pan, add the vanilla and bring just to the boil. Take off the heat and remove the vanilla. Slowly pour the cream on to the chocolate and stir until the chocolate is melted. Leave to cool.

5 Mix the egg yolks and kirsch into the cooled chocolate mixture. Put the egg whites into a large, grease-free bowl and whisk until soft peaks form, then fold carefully into the chocolate mixture until evenly incorporated. Pour the filling into the pastry cases.

6 Bake for 10–15 minutes until just set. If the filling appears to be colouring too quickly in the oven, cover with foil. Leave to cool in the tins. Don't worry if the filling seems very soft – it will become firmer on chilling. Chill for at least 5 hours or overnight.

7 Remove from the fridge 30 minutes before serving. Unmould on to plates. Arrange the raspberries on top, dust with icing sugar and serve with cream.

Banoffee Pie

Preparation Time
15 minutes, plus chilling
Cooking Time
2–3 minutes

- 100g (3½oz) butter, melted, plus extra to grease
- 200g (7oz) digestive biscuits, roughly broken
- 2 small bananas, peeled and sliced
- 8 tbsp dulce de leche toffee sauce
- 284ml carton double cream
- 1 tbsp cocoa powder to dust

NUTRITIONAL INFORMATION
Per slice 250 cals; 19g fat (of which 10g saturates); 18g carbohydrate; 0.4g salt

1 Grease the base and sides of a 23cm (9 inch) loose-based tart tin. Whizz the biscuits in a food processor until they resemble breadcrumbs. Pour in the melted butter and whizz briefly to combine. Press the mixture into the base and up the sides of the prepared tart tin, using the back of a metal spoon to level the surface, and leave to chill for 2 hours.

2 Arrange the banana slices evenly over the biscuit base and spoon the dulce de leche on top. Whip the cream until thick and spread it over the top. Dust with a sprinkling of cocoa powder and serve.

Variations
- Top with a handful of toasted flaked almonds instead of the cocoa powder.
- Whizz 25g (1oz) chopped pecan nuts into the biscuits with the butter.
- Scatter grated plain dark chocolate over the cream.

Cuts into 14 slices

Chocolate Choux Buns

Preparation Time
25 minutes
Cooking Time
40–45 minutes, plus cooling

◆ 1 quantity Choux Pastry
  (see page 331)

FILLING
◆ 300ml (½ pint) double cream
◆ 1 tsp vanilla extract
◆ 1 tsp golden caster sugar

TOPPING
◆ 200g (7oz) plain chocolate,
  broken into pieces
◆ 75g (3oz) butter, at room
  temperature

NUTRITIONAL
INFORMATION
Per bun 475 cals; 40g fat (of which 25g
saturates); 25g carbohydrate; 0.3g salt

Makes 8

1 Preheat the oven to 220°C (200°C fan oven) mark 7. Sprinkle a non-stick baking sheet with a little water. Using two dampened tablespoons, spoon the choux paste into eight large mounds on the baking sheet, spacing them well apart to allow room for expansion.

2 Bake for about 30 minutes until risen and golden brown. Remove from the oven and pierce a hole in the side of each profiterole with a metal skewer – this will allow steam to escape. Put back in the switched-off oven for 10–15 minutes to dry out. Transfer to a wire rack and leave to cool.

3 To make the filling, whip the cream with the vanilla extract and sugar until soft peaks form. Split the choux buns and fill them with the cream.

4 To make the topping, melt the chocolate with the butter in a heatproof bowl set over a pan of gently simmering water, making sure the base of the bowl doesn't touch the water. Leave to cool until beginning to thicken. Top the choux buns with the warm melted chocolate to serve.

Variation
Éclairs: (Makes 12) Insert a medium plain nozzle into a piping bag, then fill the bag with the choux pastry. Pipe fingers 9cm (3½ inches) long on the baking sheet. Trim with a wet knife. Bake at 200°C (180°C fan oven) mark 6 for about 35 minutes until crisp and golden. Using a sharp, pointed knife, make a slit down the side of each bun to release the steam, then transfer to a wire rack and leave for 20–30 minutes to cool completely. Just before serving, whip 300ml (½ pint) double cream until stiff and use it to fill the éclairs.
Break 125g (4oz) plain chocolate into a bowl set over a pan of gently simmering water, making sure the base of the bowl doesn't touch the water. Stir until melted. Pour into a wide, shallow bowl and dip the top of each filled éclair into it, drawing each one across the surface of the chocolate. Leave to set.

Profiterole Pyramid

Preparation Time
45 minutes
Cooking Time
about 50 minutes

- 75g (3oz) butter
- 100g (3½oz) plain flour
- 2 large eggs, lightly beaten

FILLING
- 450ml (¾ pint) double cream
- 40g (1½oz) icing sugar, sifted
- 2 tsp vanilla extract
- 1–2 tbsp brandy (optional)
- 100g (3½oz) caster sugar

NUTRITIONAL
INFORMATION
Per profiterole 139 cals; 11g fat
(of which 7g saturates); 8g
carbohydrate; 0.1g salt

Makes about 28 profiteroles

1 Preheat the oven to 200°C (180°C fan oven) mark 6. Melt the butter in a large pan, then add 225ml (8fl oz) water. Bring to the boil, then as soon as the mixture is bubbling rapidly, take the pan off the heat and stir in the flour. Continue stirring until the mixture comes away from the sides of the pan.

2 Transfer to a large bowl and start beating with a hand-held electric whisk. Gradually add the eggs, whisking all the time. The pastry should be thick and smooth.

3 Dollop heaped teaspoonfuls of the mixture on non-stick baking sheets, spacing them well apart (there should be about 28). Use a damp finger to smooth the mounds as much as possible. Bake for 25–30 minutes until a deep golden colour. Remove from the oven and pierce a hole in the base of each profiterole with a metal skewer – this will allow steam to escape. Lay the buns on their sides and return to the oven for 3–5 minutes to dry out. Cool completely on a wire rack.

4 Put the cream, icing sugar, vanilla and brandy, if using, into a large bowl and whisk until the cream is thick and holds a shape. Insert a 5mm (¼ inch) nozzle into a piping bag, then fill the bag with the cream and fill each profiterole through its hole.

5 Arrange the profiteroles in a pyramid on a serving plate, using a little of the cream to fix the buns in place.

6 Put the caster sugar into a large frying pan and heat gently, swirling occasionally, until the sugar dissolves and cooks to a deep caramel colour. Using a metal spoon, drizzle the caramel over the profiteroles. Allow to harden for a few minutes before serving.

Note
For convenience, complete the recipe to the end of step 3 up to one day in advance. Store the cooled buns in an airtight container. Up to three hours before serving, preheat the oven to 200°C (180°C fan oven) mark 6. Put the buns on a baking tray and reheat for 5 minutes or until crisp. Cool completely. To serve, complete the recipe up to one hour ahead.

White Chocolate and Pistachio Profiteroles

Preparation Time
30 minutes
Cooking Time
about 30 minutes, plus cooling

- 60g (2½oz) butter, cubed, plus extra to grease
- 75g (3oz) plain flour
- 2 medium eggs, well beaten
- 50g (2oz) pistachios
- 75g (3oz) white chocolate
- 450ml (¾ pint) double cream
- 3 tbsp icing sugar

NUTRITIONAL INFORMATION
Per profiterole 496 cals; 44g fat (of which 25g saturates); 20g carbohydrate; 0.3g salt

1 Put the butter and 125ml (4fl oz) water into a large pan. Gently heat to melt the butter, then bring to the boil. Take off the heat, then quickly whisk in the flour. Carry on whisking until the mixture comes away from the sides of the pan (about 30 seconds). Cool for 15 minutes.

2 Preheat the oven to 200°C (180°C fan oven) mark 6 and lightly grease two baking sheets. Gradually whisk the eggs into the pan containing the cooled flour mixture, beating after each addition. Dollop teaspoonfuls of mixture on the baking sheets, spacing them well apart (you should have about 24). Use a damp finger to smooth the tops, then bake for about 25 minutes or until puffed and a deep golden colour.

3 Remove from the oven and pierce a hole in the bottom of each profiterole with a metal skewer – this will allow steam to escape. Transfer to a wire rack and leave to cool completely.

4 Meanwhile, put the pistachios into a food processor and whizz until finely ground. Set aside. Melt half the white chocolate in a heatproof bowl set over a pan of gently simmering water, making sure the base of the bowl doesn't touch the water. Leave to cool for about 10 minutes.

5 Put the cream and icing sugar into a large bowl and whip until the mixture holds soft peaks. Whisk in half the ground pistachios and the cooled melted chocolate. Insert a 5mm (¼ inch) nozzle into a piping bag, then fill the bag with the cream and pipe into the cooled profiteroles via the steam hole.

6 Stack the profiteroles on a serving plate. Melt the remaining white chocolate as before, then drizzle over the profiteroles. Scatter the remaining pistachios over them and serve.

Note
For convenience, complete the recipe to the end of step 5 up to one day in advance, then chill. Complete the recipe up to 3 hours ahead and chill until ready to serve.

Makes 8

Makes 8-10

Eccles Cakes

Preparation Time
10 minutes, plus resting
Cooking Time
15 minutes, plus cooling

- 212g (7½oz) puff pastry, thawed if frozen
- plain flour to dust
- 25g (1oz) butter, softened
- 25g (1oz) dark soft brown sugar
- 25g (1oz) fine chopped mixed peel
- 50g (2oz) currants
- caster sugar to sprinkle

NUTRITIONAL INFORMATION
Per cake 126–158 calories; 7–9g fat (of which 1–2g saturates); 15–19g carbohydrate; 0.2–0.3g salt

1 Roll out the puff pastry on a lightly floured surface and cut into 9cm (3½ inch) rounds.

2 To make the filling, mix the butter, sugar, mixed peel and currants in a bowl.

3 Place 1 tsp of the fruit and butter mixture in the centre of each pastry round. Draw up the edges of the pastry round to enclose the filling, brush the edges with water and pinch together firmly, then reshape. Turn each round over and roll lightly until the currants just show through. Prick the top of each with a fork. Leave to rest for about 10 minutes in a cool place. Preheat the oven to 230°C (210°C fan oven) mark 8.

4 Put the pastry rounds on a damp baking sheet and bake for about 15 minutes until golden. Transfer to a wire rack and leave to cool for 30 minutes. Sprinkle with caster sugar while still warm.

Raspberry Millefeuilles

Preparation Time
40 minutes, plus chilling
Cooking Time
40 minutes, plus cooling and
standing

- 550g (1¼lb) puff pastry, thawed if frozen
- plain flour to dust
- 25g (1oz) caster sugar, plus 3 tbsp
- 50g (2oz) hazelnuts, toasted and chopped
- 225g (8oz) raspberries
- 1 tbsp lemon juice
- 1 x quantity Confectioner's Custard
- 300ml (½ pint) double cream
- 50g (2oz) icing sugar, sifted

NUTRITIONAL INFORMATION
Per cake 828 cals; 57g fat (of which 23g saturates); 65g carbohydrate; 1.4g salt

Makes 8

1 Cut the pastry into three and roll out each piece on a lightly floured surface into an 18 x 35.5cm (7 x 14 inch) rectangle. Put each on a baking sheet, prick and chill for 30 minutes.

2 Preheat the oven to 220°C (200°C fan oven) mark 7. Bake the pastry for 10 minutes, then turn the pieces over and cook for another 3 minutes. Sprinkle each sheet with 1 tbsp caster sugar and one-third of the nuts. Return to the oven for 8 minutes or until the sugar dissolves. Cool slightly, then transfer to wire racks to cool.

3 Sprinkle the raspberries with 25g (1oz) caster sugar and the lemon juice. Beat the custard until smooth. Whip the cream until thick and fold it into the custard with the raspberries and juices. Cover and chill.

4 Put the icing sugar into a bowl and stir in 2 tbsp water. Trim each pastry sheet to 15 x 30.5cm (6 x 12 inches) and drizzle with the icing. Leave for 15 minutes. Spoon half the custard over a sheet of pastry. Put another sheet on top and spoon on the remaining custard. Top with the final sheet and press down lightly. Leave for 30 minutes before slicing.

Confectioner's Custard

Scrape the vanilla seeds from 1 vanilla pod into a pan. Add the pod and 450ml (¾ pint) milk, bring to the boil, then set aside for 30 minutes. Remove the vanilla pod. Whisk 4 large egg yolks and 75g (3oz) caster sugar until pale. Mix in 50g (2oz) plain flour. Strain in a quarter of the infused milk and mix, then stir in the remainder. Return to the pan and bring to the boil over a low heat, stirring. Pour into a bowl, cover with clingfilm, cool and chill for 3–4 hours.

Apple and Cranberry Strudel

Preparation Time
20 minutes
Cooking Time
40 minutes

- 700g (1½lb) red apples, quartered, cored and thickly sliced
- 1 tbsp lemon juice
- 2 tbsp golden caster sugar
- 100g (3½oz) dried cranberries
- 6 sheets of filo pastry, thawed if frozen
- 1 tbsp olive oil
- crème fraîche or Greek-style yogurt to serve

NUTRITIONAL INFORMATION
Per cake 178 cals; 2g fat (of which trace saturates); 40g carbohydrate; 0g salt

Makes 6

1 Preheat the oven to 190°C (170°C fan oven) mark 5. Put the apples into a bowl and mix with the lemon juice, 1 tbsp sugar and the cranberries.

2 Lay three sheets of filo pastry side by side, overlapping the long edges. Brush with a little oil. Cover with three more sheets of filo and brush again. Tip the apple mixture on to the pastry, leaving a 2cm (¾ inch) border all round. Brush the border with a little water, then roll up the strudel from a long edge. Put on to a non-stick baking sheet, brush with the remaining oil and sprinkle with the remaining sugar.

3 Bake in the oven for 40 minutes or until the pastry is golden and the apples are soft. Serve with crème fraîche or yogurt.

Pistachio Baklava

Preparation Time
30 minutes
Cooking Time
40–45 minutes, plus cooling

- 175g (6oz) shelled, unsalted pistachio nuts
- 125g (4oz) pinenuts
- 1 tsp ground cinnamon
- ½ tsp ground cloves
- a pinch of freshly grated nutmeg
- 2 tbsp caster sugar
- 225g (8oz) filo pastry, thawed if frozen
- 75g (3oz) unsalted butter, melted

SYRUP
- grated zest and juice of ½ lemon
- 225g (8oz) clear honey
- 2 cardamom pods, bruised
- 2 tbsp rosewater (optional)

NUTRITIONAL INFORMATION
Per baklava 479 cals; 31g fat (of which 7g saturates); 45g carbohydrate; 0.4g salt

Makes 8

1 Preheat the oven to 180°C (160°C fan oven) mark 4. Put the pistachio nuts, pinenuts, cinnamon, cloves and nutmeg into a food processor and pulse briefly until coarsely ground. Stir in the sugar.

2 Brush a sheet of filo pastry with melted butter and press into an 18 x 25.5cm (7 x 10 inch) baking tin. Continue to brush and layer half the filo. Scatter the nut mixture over it, then top with the remaining filo sheets, brushing each with butter. Score through the pastry in a diamond pattern. Drizzle with any remaining butter and bake for 20 minutes. Lower the oven setting to 170°C (150°C fan oven) mark 3 and bake for a further 20–25 minutes until crisp and golden.

3 To make the syrup, put the lemon zest and juice, honey, cardamom pods and 150ml (¼ pint) water into a pan and simmer gently for 5 minutes. Remove from the heat and stir in the rosewater, if you like. Pour half the honey syrup evenly over the hot baklava. Leave in the tin until completely cold. Cut into diamond shapes and drizzle with the remaining syrup.

Oven Scones

Preparation Time
15 minutes
Cooking Time
10 minutes, plus cooling

- 40g (1½oz) butter, diced, plus extra to grease
- 225g (8oz) self-raising flour, plus extra to dust
- a pinch of salt
- 1 tsp baking powder
- about 150ml (¼ pint) milk
- beaten egg or milk to glaze
- whipped cream, or butter and jam to serve

NUTRITIONAL INFORMATION

Per scone 140 cals; 5g fat (of which 3g saturates); 22g carbohydrate; 0.7g salt

Makes 8

1 Preheat the oven to 220°C (200°C fan oven) mark 7. Grease a baking sheet. Sift the flour, salt and baking powder into a bowl. Rub in the butter until the mixture resembles fine breadcrumbs. Using a knife to stir it in, add enough milk to give a fairly soft dough.

2 Gently roll or pat out the dough on a lightly floured surface to a 2cm (¾ inch) thickness and then, using a 6cm (2½ inch) plain cutter, cut out rounds.

3 Put on the baking sheet and brush the tops with beaten egg or milk. Bake for about 10 minutes until golden brown and well risen. Transfer to a wire rack and leave to cool.

4 Serve warm, split and filled with cream, or butter and jam.

Note
To ensure a good rise, avoid heavy handling and make sure the rolled-out dough is at least 2cm (¾ inch) thick.

Breads

White Farmhouse Loaf

BREAD MACHINE RECIPE
Preparation Time
10 minutes, plus kneading
Cooking Time
as per your machine, plus
cooling

- 1 tsp easy-blend dried yeast
- 500g (1lb 2oz) strong white bread flour, plus extra to sprinkle
- 1 tbsp caster sugar
- 2 tbsp milk powder
- 1½ tsp salt
- 25g (1oz) butter
- 350ml (12fl oz) water

NUTRITIONAL INFORMATION
Per slice 180 cals; 3g fat (of which 1g saturates); 34g carbohydrate; 0.9g salt

Makes 1 loaf – cuts into about 12 slices

1 Put the ingredients into the bread-maker's bucket, following the order and method specified in the manual.

2 Fit the bucket into the bread-maker and set to the basic program with a crust of your choice. Press Start.

3 Just before baking starts, brush the top of the dough with water and sprinkle with flour. If preferred, slash the top of the bread lengthways with a sharp knife, taking care not to scratch the bucket.

4 After baking, remove the bucket from the machine, then turn out the loaf on to a wire rack to cool.

Brown Loaf

Preparation Time
25 minutes, plus 'sponging' and
rising
Cooking Time
45–50 minutes, plus cooling

- ◆ 300g (11oz) strong plain
  white flour, sifted, plus extra
  to dust
- ◆ 200g (7oz) strong plain
  wholemeal flour
- ◆ 15g (½oz) fresh yeast or 1 tsp
  traditional dried yeast
- ◆ 2 tsp salt
- ◆ vegetable oil to grease

**NUTRITIONAL
INFORMATION**
Per slice 100 cals; 1g fat (of which
0.1g saturates); 22g carbohydrate;
0.6g salt

Makes 1 loaf –
cuts into 16 slices

1 Put both flours into a large bowl, make a well in the centre and pour in 300ml (11fl oz) tepid water. Crumble the fresh yeast into the water (if using dried yeast, just sprinkle it on top). Draw a little of the flour into the water and yeast and mix to form a batter. Sprinkle the salt over the remaining dry flour, so that it doesn't come into contact with the yeast. Cover with a clean tea towel and leave to 'sponge' for 20 minutes.

2 Combine the flour and salt with the batter to make a soft dough and knead for at least 10 minutes or until the dough feels smooth and elastic. Shape into a ball, put into an oiled bowl, cover with the tea towel and leave to rise at a warm room temperature until doubled in size (2–3 hours).

3 Knock back the dough, knead briefly and shape into a round on a lightly floured baking sheet. Slash the top with a sharp knife and dust with flour. Cover and leave to rise for 45 minutes–1½ hours until doubled in size and spongy.

4 Preheat the oven to 200°C (180°C fan oven) mark 6. Bake the loaf for 45–50 minutes until it sounds hollow when tapped underneath. Transfer to a wire rack and leave to cool.

Note
The 'sponging' process in step 1 adds a fermentation stage, which gives a slightly lighter loaf.

Wholemeal Bread

Preparation Time
15 minutes, plus rising
Cooking Time
30–35 minutes, plus cooling

- 225g (8oz) strong plain white flour, plus extra to dust
- 450g (1lb) strong plain wholemeal flour
- 2 tsp salt
- 1 tsp golden caster sugar
- 2 tsp fast-action dried yeast (see Note)
- vegetable oil to grease

NUTRITIONAL INFORMATION
Per slice 140 cals; 1g fat (of which 0.1g saturates); 29g carbohydrate; 0.6g salt

1 Sift the white flour into a large bowl and stir in the wholemeal flour, salt, sugar and yeast. Make a well in the centre and add about 450ml (¾ pint) warm water. Work to a smooth, soft dough, adding a little extra water if necessary.

2 Knead for 10 minutes or until smooth, then shape the dough into a ball and put into an oiled bowl. Cover and leave to rise in a warm place for about 2 hours until doubled in size.

3 Knock back the dough on a lightly floured surface and shape into an oblong. Press into an oiled 900g (2lb) loaf tin, cover and leave to rise for a further 30 minutes.

4 Preheat the oven to 230°C (210°C fan oven) mark 8. Bake the loaf for 15 minutes. Lower the oven setting to 200°C (180°C fan oven) mark 6 and bake for a further 15–20 minutes until the bread is risen and sounds hollow when tapped underneath. Leave in the tin for 10 minutes, then turn out on to a wire rack and leave to cool.

Note
If available, use 40g (1½oz) fresh yeast instead of dried. Proceed as for Brown Loaf (see step 1, page 231).

Makes 1 loaf –
cuts into 16 slices

Makes 1 loaf –
cuts into about 16 slices

Dark Rye Bread

Preparation Time
20 minutes, plus rising
Cooking Time
about 50 minutes, plus cooling

- 350g (12oz) rye flour, plus extra to dust
- 50g (2oz) plain wholemeal flour
- zest of 1 lemon
- 1 tsp salt
- 25g (1oz) butter
- 1 tsp caraway seeds, lightly crushed (optional)
- 125g (4oz) cool mashed potato
- 15g (½oz) fresh yeast or 1½ tsp traditional dried yeast and 1 tsp sugar
- 1 tsp sugar
- 50g (2oz) molasses or black treacle
- oil to grease

NUTRITIONAL INFORMATION
Per slice 112 calories; 2g fat (of which 1g saturates); 22g carbohydrate; 0.4g salt

1 Mix together the flours, lemon zest and salt. Rub in the butter, caraway seeds, if you like, and mashed potato.

2 Blend the fresh yeast with 150ml (¼ pint) tepid water. If using dried yeast, sprinkle it into the water with 1 tsp sugar and leave in a warm place for 15 minutes or until frothy. Heat the other 1 tsp sugar, the molasses and 2 tbsp water together, then cool until tepid.

3 Pour the yeast liquid and molasses mixture on to the dry ingredients and beat well to form a firm dough. Knead on a lightly floured surface for 10 minutes or until smooth and no longer sticky. Place in an oiled bowl, cover with oiled clingfilm and leave to rise in a warm place for about 1½ hours until doubled in size.

4 Knead again for 5 minutes, then shape into a large round, about 18cm (7 inches) in diameter. Place on a baking sheet. Cut a criss-cross pattern on the surface of the loaf to a depth of 5mm (¼ inch). Dust with a little more flour. Leave to rise in a warm place for 10–15 minutes. Preheat the oven to 200°C (180°C fan oven) mark 6.

5 Bake the loaf in the oven for about 50 minutes. Turn out on to a wire rack and leave to cool completely.

Freezing tip
To freeze, complete the recipe. Once the bread is cold, slice, if you like, for convenience, then pack, seal and freeze. To use, thaw at a cool room temperature.

Oatmeal Soda Bread

Preparation Time
15 minutes
Cooking Time
25 minutes, plus cooling

- 25g (1oz) butter, plus extra to grease
- 275g (10oz) plain wholemeal flour
- 175g (6oz) coarse oatmeal
- 2 tsp cream of tartar
- 1 tsp salt
- about 300ml (10fl oz) milk and water, mixed

NUTRITIONAL INFORMATION
Per slice 183 cals; 4g fat (of which 2g saturates); 31g carbohydrate; 0.6g salt

Makes 1 loaf – cuts into about 10 slices

1 Preheat the oven to 220°C (200°C fan oven) mark 7. Grease and base-line a 900g (2lb) loaf tin.

2 Mix together all the dry ingredients in a bowl. Rub in the butter, then add the milk and water to bind to a soft dough. Spoon into the prepared tin.

3 Bake in the oven for about 25 minutes until golden brown and well risen. Turn out on to a wire rack and leave to cool slightly. This bread is best eaten on the day it is made.

Cornbread

Preparation Time
5 minutes
Cooking Time
25–30 minutes

- oil to grease
- 125g (4oz) plain flour
- 175g (6oz) polenta (see Note) or cornmeal
- 1 tbsp baking powder
- 1 tbsp caster sugar
- ½ tsp salt
- 300ml (½ pint) buttermilk, or equal quantities of natural yogurt and milk, mixed together
- 2 medium eggs
- 4 tbsp extra virgin olive oil

NUTRITIONAL INFORMATION
Per wedge 229 cals; 8g fat (of which 1g saturates); 33g carbohydrate; 1.3g salt

Makes 1 loaf – cuts into 8 wedges

1 Preheat the oven to 200°C (180°C fan oven) mark 6. Generously oil a shallow 20.5cm (8 inch) square tin.

2 Put the flour into a large bowl, then add the polenta or cornmeal, the baking powder, sugar and salt. Make a well in the centre and pour in the buttermilk or yogurt and milk mixture. Add the eggs and olive oil and stir together until evenly mixed.

3 Pour into the tin and bake for 25–30 minutes until firm to the touch. Insert a skewer into the centre – if it comes out clean, the cornbread is done.

4 Leave the cornbread to rest in the tin for 5 minutes, then turn out and cut into chunky triangles. Serve warm with butter.

Note
Use dried polenta grains for this recipe.

Black Olive Bread

Preparation Time
40 minutes, plus rising
Cooking Time
30–35 minutes

- ◆ 2 tsp traditional dried yeast
- ◆ 500g (1lb 2oz) strong white bread flour, plus extra to dust
- ◆ 2 tsp coarse salt, plus extra to sprinkle
- ◆ 6 tbsp extra virgin olive oil, plus extra to grease
- ◆ 100g (3½oz) black olives, pitted and chopped

NUTRITIONAL INFORMATION
Per loaf 600 cals; 21g fat (of which 3g saturates); 97g carbohydrate; 3.8g salt

Makes 2 loaves

1 Put 150ml (¼ pint) hand-hot water into a jug, stir in the yeast and leave for 10 minutes or until frothy. Put the flour into a bowl or a food processor, then add the salt, yeast mix, 200ml (7fl oz) warm water and 2 tbsp olive oil. Using a wooden spoon or the dough hook, mix for 2–3 minutes to make a soft, smooth dough. Put the dough into a lightly oiled bowl, cover with oiled clingfilm and leave in a warm place for 45 minutes or until doubled in size.

2 Punch the dough to knock out the air, then knead on a lightly floured surface for 1 minute. Add the

olives and knead until combined. Divide in half, shape into rectangles and put into two greased tins, each about 25.5 x 15cm (10 x 6 inches). Cover with clingfilm and leave in a warm place for 1 hour or until the dough is puffy.

3 Preheat the oven to 200°C (180°C fan oven) mark 6. Press your finger into the dough 12 times, drizzle 2 tbsp oil over the surface and sprinkle with salt. Bake for 30–35 minutes until golden. Drizzle with the remaining oil. Slice and serve warm.

Toasted Seed and Nut Bread

BREAD MACHINE RECIPE
Preparation Time
10 minutes, plus kneading
Cooking Time
as per your machine, plus
cooling

- 75g (3oz) unblanched hazelnuts, finely chopped
- 2 tbsp each of poppy, sesame, sunflower and pumpkin seeds
- 1 tsp easy-blend dried yeast
- 375g (13oz) strong white bread flour
- 25g (1oz) wheat bran
- 1 tsp salt
- 2 tsp light muscovado sugar
- 2 tbsp hazelnut or sunflower oil

NUTRITIONAL INFORMATION
Per slice 256 cals; 13g fat (of which 1g saturates); 31g carbohydrate; 0.5g salt

Makes 1 medium loaf – cuts into about 10 slices

1 Toast the chopped hazelnuts in a dry frying pan over a gentle heat, stirring, until they begin to colour (about 2 minutes). Add the seeds and fry gently for a further 1 minute. Take off the heat.

2 Put all the remaining ingredients in the bread-maker's bucket with 300ml (½ pint) water, following the order and method specified in the manual. Set aside 2 tbsp of the toasted nut mixture; add the rest to the bucket.

3 Fit the bucket into the bread-maker and set to the basic program with a crust of your choice. Press Start.

4 Just before baking starts, brush the top of the dough with 1 tbsp water and sprinkle with the reserved nuts and seeds.

5 After baking, remove the bucket from the machine, then turn out the loaf on to a wire rack to cool.

Floury Baps

BREAD MACHINE RECIPE
Preparation Time
10 minutes, plus kneading and
rising
Cooking Time
18–20 minutes, plus cooling

- 1 tsp easy-blend dried yeast
- 450g (1lb) strong white bread flour, plus extra to dust
- 1 tsp salt
- 1 tsp golden caster sugar
- 15g (½oz) butter
- 150ml (¼ pint) milk, plus extra to brush
- oil to grease

NUTRITIONAL INFORMATION
Per bap 220 cals; 3g fat (of which 1g saturates); 45g carbohydrate; 0.7g salt

1 Put all the ingredients except the oil into the bread-maker's bucket with 125ml (4fl oz) water, following the order and method specified in the manual.

2 Fit the bucket into the bread-maker and set to the dough program. Press Start. Lightly oil a large baking sheet.

3 Once the dough is ready, turn it out on to a floured surface and punch it down to deflate. Divide into eight even-sized pieces. Shape each piece into a round and flatten with the palm of your hand until about 10cm (4 inches) in diameter.

4 Space slightly apart on the prepared baking sheet and brush lightly with milk. Sprinkle generously with flour, cover loosely with a cloth and leave to rise for 30–40 minutes until doubled in size.

5 Preheat the oven to 200°C (180°C fan oven) mark 6. Using your thumb, make a deep impression in the centre of each bap. Dust with a little more flour and bake for 18–20 minutes until risen and pale golden around the edges. Eat warm or transfer to a wire rack to cool.

Makes 8 baps

Makes 1 small loaf –
cuts into about 10 thick slices

Basic Gluten-free White Bread

BREAD MACHINE RECIPE
Preparation Time
5 minutes, plus kneading
Cooking Time
as per your machine, plus cooling

- 1 tsp easy-blend dried yeast
- 350g (12oz) gluten-free bread flour, for bread machines
- ½ tsp salt
- 1 tbsp olive oil

NUTRITIONAL INFORMATION
Per slice 130 cals; 2g fat (of which 0.2g saturates); 27g carbohydrate; 0.2g salt

1 Put all the ingredients into the bread-maker's bucket with 300ml (½ pint) water, following the order and method specified in the manual.

2 Fit the bucket into the bread-maker and set to the program and crust recommended for gluten-free breads. Press Start.

3 After baking, remove the bucket from the machine, then turn out the loaf on to a wire rack to cool.

Freezing tip
To freeze, complete the recipe. Once the bread is cold, slice, if you like, for convenience, then pack, seal and freeze. To use, thaw at a cool room temperature.

Pitta Bread

Preparation Time
20 minutes, plus rising
Cooking Time
5–8 minutes per batch, plus
cooling

- 15g (½oz) fresh yeast or
  1½ tsp traditional dried yeast
  and 1 tsp sugar
- 700g (1½lb) strong white
  flour, plus extra to dust
- 1 tsp salt
- 1 tbsp caster sugar
- 1 tbsp olive oil, plus extra to
  grease

**NUTRITIONAL
INFORMATION**
Per pitta 159 calories; 1g fat (of
which 0.2g saturates); 34g
carbohydrate; 0.3g salt

Makes 16 pitta breads

1 Blend the fresh yeast with 450ml (¾ pint) tepid water. If using dried yeast, sprinkle it into the water with the sugar and leave in a warm place for 15 minutes or until frothy.

2 Put the flour, salt and sugar into a bowl, make a well in the centre and pour in the yeast liquid with the olive oil. Mix to a smooth dough, then turn out on to a lightly floured surface and knead for 10 minutes or until smooth and elastic.

3 Place the dough in a large bowl, cover with oiled clingfilm and leave to rise in a warm place until doubled in size.

4 Divide the dough into 16 pieces and roll each into an oval shape about 20.5cm (8 inches) long. Place on floured baking sheets, cover with oiled clingfilm and leave in a warm place for about 30 minutes until slightly risen and puffy. Preheat the oven to 240°C (220°C fan oven) mark 9.

5 Bake the pittas in batches for 5–8 minutes only. They should be just lightly browned on top. Remove from the oven and wrap in a clean tea towel. Repeat with the remaining pittas.

6 When the pittas are warm enough to handle, but not completely cold, transfer them to a plastic bag and leave until cold. This will ensure that they have a soft crust.

7 To serve, warm in the oven, or toast lightly. Split and fill with salad, cheese, cold meats or your favourite sandwich filling. Or, cut into strips and serve with dips.

Focaccia

BREAD MACHINE RECIPE
Preparation Time
10 minutes, plus kneading and
rising
Cooking Time
20–25 minutes, plus cooling

- 1 tsp easy-blend dried yeast
- 475g (1lb 1oz) strong white
  bread flour, plus extra to dust
- 1½ tsp salt
- 3 tbsp olive oil, plus extra to
  grease

TOPPING AND DECORATION
- fresh rosemary sprigs
- 2 tbsp olive oil
- sea salt flakes

NUTRITIONAL
INFORMATION
Per wedge 264 cals; 8g fat (of
which 1g saturates); 45g
carbohydrate; 1.2g salt

Makes 1 large focaccia –
cuts into 6 wedges

1 Put all the dough ingredients into the bread-maker's bucket with 300ml (½ pint) water, following the order and method specified in the manual.

2 Fit the bucket into the bread-maker and set to the dough program. Press Start. Grease a 28cm (11 inch) metal flan ring (see Notes) and place on a greased baking sheet.

3 Once the dough is ready, turn it out on to a floured surface and punch it down to deflate. Roll out to a 25.5cm (10 inch) round and place inside the flan ring, pushing the dough to the edges. (Don't worry if it shrinks back: the dough will expand to fill the ring as it proves.) Cover loosely with oiled clingfilm and leave to rise in a warm place for 30 minutes.

4 Using fingertips dipped in flour, make deep dimples all over the dough. Scatter with small rosemary sprigs, drizzle with the olive oil and sprinkle generously with sea salt flakes. Re-cover with oiled clingfilm and leave for a further 10 minutes, as the dough might have shrunk back when dimpled. Preheat the oven to 200°C (180°C fan oven) mark 6.

5 Drizzle the dough with water. (This is not essential but helps the crust to stay soft during baking.) Bake for 20–25 minutes until just firm and a pale golden colour. Transfer to a wire rack and leave to cool.

Notes
- The flan ring helps the bread to rise and bake in a perfect round, but don't worry if you haven't got one: just lay the dough, pizza-style, on the baking sheet.
- Other toppings include finely chopped garlic, thinly sliced onions, roughly chopped olives and ground black pepper.

Crumpets

Preparation Time
20 minutes, plus rising
Cooking Time
about 35 minutes

- 350g (12oz) strong plain white flour
- ½ tsp salt
- ½ tsp bicarbonate of soda
- 1½ tsp fast-action dried yeast
- 250ml (9fl oz) warm milk
- a little vegetable oil to fry
- butter to serve

NUTRITIONAL INFORMATION
Per crumpet 60 cals; 1g fat (of which 0.1g saturates); 12g carbohydrate; 0.2g salt

1 Sift the flour, salt and bicarbonate of soda into a large bowl and stir in the yeast. Make a well in the centre, then pour in 300ml (½ pint) warm water and the milk. Mix to a thick batter.

2 Using a wooden spoon, beat the batter vigorously for about 5 minutes. Cover and leave in a warm place for about 1 hour until sponge-like in texture. Beat the batter for a further 2 minutes, then transfer to a jug.

3 Put a large, non-stick frying pan over a high heat and brush a little oil over the surface. Oil the insides of four crumpet rings or 7.5cm (3 inch) plain metal cutters. Put the rings, blunt-edge down, on the hot pan's surface and leave for about 2 minutes until very hot.

4 Pour a little batter into each ring to a depth of 1cm (½ inch). Cook the crumpets for 4–5 minutes until the surface is set and appears honeycombed with holes.

5 Carefully remove each metal ring. Flip the crumpets over and cook the other side for 1 minute only. Transfer to a wire rack. Repeat to use all of the batter.

6 To serve, toast the crumpets on both sides and serve with butter.

Note
The pan and metal rings must be well oiled each time, and heated between frying each batch.

Makes about 24

Roasted Red Onion and Gruyère Bread

BREAD MACHINE RECIPE
Preparation Time
20 minutes, plus kneading and rising
Cooking Time
25–30 minutes

- 2 tsp fennel seeds
- 1 tsp easy-blend dried yeast
- 300g (11oz) strong white bread flour, plus extra to dust
- ½ tsp celery salt
- 1 tsp golden caster sugar
- 2 tbsp olive oil

TOPPING

- 3 tbsp olive oil, plus extra to grease
- 450g (1lb) red onions, peeled and thinly sliced
- several fresh thyme sprigs, chopped
- 100g (3½oz) Gruyère cheese, thinly sliced
- salt and ground black pepper

NUTRITIONAL INFORMATION
Per wedge 348 cals; 16g fat
(of which 5g saturates); 44g
carbohydrate; 0.7g salt

Makes 1 round bread –
cuts into 6 large wedges

1 Lightly crush the fennel seeds, using a pestle and mortar. Put all the dough ingredients into the bread-maker's bucket with 200ml (7fl oz) water, following the order and method specified in the manual, adding the crushed fennel seeds with the flour.

2 Fit the bucket into the bread-maker and set to the dough program with pizza setting, if available, if not then the dough setting. Press Start.

3 While the dough is in the bread-maker, prepare the topping. Heat the oil in a frying pan, add the onions and fry gently for about 10 minutes until golden, stirring frequently. Stir in the thyme and seasoning.

4 Place a 28cm (11 inch) round metal flan ring on a baking sheet (see Note). Brush the inside of the ring and baking sheet with oil.

5 Once the dough is ready, turn it out on to a floured surface, knead lightly and roll out to a 28cm (11 inch) round. Lift the dough round into the ring on the baking sheet. Arrange the fried onion and cheese slices over the surface to within 1cm (½ inch) of the edges. Cover loosely with oiled clingfilm and leave in a warm place for 20 minutes. Preheat the oven to 220°C (200°C fan oven) mark 7.

6 Bake for 25–30 minutes until the crust is slightly risen and golden. Serve warm, cut into wedges.

Note
If you do not have a suitably sized metal flan ring, simply roll the dough to a large round and place directly on the baking sheet.

Sweet Cherry Bread

Preparation Time
40 minutes, plus rising
Cooking Time
40 minutes, plus cooling

- oil to grease
- 350g (12oz) strong white bread flour, plus extra to dust
- ½ tsp salt
- 2 tsp ground mixed spice
- 1 tsp ground cinnamon
- 25g (1oz) caster sugar
- 1 tbsp fast-action dried yeast
- 75g (3oz) unsalted butter, diced
- 200ml (7fl oz) warm milk
- 125g (4oz) white almond paste, roughly chopped
- 125g (4oz) glacé cherries
- 3 tbsp honey, warmed
- 75g (3oz) icing sugar, sifted

NUTRITIONAL INFORMATION
Per slice 310 cals; 4g fat (of which trace saturates); 66g carbohydrate; 0.4g salt

Cuts into 8 slices

1 Grease a deep 20.5cm (8 inch) round cake tin and base-line with greaseproof paper.

2 Sift the flour, salt, spices and caster sugar into a bowl. Add the yeast, then rub in the butter. Add the milk to make a dough (if the dough is too dry, add a little more milk). Turn out on to a lightly floured surface and knead for 10 minutes. Put the dough into a lightly oiled bowl, cover with oiled clingfilm and leave in a warm place for 2 hours or until doubled in size.

3 Turn out the dough on to a lightly floured surface and knead lightly. Shape into an oval, 60cm (24 inches) long. Scatter the almond paste and

cherries over the surface and roll up the dough lengthways, then form it into a tight coil. Put in the cake tin, cover and leave in a warm place for 30 minutes or until doubled in size. Preheat the oven to 180°C (160°C fan oven) mark 4.

4 Bake for 40 minutes or until golden; it should sound hollow when tapped underneath. Turn out on to a wire rack and leave to cool completely. When cool, brush with honey. Mix the icing sugar with a few drops of water and drizzle over the bread.

Makes 2 loaves –
each cuts into about 10 slices

Apricot and Hazelnut Bread

Preparation Time
25 minutes, plus rising
Cooking Time
30–35 minutes, plus cooling

- 75g (3oz) hazelnuts
- 450g (1lb) strong granary bread flour, plus extra to dust
- 1 tsp salt
- 25g (1oz) unsalted butter, diced
- 75g (3oz) ready-to-eat dried apricots, chopped
- 2 tsp fast-action dried yeast
- 2 tbsp molasses
- oil to grease
- milk to glaze

NUTRITIONAL INFORMATION
Per slice 118 cals; 4g fat (of which 0.9g saturates); 18g carbohydrate; 0.3g salt

1 Spread the hazelnuts on a baking sheet. Toast under a hot grill until golden brown, turning frequently. Put the hazelnuts in a clean tea towel and rub off the skins. Leave to cool. Chop and put to one side.

2 Put the flour into a large bowl. Add the salt, then rub in the butter. Stir in the hazelnuts, apricots and yeast. Make a well in the centre and gradually work in the molasses and about 225ml (8fl oz) hand-hot water to form a soft dough, adding a little more water if the dough feels dry. Knead for 8–10 minutes until smooth, then transfer the dough to an oiled bowl, cover and leave to rise in a warm place for 1–1¼ hours until doubled in size.

3 Punch the dough to knock back, then divide in half. Shape each portion into a small, flattish round and put on a well-floured baking sheet. Cover loosely and leave to rise for a further 30 minutes.

4 Preheat the oven to 220°C (200°C fan oven) mark 7 and put a large baking sheet on the top shelf to heat up.

5 Using a sharp knife, cut several slashes in each round, brush with a little milk and transfer to the heated baking sheet. Bake for 15 minutes, then lower the oven setting to 190°C (170°C fan oven) mark 5 and bake for a further 15–20 minutes until the bread is risen and sounds hollow when tapped underneath. Turn out on to a wire rack and leave the loaf to cool completely.

Variation
Replace the hazelnuts with walnuts or pecan nuts and use sultanas instead of apricots.

Fruited Muesli Loaf

BREAD MACHINE RECIPE
Preparation Time
10 minutes, plus kneading
Cooking Time
as per your machine, plus cooling

- 1½ tsp easy-blend dried yeast
- 225g (8oz) strong white bread flour
- 100g (3½oz) strong brown bread flour
- 100g (3½oz) natural (no added sugar or salt) muesli
- 1 tsp salt
- 1 tbsp clear honey, plus 2 tbsp clear honey to glaze
- 50g (2oz) raisins
- 25g (1oz) butter

NUTRITIONAL INFORMATION
Per slice 200 cals; 3g fat (of which 2g saturates); 39g carbohydrate; 0.6g salt

1 Put all the ingredients except the honey to glaze into the bread-maker's bucket with 250ml (9fl oz) water, following the order and method specified in the manual.

2 Fit the bucket into the bread-maker and set to the program that is recommended in the manual – usually multigrain. Select the crust of your choice and press Start.

3 After baking, remove the bucket from the machine, then turn out the loaf on to a wire rack to cool. Brush the top of the loaf with honey to glaze.

Freezing tip
To freeze, complete the recipe. Once the bread is cold, slice, if you like, for convenience, then pack, seal and freeze. To use, thaw at a cool room temperature.

Makes 1 medium loaf –
cuts into about 10 slices

Chocolate Macadamia Loaf

BREAD MACHINE RECIPE
Preparation Time
15 minutes, plus kneading
Cooking Time
15 minutes, plus baking time as
per your machine, and cooling
and setting

- 100g (3½oz) macadamia nuts,
  roughly chopped
- 1 large egg, plus 2 egg yolks
- 75g (3oz) unsalted butter,
  melted
- 2 tsp finely chopped fresh
  rosemary
- 1¼ tsp easy-blend dried yeast
- 400g (14oz) strong white
  bread flour
- ¾ tsp salt
- 50g (2oz) golden caster sugar
- 75g (3oz) plain chocolate,
  chopped
- 175g (6oz) white chocolate,
  chopped

**NUTRITIONAL
INFORMATION**
Per slice 450 cals; 25g fat (of
which 10g saturates); 52g
carbohydrate; 0.6g salt

Makes 1 medium loaf –
cuts into about 10 slices

1 Lightly toast the nuts in a frying pan over a low heat for about 3 minutes, shaking the pan frequently. Tip on to a plate and set aside.

2 Mix together the egg, egg yolks, butter, rosemary and 175ml (6fl oz) water. Put all the ingredients except the nuts and chocolate into the bread-maker's bucket, following the order and method specified in the manual.

3 Fit the bucket into the bread-maker and set to the basic program with raisin setting, if available. Select a light crust and press Start. Add the nuts, plain chocolate and 125g (4oz) white chocolate when the machine beeps, or halfway through the kneading program.

4 After baking, remove the bucket from the machine, then turn out the loaf on to a wire rack to cool. Once the bread has cooled, melt the remaining white chocolate carefully in a heatproof bowl set over a pan of hot water on the stove, simmering gently, making sure the base of the bowl doesn't touch the water. Stir until smooth, then spread over the top of the loaf. Leave to set.

Note
Macadamia nuts are mildly flavoured with an almost buttery taste – not a coincidence, as the nut has a high oil content.

Sticky Currant Buns

BREAD MACHINE RECIPE
Preparation Time
10 minutes, plus kneading and rising
Cooking Time
10–15 minutes, plus cooling

- 1 tsp easy-blend dried yeast
- 350g (12oz) strong white bread flour, plus extra to dust
- ½ tsp salt
- 1 tsp ground mixed spice
- 15g (½oz) butter, plus extra to grease
- finely grated zest of 1 orange
- 25g (1oz) light muscovado sugar
- 200ml (7fl oz) milk
- 75g (3oz) currants
- oil to grease

TOPPING

- 25g (1oz) light muscovado sugar
- 50g (2oz) rough sugar pieces, lightly crushed

NUTRITIONAL INFORMATION
Per bun 250 cals; 3g fat (of which 1g saturates); 53g carbohydrate; 0.4g salt

Makes 8

1 Put all the dough ingredients except the currants and oil into the bread-maker's bucket, following the order and method specified in the manual.

2 Fit the bucket into the bread-maker and set to the dough program with raisin setting, if available. Add the currants when the machine beeps, or halfway through the kneading cycle. Lightly grease a large baking sheet.

3 Once the dough is ready, turn out on to a floured surface and punch it down to deflate. Divide into eight evenly sized pieces, scrunch into rounds and space slightly apart on the prepared baking sheet. Cover with oiled clingfilm and leave to rise in a warm place for 30 minutes until doubled in size. Preheat the oven to 220°C (200°C fan oven) mark 7.

4 Bake the buns for 10–15 minutes until golden. Meanwhile, put the muscovado sugar in a small pan with 2 tbsp water and heat gently over a low heat until the sugar dissolves.

5 Transfer the buns to a wire rack and brush with the glaze, sprinkling them with the crushed sugar as you work. Leave to cool.

Note
It's the rough, craggy appearance of these buns that makes them so inviting, so don't waste time rolling and shaping them carefully.

Cuts into about 10 slices

Panettone

Preparation Time
20 minutes, plus standing
Cooking Time
1 hour

- 450g (1lb) plain white flour
- 20g (¾oz) fresh yeast or
  2¼ tsp traditional dried yeast
- 225ml (8fl oz) tepid milk
- 125g (4oz) butter, softened,
  plus extra to grease
- 2 medium egg yolks
- 50g (2oz) caster sugar
- 75g (3oz) chopped mixed
  candied peel
- 50g (2oz) sultanas
- a pinch of freshly grated
  nutmeg
- egg yolk to glaze

NUTRITIONAL INFORMATION

Per slice 285 calories; 12g fat (of which 7g saturates); 41g carbohydrate; 0.3g salt

1 Sift the flour into a large bowl and make a well in the centre. Blend the fresh yeast with the milk. If using dried yeast, sprinkle it on to the milk and leave in a warm place for 15 minutes or until frothy. Add the yeast liquid to the flour and mix well together, gradually drawing in the flour from the sides of the bowl. Leave to stand in a warm place for 45 minutes or until doubled in size.

2 Add the softened butter to the dough with the 2 egg yolks, the sugar, candied peel, sultanas and nutmeg. Mix well. Leave to stand again in a warm place for a further 45 minutes or until doubled in size.

3 Meanwhile, line an 18cm (7 inch) circular tin with baking parchment. Place the dough inside the tin and leave in a warm place for about 1 hour until risen to the top. Preheat the oven to 200°C (180°C fan oven) mark 6.

4 Brush the top of the dough with egg yolk to glaze. Bake on the lowest shelf of the oven for 20 minutes, then lower the oven setting to 180°C (160°C fan oven) mark 4 and cook for a further 40 minutes or until a fine warmed skewer inserted into the centre comes out clean. Leave to cool in the tin.

Brioche

Preparation Time
20 minutes, plus rising
Cooking Time
15–20 minutes, plus cooling

- 15g (½oz) fresh yeast or 1½ tsp fast-action dried yeast
- 225g (8oz) strong plain white flour, plus extra to dust
- a pinch of salt
- 1 tbsp golden caster sugar
- 2 extra-large eggs, beaten
- 50g (2oz) butter, melted and cooled until tepid
- vegetable oil to grease
- beaten egg to glaze

NUTRITIONAL INFORMATION
Per slice 140 cals; 6g fat (of which 3g saturates); 19g carbohydrate; 0.2g salt

Cuts into 10 slices

1 If using fresh yeast, blend with 2 tbsp tepid water. Mix the flour, salt and sugar together in a large bowl. (Stir in the fast-action dried yeast if using.)

2 Make a well in the centre and pour in the yeast liquid (or 2 tbsp tepid water if using fast-action dried yeast) plus the eggs and melted butter. Work the ingredients together to a soft dough.

3 Turn out on to a lightly floured surface and knead for about 5 minutes until smooth and elastic. Put the dough into a large oiled bowl, cover and leave in a warm place for about 1 hour until doubled in size.

4 Knock back the dough on a lightly floured surface. Shape three-quarters of it into a ball and put into an oiled 1.2 litre (2 pint) brioche mould. Press a hole

through the centre. Shape the remaining dough into a round, put on top of the brioche and press down lightly. Cover and leave in a warm place until the dough is puffy and nearly risen to the top of the mould.

5 Preheat the oven to 230°C (210°C fan oven) mark 8. Brush the brioche dough lightly with beaten egg and bake for 15–20 minutes until golden.

6 Turn out on to a wire rack and leave to cool. Serve warm or cold.

Note

For individual brioches, divide the dough into ten pieces. Shape as above. Bake in individual tins, for 10 minutes.

Pistachio and Rosewater Stollen

BREAD MACHINE RECIPE
Preparation Time
15 minutes, plus kneading and rising
Cooking Time
20–25 minutes, plus cooling

- 1¼ tsp easy-blend dried yeast
- 350g (12oz) strong white bread flour
- ½ tsp salt
- 1 tsp ground mixed spice
- 25g (1oz) golden caster sugar
- 50g (2oz) butter, melted
- 150ml (¼ pint) milk
- 3 tbsp rosewater
- 75g (3oz) sultanas
- 50g (2oz) pistachio nuts
- 50g (2oz) chopped mixed candied peel
- icing sugar to dust

MARZIPAN

- 150g (5oz) pistachio nuts, skinned (see Note)
- 40g (1½oz) golden caster sugar
- 40g (1½oz) golden icing sugar
- 2 medium egg yolks
- oil to grease

NUTRITIONAL
INFORMATION
Per slice 380 cals; 17g fat (of which 5g
saturates); 51g carbohydrate; 0.7g salt

Makes 1 stollen – cuts into about 10 thick slices

1 Put all the dough ingredients except the sultanas, pistachio nuts, candied peel and icing sugar into the bread-maker's bucket, following the order and method specified in the manual.

2 Fit the bucket into the bread-maker and set to the dough program with raisin setting, if available. Press Start. Add the sultanas, pistachio nuts and candied peel when the machine beeps, or halfway through the kneading cycle.

3 Meanwhile, make the marzipan. Put the pistachio nuts in a food processor and blend until finely ground. Add the sugars and egg yolks and blend to a paste. Turn out on to the worksurface and shape into a log, 24cm (9½ inches) long. Grease a large baking sheet.

4 Once the dough is ready, turn out on to a floured surface and punch it down to deflate. Roll out to an oblong, 28 x 15cm (11 x 6 inches). Lay the marzipan on the dough, slightly to one side of the centre. Brush the long edges of the dough with water, then fold the wider piece of dough over the paste, sealing well.

5 Transfer to the prepared baking sheet, cover loosely with oiled clingfilm and leave in a warm place for about 40 minutes until doubled in size. Preheat the oven to 200°C (180°C fan oven) mark 6.

6 Bake for 20–25 minutes until risen and golden. Transfer to a wire rack to cool. Serve lavishly dusted with icing sugar.

Note
For a vibrantly coloured marzipan, it's best to skin the pistachios first – soak them in boiling water for a couple of minutes, then rub between pieces of kitchen paper to remove the skins.

Strawberry Doughnuts

Preparation Time
25 minutes, plus rising
Cooking Time
about 20 minutes

- 250g (9oz) plain flour, plus extra to dust
- 1 x 7g sachet fast-action dried yeast
- 100g (3½oz) caster sugar
- 100ml (3½fl oz) milk
- 25g (1oz) butter
- 1 medium egg
- sunflower oil to deep-fry
- 175g (6oz) 'no bits' strawberry jam
- ½ tsp ground cinnamon

NUTRITIONAL INFORMATION
Per doughnut 261 cals; 13g fat (of which 3g saturates); 35g carbohydrate; 0.1g salt

Makes 12

1 Put the flour, yeast and half the sugar into a large bowl. Heat the milk and butter in a small pan until just warm. Tip into a jug and beat in the egg. Working quickly, pour the liquid into the flour mixture and stir to make a soft dough. Tip on to a floured surface and knead for 5 minutes or until smooth and elastic. Return the dough to the bowl, cover with clingfilm and leave to rise in a warm place for 30–40 minutes.

2 Line a baking sheet with baking parchment. When the dough is ready, tip on to a lightly floured surface. Gently pat out into a rough rectangle 1cm (½ inch) thick and, using a 5.5cm (2¼ inch) round pastry cutter, stamp out 12 rounds. Transfer to the prepared baking sheet, cover loosely with clingfilm and leave to rise in a warm place for 20 minutes.

3 Fill a large pan one-third full with oil and heat to 150°C, using a thermometer. Fry the doughnuts in batches of four until deep golden brown (about 7 minutes), turning over halfway through the cooking

time. Using a slotted spoon, lift the doughnuts on to kitchen paper to drain and leave to cool for 5 minutes. Cook the remaining doughnuts in the same way.

4 Insert a 5mm (¼ inch) plain nozzle into a piping bag, then fill the bag with the jam. Use a skewer to poke a hole into the centre of each doughnut through the side, then push the piping nozzle in and squirt in some jam. Mix the remaining caster sugar with the cinnamon and tip on to a plate. Roll the filled doughnuts in the sugar mixture and serve warm.

Note
To oven-bake your doughnuts, complete the recipe to the end of step 2. Next, preheat the oven to 200°C (180°C fan oven) mark 6 and bake the doughnuts for 15 minutes or until puffed and golden. Complete the recipe from step 4, brushing the doughnuts with oil before coating in the sugar mixture.

Kugelhopf

Preparation Time
45 minutes, plus soaking, overnight
chilling and rising
Cooking Time
50–55 minutes, plus cooling

- 200g (7oz) raisins, black seedless
  if possible
- 3 tbsp light rum
- 2 tsp fast-action dried yeast
- 300g (11oz) plain white flour, plus
  extra to dust
- 4 large eggs
- 100ml (3½fl oz) milk
- 225g (8oz) unsalted butter,
  softened, plus extra to grease
- 75g (3oz) caster sugar
- a pinch of salt
- zest of 1 lemon
- 100g (3½oz) split blanched
  almonds, lightly toasted
- whole glacé fruits and nuts to
  decorate
- icing sugar to dust

**NUTRITIONAL
INFORMATION**
Per slice 382 cals; 22g fat (of which 11g
saturates); 39g carbohydrate; 0.4g salt

Cuts into 12 slices

1 Combine the raisins and rum, cover and soak overnight. Put the yeast and flour into a food mixer. Lightly whisk the eggs and milk and then, with the machine running on a slow speed, pour in the egg mixture and mix for 10 minutes or until the dough is very smooth, shiny and elastic. In another bowl, beat the butter, caster sugar, salt and lemon zest and then, with the mixer running, add to the dough, a spoonful at a time, until evenly incorporated. Turn the mixture into a large, lightly floured bowl. Cover with clingfilm and chill overnight.

2 Generously butter a 2 litre (3½ pint) kugelhopf ring mould. Press one-third of the almonds on to the sides of the mould. Chill. Roughly chop the remaining almonds. Mix by hand into the dough with the raisins and rum, then put into the mould, cover and leave for 3 hours in a warm place until it feels spongy and has risen to within 2cm (¾ inch) of the top of the mould.

3 Preheat the oven to 200°C (180°C fan oven) mark 6. Bake the kugelhopf on a shelf below the centre of the oven for 10 minutes. Cover with greaseproof paper, lower the oven setting to 190°C (170°C fan oven) mark 5 and bake for 40–45 minutes until the kugelhopf sounds hollow when you tap the mould. Cool in the tin for 15 minutes, then turn out on to a wire rack and leave to cool completely. Decorate with glacé fruits and nuts and serve dusted with icing sugar.

Notes
- If you don't have a mixer with a beater attachment, use a food processor with a flat plastic blade.
- This cake is made with yeast, so it's best eaten within two days or it will go stale. If you have any left over, wrap and freeze in slices – toast or use for making bread and butter pudding.

Lemon-glazed Chelsea Buns

BREAD MACHINE RECIPE
Preparation Time
15 minutes, plus kneading and
rising
Cooking Time
25–30 minutes, plus cooling

- 1 large egg
- 50g (2oz) unsalted butter,
  melted, plus extra to grease
- 225ml (8fl oz) milk
- 1½ tsp easy-blend dried yeast
- 400g (14oz) strong white
  bread flour, plus extra to dust
- 100g (3½oz) strong soft grain
  or granary flour
- 1 tsp salt
- 75g (3oz) light muscovado
  sugar

FILLING AND TOPPING

- 2 pieces preserved stem
  ginger, plus 3 tbsp syrup
- 100g (3½oz) raisins
- 100g (3½oz) sultanas
- 50g (2oz) light muscovado
  sugar
- 2 tsp ground mixed spice
- finely grated zest and juice of
  1 lemon
- 40g (1½oz) unsalted butter,
  cut into pieces

**NUTRITIONAL
INFORMATION**
Per bun 310 cals; 8g fat (of which
4g saturates); 56g carbohydrate;
0.6g salt

1 In a bowl, whisk the egg, butter and milk together with a fork. Put all the dough ingredients into the bread-maker's bucket, following the order and method specified in the manual.

2 Fit the bucket into the bread-maker and set to the dough program. Press Start.

3 Grease a 23cm (9 inch) square cake tin, 7.5cm (3 inches) deep. To make the filling, finely chop the stem ginger and mix in a bowl with the raisins, sultanas, 25g (1oz) sugar, the spice and lemon zest.

4 Once the dough is ready, turn out on to a floured surface and punch it down to deflate. Roll out to a 30.5cm (12 inch) square and spread with the filling to within 1cm (½ inch) of the edges. Dot with the butter. Roll up the dough to enclose the filling, then cut into slices 2.5cm (1 inch) thick.

5 Pack the slices, cut-sides uppermost, into the prepared tin, spacing them evenly apart. Cover with oiled clingfilm and leave to rise in a warm place for about 45 minutes until doubled in size and rising up towards the top of the tin. Preheat the oven to 200°C (180°C fan oven) mark 6.

6 Bake the buns for 20 minutes, then lower the oven setting to 180°C (160°C fan oven) mark 4 and bake for a further 5–10 minutes until risen and a deep golden colour. Meanwhile, mix together the remaining sugar, lemon juice and stem ginger syrup to make a glaze. Transfer the buns to a wire rack and brush with the glaze. Leave to cool until just warm.

Note
Like most fruity breads, these are best eaten warm, so if you make them ahead, pop them in the oven for a few minutes before serving.

Makes 12

Makes 15

Hot Cross Buns

Preparation Time
30 minutes, plus 'sponging' and
rising
Cooking Time
15–18 minutes, plus cooling

- 100ml (3½fl oz) warm milk, plus extra to glaze
- 15g (½oz) fresh yeast or 7g sachet (2 tsp) traditional dried yeast
- 50g (2oz) golden caster sugar, plus extra to glaze
- 350g (12oz) strong plain white flour, sifted, plus extra to dust
- a pinch of salt
- a pinch of ground cinnamon
- a pinch of freshly grated nutmeg
- 25g (1oz) chopped mixed candied peel
- 125g (4oz) mixed raisins, sultanas and currants
- 25g (1oz) butter, melted and cooled until tepid
- 1 medium egg, beaten
- vegetable oil to grease

NUTRITIONAL INFORMATION
Per bun 140 cals; 2g fat (of which 1g saturates); 28g carbohydrate; 0.2g salt

1 Mix the warm milk with an equal quantity of warm water. Put the yeast into a small bowl with 1 tbsp of the warm liquid and 1 tsp sugar and set aside for 5 minutes.

2 Put 225g (8oz) flour and the salt into a large bowl, make a well in the centre and pour in the yeast mixture. Cover with a clean tea towel and leave in a warm place for 20 minutes to 'sponge'.

3 Mix the remaining flour and sugar together with the spices, peel and dried fruit. Add to the yeast mixture with the melted butter and egg. Mix thoroughly to form a soft dough, adding a little more liquid if needed. Put the dough into a lightly oiled bowl, cover and leave to rise in a warm place for 1–1½ hours until doubled in size.

4 Knock back the dough and knead lightly on a lightly floured surface for 1–2 minutes. Divide the dough into 15 equal-sized pieces and shape into buns. Put well apart on a large oiled baking sheet. Make a deep cross on the top of each one with a sharp knife, then cover with a tea towel and leave in a warm place for about 30 minutes until doubled in size.

5 Preheat the oven to 220°C (200°C fan oven) mark 7. Brush the buns with milk and sprinkle with sugar, then bake for 15–18 minutes until they sound hollow when tapped underneath. Transfer to a wire rack and leave to cool. Serve warm.

Variation
Rather than mark crosses on the buns, brush with beaten egg to glaze, then top each with a pastry cross and glaze again. Bake as above.

Strawberry Savarin

Preparation Time
15 minutes, plus standing
Cooking Time
40–45 minutes, plus cooling

- oil to grease
- 15g (½oz) fresh yeast or 1½ tsp dried yeast
- 3 tbsp tepid milk
- 2 medium eggs, lightly beaten
- 50g (2oz) butter, melted and cooled
- 200g (7oz) plain white flour
- 1 tbsp caster sugar
- 25g (1oz) desiccated coconut
- 6 tbsp redcurrant jelly or sieved strawberry jam
- 5 tbsp lemon juice
- 450g (1lb) strawberries, hulled and quartered
- soured cream to serve

NUTRITIONAL INFORMATION
Per slice 275 cals; 12g fat (of which 7g saturates); 39g carbohydrate; 0.2g salt

1 Lightly oil a 1.3 litre (2¼ pint) savarin tin or ring mould and turn it upside down on kitchen paper to drain off the excess oil.

2 Blend the fresh yeast with the milk. If using dried yeast, sprinkle it on to the milk and leave in a warm place for 30 minutes or until frothy. Gradually beat the eggs and butter into the yeast liquid.

3 Mix the flour in a bowl with the sugar and coconut. With a wooden spoon, gradually stir in the yeast mixture to form a thick, smooth batter. Beat together thoroughly.

4 Turn into the prepared tin, cover with oiled clingfilm and leave in a warm place for about 1 hour until the savarin is nearly doubled in size. Preheat the oven to 190°C (170°C fan oven) mark 5.

5 Bake the savarin for 35–40 minutes until golden. Turn out on to a wire rack placed over a large plate. Put the jelly or jam and lemon juice into a small pan over a low heat.

6 When the jelly or jam is melted, spoon it over the warm savarin until well glazed, allowing any excess to collect on the plate under the wire rack. Transfer the savarin to a serving plate.

7 Return the excess jelly mixture to the pan, add the strawberries and stir to coat. Remove from the heat and cool for 15–20 minutes until almost set, then spoon into the middle of the savarin. Serve warm or cold with soured cream.

Variations

Strawberry Babas: Divide the yeast batter among six 9cm (3½ inch) ring tins. Leave to rise until the moulds are nearly two-thirds full, then bake for 15–20 minutes. Replace the lemon juice with brandy, soak each baba well and place on individual plates. Finish with strawberries and soured cream as above.

Rum Babas: Make as Strawberry Babas but soak the warm babas in a rum syrup made with 8 tbsp clear honey, 8 tbsp water and rum or rum essence to taste. Serve filled with whipped cream.

Cuts into 6 slices

Special Occasion Cakes

Chocolate Birthday Cake

EGG FREE
Preparation Time
30 minutes, plus cooling
Cooking Time
1–1¼ hours, plus cooling

- 150ml (¼ pint) sunflower oil, plus extra to grease
- 75g (3oz) creamed coconut
- 25g (1oz) plain chocolate, broken into pieces
- 50g (2oz) cocoa powder
- 350g (12oz) self-raising flour
- 1 tsp baking powder
- a pinch of salt
- 175g (6oz) light muscovado sugar

ICING
- 350g (12oz) plain chocolate, broken into small pieces
- 150ml (¼ pint) double cream
- white and milk chocolate Maltesers to decorate

NUTRITIONAL INFORMATION
Per slice 515 cals; 31g fat (of which 15g saturates); 59g carbohydrate; 0.4g salt

1 Grease a 1.7 litre (3 pint), 30.5 x 10cm (12 x 4 inch) loaf tin and line with greaseproof paper. Put the coconut into a heatproof bowl, pour on 425ml (14½fl oz) boiling water and stir to dissolve. Set aside to cool for 30 minutes.

2 Melt the chocolate in a heatproof bowl set over a pan of gently simmering water, making sure the base of the bowl doesn't touch the water. Stir until smooth, then remove the bowl from the pan and leave to cool slightly. Preheat the oven to 180°C (160°C fan oven) mark 4.

3 Sift the cocoa powder, flour, baking powder and salt into a bowl. Stir in the sugar and make a well in the middle. Add the coconut mixture, melted chocolate and oil and beat to make a smooth batter. Pour the cake batter into the prepared tin.

4 Bake for 1–1¼ hours or until risen and just firm to the touch (if necessary, after about 40 minutes, lightly cover the top of the cake with foil if it appears to be browning too quickly). Leave in the tin for 10 minutes, then transfer to a wire rack and leave to cool completely. When cold, peel off the lining paper and trim to neaten the edges.

5 To make the icing, put the chocolate into a heatproof bowl. Heat the cream to just below boiling point. Pour on to the chocolate and stir until melted. Leave to cool, beating occasionally, until thick – pop it into the fridge for 30 minutes to help thicken, if necessary.

6 Cut the cold cake in half horizontally and sandwich the layers together with one-third of the icing. Spread the rest evenly over the top and sides of the cake. Decorate the top of the cake with alternate rows of milk and white Maltesers. Lay an edging of alternate milk and white Maltesers around the base of the cake to decorate.

Cuts into 12 slices

Cuts into 12 slices

Afternoon Tea Carrot Cake

Preparation Time
15 minutes
Cooking Time
40 minutes, plus cooling

- 250ml (9fl oz) sunflower oil, plus extra to grease
- 225g (8oz) light muscovado sugar
- 3 large eggs
- 225g (8oz) self-raising flour
- a large pinch of salt
- ½ tsp each ground mixed spice, grated nutmeg and ground cinnamon
- 250g (9oz) carrots, peeled and coarsely grated

FROSTING
- 50g (2oz) butter, preferably unsalted, at room temperature
- 225g pack cream cheese
- 25g (1oz) golden icing sugar
- ½ tsp vanilla extract
- 8 pecan halves, roughly chopped

NUTRITIONAL INFORMATION
Per slice 383 cals; 32g fat (of which 10g saturates); 24g carbohydrate; 0.3g salt

1 Preheat the oven to 180°C (160°C fan oven) mark 4. Grease two 18cm (7 inch) sandwich tins and base-line with greaseproof paper, then grease the paper lightly.

2 Using a hand-held electric whisk, whisk the oil and muscovado sugar together to combine, then whisk in the eggs, one at a time.

3 Sift the flour, salt and spices into the mixture and, using a large metal spoon, gently fold in. Tip the carrots into the bowl and fold in.

4 Divide the cake mixture between the prepared tins and bake for 30–40 minutes until golden and a skewer inserted into the centre comes out clean. Remove from the oven and leave in the tins for 10 minutes, then turn out on to a wire rack and leave to cool completely. Peel off the lining paper.

5 To make the frosting, beat the butter and cream cheese together in a bowl until light and fluffy. Sift in the icing sugar, add the vanilla extract and beat well until smooth. Spread one-third of the frosting over one cake and sandwich together with the other cake. Spread the remaining frosting on top and sprinkle with the pecans.

Black Forest Birthday Gateau

Preparation Time
30 minutes
Cooking Time
50 minutes, plus cooling

- 125g (4oz) unsalted butter, melted
- 200g (7oz) plain flour
- 50g (2oz) cornflour
- 50g (2oz) cocoa powder, plus extra to dust
- 2 tsp espresso instant coffee powder
- 1 tsp baking powder
- 4 large eggs, separated
- 300g (11oz) golden caster sugar
- 2 × 300g jars morello cherries in syrup
- 2 tbsp kirsch
- 200ml (7fl oz) double cream
- 2 tbsp icing sugar, sifted

DECORATION
- fresh cherries
- Chocolate Curls

NUTRITIONAL INFORMATION
Per slice 440 cals; 22g fat (of which 12g saturates); 59g carbohydrate; 0.8g salt

1 Preheat the oven to 180°C (160°C fan oven) mark 4. Brush a little of the melted butter over the base and sides of a 20.5 x 9cm (8 x 3½ inch) round cake tin. Line the base and sides with baking parchment.

2 Sift the flour, cornflour, cocoa powder, coffee powder and baking powder together three times – this helps to add air and makes sure the ingredients are well mixed.

3 Put the egg yolks, caster sugar and 100ml (3½fl oz) cold water into a freestanding mixer and whisk for 8 minutes or until the mixture leaves a trail for 3 seconds when the whisk is lifted.

4 Add the rest of the melted butter, pouring it around the edge of the bowl so that the mixture doesn't lose any air, then quickly fold it in, followed by the sifted flour mixture in two batches.

5 In another grease-free bowl, whisk the egg whites until stiff peaks form, then fold a spoonful into the cake mixture to loosen. Carefully fold in the rest of the egg whites, making sure that there are no white blobs left. Pour into the prepared tin and bake in the oven for 45–50 minutes until a skewer inserted into the centre comes out clean. Leave in the tin for 10 minutes, then turn out on to a wire rack to cool completely.

6 When the cake is cold, peel off the lining paper and trim the top to make a flat surface. Turn the cake over so that the top becomes the base. Using a long serrated bread knife, carefully cut horizontally into three. Drain the cherries, reserving 250ml (9fl oz) of the syrup. Put the syrup into a pan and simmer to reduce by half. Stir in the kirsch. Brush the hot syrup on each layer of the cake – including the top – using up all the liquid.

7 Lightly whip the cream with the icing sugar. Spread one-third over the bottom layer of cake and cover with half the cherries. Top with the next cake layer and repeat with another third of the cream and the remaining cherries. Top with the final cake layer and spread the remaining cream over it. Decorate with fresh cherries, chocolate curls and a dusting of cocoa powder.

Note
Make the gateau up to two hours ahead to allow the flavours to mingle and the syrup to moisten the cake.

Cuts into 12 slices

Cuts into 8 slices

Toasted Hazelnut Meringue Birthday Cake

Preparation Time
10 minutes
Cooking Time
30 minutes, plus cooling

- oil to grease
- 175g (6oz) skinned hazelnuts, toasted
- 3 large egg whites
- 175g (6oz) golden caster sugar
- 250g carton mascarpone cheese
- 285ml (9½fl oz) double cream
- 3 tbsp Bailey's Irish Cream liqueur, plus extra to serve
- 140g (4½oz) frozen raspberries
- 340g jar redcurrant jelly

NUTRITIONAL INFORMATION
Per slice 598 cals; 38g fat (of which 16g saturates); 57g carbohydrate; 0.1g salt

1 Preheat the oven to 190°C (170°C fan oven) mark 5. Lightly oil two 18cm (7 inch) sandwich tins and base-line with baking parchment. Whizz the hazelnuts in a food processor until finely chopped.

2 Put the egg whites into a large, grease-free bowl and whisk until stiff peaks form. Whisk in the sugar, a spoonful at a time. Using a metal spoon, fold in half the nuts. Divide the mixture equally between the tins and spread evenly. Bake in the middle of the oven for about 30 minutes, then leave to cool in the tins for 30 minutes.

3 To make the filling, put the mascarpone cheese in a bowl. Beat in the cream and liqueur until smooth. Put the raspberries and redcurrant jelly into a pan and heat gently until the jelly has melted. Sieve, then cool.

4 Use a palette knife to loosen the edges of the meringues, then turn out on to a wire rack. Peel off the lining paper and discard. Put a large sheet of baking parchment on a board and sit one meringue on top, flat-side down. Spread one-third of the mascarpone mixture over the meringue, then drizzle with raspberry purée. Top with the other meringue, then cover the whole cake with the rest of the mascarpone mixture. Sprinkle with the remaining hazelnuts. Carefully put the cake on a serving plate and drizzle with more liqueur, if you like.

Easter Chocolate Fudge Cake

Preparation Time
30 minutes
Cooking Time
50 minutes, plus cooling

- 175g (6oz) unsalted butter, softened, plus extra to grease
- 150g (5oz) plain flour
- 50g (2oz) cocoa powder
- 1 tsp baking powder
- a pinch of salt
- 150g (5oz) light muscovado sugar
- 3 medium eggs, beaten
- 250ml (9fl oz) soured cream
- 1 tsp vanilla extract

ICING AND DECORATION
- 100g (3½oz) plain chocolate, finely chopped
- 150g (5oz) unsalted butter, softened
- 125g (4oz) cream cheese
- 175g (6oz) icing sugar, sifted
- 50g (2oz) Chocolate Curls, lightly crushed
- foil-covered chocolate eggs

NUTRITIONAL INFORMATION
Per slice 590 cals; 42g fat (of which 25g saturates); 50g carbohydrate; 0.7g salt

1 Preheat the oven to 180°C (160°C fan oven) mark 4. Grease a 20.5cm (8 inch) springform tin and line with greaseproof paper, then grease the paper lightly. Sift the flour, cocoa powder, baking powder and salt into a large bowl.

2 Using an electric mixer or electric beaters, mix the butter and muscovado sugar in a separate bowl until pale and fluffy – this will take about 5 minutes. Gradually add the beaten eggs, mixing well after each addition. Add a little of the flour mixture if the butter mixture looks like curdling. In one go, add the remaining flour mixture, the soured cream and vanilla extract, then fold in everything gently with a metal spoon. Spoon into the prepared tin and bake for 40–50 minutes until a skewer inserted into the centre comes out clean. Cool in the tin.

3 To make the icing, melt the chocolate in a heatproof bowl set over a pan of gently simmering water, making sure the base of the bowl doesn't touch the water. Leave to cool for 15 minutes. In a separate bowl, beat the butter and cream cheese with a wooden spoon until combined. Beat in the icing sugar, then the cooled chocolate. Take care not to over-beat the mixture – it should be fudgey, not stiff.

4 Remove the cake from the tin and peel off the lining paper, then cut in half horizontally and use some icing to sandwich the layers together. Transfer to a cake stand, then ice the top and sides, smoothing with a palette knife. Decorate with crushed curls and chocolate eggs.

Cuts into 12 slices

Cuts into 10 slices

White Chocolate Cappuccino Mother's Day Cake

Preparation Time
45 minutes
Cooking Time
about 50 minutes, plus cooling

- 300g (11oz) unsalted butter, at room temperature, plus extra to grease
- 250g (9oz) self-raising flour, plus extra to dust
- 200g (7oz) caster sugar
- 3 large eggs, at room temperature, beaten
- 1½ tsp baking powder
- 50ml (2fl oz) milk
- 1 tsp vanilla extract
- 125g (4oz) white chocolate
- 125ml (4fl oz) double cream
- 1½–2 tbsp espresso coffee, cooled
- 75g (3oz) icing sugar, sifted, plus extra to dust
- 50g (2oz) plain chocolate, grated
- 40g (1½oz) hazelnuts, roasted and chopped
- fresh small roses to decorate

NUTRITIONAL INFORMATION
Per slice 659 cals; 45g fat (of which 25g saturates); 60g carbohydrate; 0.3g salt

1 Preheat the oven to 180°C (160°C fan oven) mark 4. Grease a deep, non-stick 20.5cm (8 inch) cake tin and dust with flour.

2 Beat together the caster sugar and 175g (6oz) butter until pale and creamy. Gradually add the eggs, beating well after each addition. Add 1 tbsp flour if the mix looks like curdling. Fold in the remaining flour and the baking powder, followed by the milk and vanilla extract. Spoon into the prepared tin and level the surface. Bake for 40–50 minutes until a skewer inserted into the centre comes out clean. Cool in the tin for 5 minutes, then turn out on to a wire rack and leave to cool completely.

3 Cut the cake in half horizontally. Grate 25g (1oz) white chocolate, then beat together with the cream and coffee until the mixture holds its shape. Use to sandwich the two cake halves together.

4 Melt the remaining white chocolate in a bowl set over a pan of gently simmering water, making sure the base of the bowl doesn't touch the water. Leave to cool for 10 minutes. Beat together the remaining butter and the icing sugar until pale and creamy. Beat in the cooled white chocolate, then spread over the sides and top of the cake.

5 Mix the plain chocolate with the nuts and press around the side of the cake. Decorate with small roses dusted with icing sugar.

Note
For convenience, complete the recipe to the end of step 2 up to 24 hours ahead. Return to the tin when cool and wrap in clingfilm. Complete the recipe to serve.

Simnel Cake

Preparation Time
30 minutes, plus cooling
Cooking Time
about 1 hour 25 minutes

- 225g (8oz) butter, softened, plus extra to grease
- 225g (8oz) self-raising flour
- 2 tsp ground mixed spice
- 400g (14oz) mixed dried fruit
- 150g (5oz) light muscovado sugar
- 50g (2oz) golden syrup
- finely grated zest of 2 lemons
- 4 medium eggs, lightly beaten

DECORATION
- icing sugar to dust
- 500g (1lb 2oz) marzipan
- 2 tbsp apricot jam
- length of yellow ribbon

NUTRITIONAL INFORMATION
Per slice 546 cals; 23g fat (of which 11g saturates); 83g carbohydrate; 0.6g salt

1 Preheat the oven to 170°C (150°C fan oven) mark 3. Grease a 20.5cm (8 inch) round cake tin with butter and line with baking parchment.

2 Put the flour, mixed spice and dried fruit into a large bowl and stir together until combined. Put the butter, muscovado sugar, syrup and lemon zest into a separate large bowl and, using a hand-held electric whisk, beat together until pale and fluffy (about 3 minutes). Gradually beat in the eggs, whisking well after each addition. Add the flour mixture and fold everything together with a large metal spoon.

3 Empty the mixture into the prepared tin and bake, covering with foil after 1 hour of cooking, for 1 hour 25 minutes, or until the cake is risen and springy to the touch. A skewer inserted into the centre should come out clean, but don't be tempted to test too early or the cake may sink. Leave the cake to cool completely in the tin.

4 Take the cake out of the tin, peel off the lining paper and transfer to a serving plate. To decorate, dust the worksurface with icing sugar and roll out two-thirds of the marzipan until large enough for a 20.5cm (8 inch) circle (cut around the base of the cake tin). Heat the jam with 1 tsp water in a small pan over a medium heat until runny. Brush the top of the cake with some jam, then lay the marzipan circle on top and gently press down to stick it to the cake. Using a small knife, score lines on top of the cake to make a diamond pattern. Crimp the edge of the marzipan using the thumb and forefinger of one hand, and the index finger of the other.

5 Roll the remaining marzipan into 11 equal-sized balls. Brush the underside of each with a little jam or water and stick to the top of the cake. If you like, use a blowtorch to lightly brown the marzipan. To finish, secure a yellow ribbon around the cake. Serve in slices.

Note
Simnel cake is the classic Easter celebration cake, its marzipan balls representing the disciples – either 11 or 12, depending on whether you think Judas should be included.

Cuts into 12 slices

Cuts into 30 slices

White Chocolate and Orange Wedding Cake

Preparation Time
1½ hours, plus chilling
Cooking Time
1 hour, plus cooling

- butter to grease
- 550g (1¼lb) strawberries, hulled and thinly sliced

LARGE CAKE
- 6 large eggs, separated
- 250g (9oz) golden caster sugar
- 150g (5oz) self-raising flour
- 150g (5oz) ground almonds
- grated zest of 2 oranges

MEDIUM AND SMALL CAKES
- 4 large eggs, separated
- 165g (5½oz) golden caster sugar
- 125g (4oz) self-raising flour
- 125g (4oz) ground almonds
- grated zest of 1¼ oranges

SYRUP
- 200g (7oz) golden granulated sugar
- 500ml (18fl oz) sweet white wine
- juice of 6 large oranges

WHITE CHOCOLATE GANACHE
- 400g (14oz) white chocolate, chopped
- 600ml, 300ml and 150ml cartons double cream

NUTRITIONAL INFORMATION
Per slice 530 cals; 34g fat (of which 17g saturates); 49g carbohydrate; 0.3g salt

1 Preheat the oven to 180°C (160°C fan oven) mark 4. Grease a deep, round 23cm (9 inch) cake tin, a 15cm (6 inch) cake tin and a clean 200g baked bean tin and base-line with greaseproof paper.

2 To make the large cake, put the egg whites into a large, grease-free bowl and whisk until soft peaks form. Gradually beat in 50g (2oz) sugar. Whisk until the mixture stands in stiff peaks and looks glossy. Put the egg yolks and remaining sugar in another bowl and whisk until soft and mousse-like. Carefully stir in the flour to make a paste.

3 Using a clean metal spoon, add a third of the egg white to the paste and fold in carefully. Put the remaining egg white, the ground almonds and orange zest into the bowl and fold in, taking care not to knock too much volume out of the egg white. You should end up with a smooth batter.

4 Spoon into the prepared 23cm (9 inch) tin and bake for 35 minutes or until a skewer inserted into the centre comes out clean. Cool in the tin for 10 minutes, then turn out on to a wire rack and leave to cool completely.

5 Make the other two cakes in the same way, gradually beating in 25g (1oz) of the sugar at step 2. Pour a quarter of the batter into the baked bean tin and the remaining mixture into the 15cm (6 inch) cake tin. Bake the medium cake for 30–35 minutes and the small cake for 25–30 minutes.

6 Put the syrup ingredients into a pan and stir over a gentle heat until the sugar has dissolved. Bring to the boil and bubble for 5 minutes or until syrupy. Set aside to cool.

7 To make the ganache, put the chocolate into a heatproof bowl with half the cream. Set over a pan of gently simmering water, making sure that the base of the bowl doesn't touch the water, and leave until the chocolate has melted, then stir (don't stir until melted). Leave to cool until beginning to thicken, then beat with a wooden spoon until cold and thick. Put the remaining double cream into a bowl and whip lightly. Beat a large spoonful of the whipped cream into the chocolate cream to loosen it, then fold in the remainder. Cover and leave to chill for 2 hours.

8 Remove the lining paper from the cakes, then cut each cake in half horizontally, pierce all over with a skewer and put them, cut-sides up, on an edged tray or baking sheet. Spoon on the syrup and leave to soak in.

9 Spread a quarter of the ganache over the base of each cake and scatter with 425g (15oz) strawberries. Cover with the top half of each cake and press down lightly. Using a palette knife, smooth the remaining ganache over the top and sides of the cakes. Assemble up to 4 hours ahead, wrap loosely and keep chilled in the fridge. Decorate with the remaining strawberries and serve.

Sleeping Beauty's Castle

Preparation Time
1 hour

◆ 1 x white ready-iced 23cm
  (9 inch) square sponge cake
◆ 5 raspberry or strawberry
  Swiss rolls, about 9cm
  (3½ inches) long
◆ 450g (1lb) white sugarpaste
◆ icing sugar to dust
◆ Apricot Glaze (see page 313)
◆ 1 x white ready-iced 15cm
  (6 inch) round sponge cake
◆ 2 x quantities of pink
  buttercream icing (see page
  314)
◆ 5 ice cream sugar cones

DECORATION
◆ multicoloured sprinkles
◆ red, pink, yellow, green and
  white writing icing
◆ sugar flowers
◆ small round pink sweets or
  pink edible balls
◆ paper flag

NUTRITIONAL
INFORMATION
Per slice 425 cals; 8g fat (of which
3g saturates); 86g carbohydrate;
0.2g salt

1 Put the square cake on a 30.5cm (12 inch) square cake board. Measure the circumference of a Swiss roll with a piece of string. Divide the sugarpaste into five pieces. Lightly dust a worksurface with icing sugar, then roll out each piece of sugarpaste thinly into a rectangle the length of the Swiss roll by the length of the piece of string. Neaten the edges with a sharp knife. Brush each piece of icing with apricot glaze and roll around a Swiss roll, gently working the edges together to seal.

2 Put the round cake in the centre of the square cake. Put a dollop of buttercream at each corner of the square cake and position four of the Swiss rolls, with the sealed edge facing inwards, to make towers. Smooth pink buttercream over four of the cones and spread a little on top of each tower. Dip the tips of the cones in sprinkles, then fix on top of the towers. Using red writing icing, draw a simple window, divided by four panes, at the top of each tower.

3 At the front of the castle, use red writing icing to draw a door with a doorknob. Use pink and yellow writing icing to draw small flowers around the castle and below the windows. Fix a few sugar flowers to the walls with writing icing. Connect the flowers with green writing icing to represent stems. Use the green writing icing to draw clumps of grass around the base of the wall. Stick a sugar flower to the paper flag with writing icing.

4 Position the remaining Swiss roll in the centre of the round cake. Cover the remaining cone with buttercream, dip in sprinkles and position on top of the round cake, fixing with a little buttercream. Draw on windows and decorate with sugar flowers as before. Make blobs of white writing icing, just touching each other, around the edges of the cones and decorate with pink sweets or edible balls. Stick the paper flag into the central tower.

Note
For convenience, complete the recipe up to one day ahead.

Cuts into 35 small slices

Cuts into 12 slices

Creepy-crawly Cake

Preparation Time
1½ hours
Cooking Time
25–30 minutes, plus cooling and drying

- butter to grease
- 1 x 4-egg quantity of chocolate Victoria Sponge mixture (see page 10)
- ½ x quantity of chocolate buttercream icing (see page 314)

DECORATION

- 225g (8oz) white sugarpaste
- assorted food colourings, including brown and black
- red and black liquorice bootlaces and jelly creepy-crawly sweets, such as snakes and frogs
- a little glacé icing (see page 312)
- a chocolate matchstick (optional)

ICING

- 450g (1lb) icing sugar, sifted
- 225g (8oz) butter, softened
- a few drops of vanilla extract
- green food colouring

NUTRITIONAL INFORMATION
Per slice 534 cals; 26 fat (of which 17g saturates); 76g carbohydrate; 0.6g salt

1 To make a trap door, use 125g (4oz) sugarpaste. Knead in a few drops of brown food colouring and roll out to a thickness of 5mm (¼ inch), then use a small tumbler to cut out a circle. Place on a baking tray lined with baking parchment and leave in a cool place overnight to dry.

2 Use the remaining white and brown icing to make a selection of spiders and beetles, colouring the icing accordingly. Use the liquorice to make spiders' legs. Pipe eyes on the creatures with white glacé icing. Allow to dry overnight.

3 The next day, preheat the oven to 190°C (170°C fan oven) mark 5. Grease two 20.5cm (8 inch) round sandwich tins and line with greaseproof paper, then grease the paper lightly. Make and bake the sponge mixture according to the instructions on page 10. Cool in the tins for 5 minutes, then turn out on to a wire rack, remove the lining paper and leave to cool completely.

4 Sandwich the cold cakes together with chocolate buttercream. Cut out a hole 1cm (½ inch) deep and 6.5cm (2½ inches) wide in the centre of the cake. Discard (or eat) the trimmings.

5 For the icing, beat the icing sugar into the butter with the vanilla. Beat in the food colouring. Put the cake on a board or plate and cover with the icing. Secure the trap door over the hole in the middle of the cake. Prop open with a cocktail stick painted with brown food colouring, or a chocolate matchstick. Arrange the creatures over the cake, with some creepy-crawlies crawling out of the trap door. Leave to dry.

Clown Cake

Preparation Time
45 minutes

- 25g (1oz) each of white, green, black and blue sugarpaste
- 50g (2oz) red sugarpaste
- black and yellow writing icing
- 1 x white ready-iced 20.5cm (8 inch) sponge cake

NUTRITIONAL INFORMATION
Per slice 300 cals; 8g fat (of which 2g saturates); 55g carbohydrate; 0.1g salt

1 First make the shapes for the clown's face. Roll out the white sugarpaste and cut out two ovals for eyes. Roll out half the red sugarpaste and cut out a crescent shape for the mouth. Mark a smiley line along the centre of the mouth with black writing icing. Knead the trimmings and the other piece of red icing together and roll into a ball for his nose. Roll out a small piece of green icing and, using a star-shaped cutter, stamp out two stars to decorate his cheeks.

2 Brush the backs of the shapes with water and position on the cake. Roll out the black icing and cut out two small circles to make pupils for the eyes, then stick on to the white ovals. Use the black and yellow writing icing to give him eyebrows and a swirl of hair.

3 Roll out the blue icing and cut out two sides of a bow tie. Roll the trimmings into a ball and flatten slightly to make the centre knot. Fix the two bow-tie pieces to the bottom edge of the cake with writing icing. Position the knot on top. Use the yellow writing icing to pipe polka dots on the tie.

Cuts into 15 slices

Cuts into 12 slices

Toadstool

Preparation Time:
1½ hours
Cooking Time
40 minutes, plus cooling

- unsalted butter to grease
- 1 x 3-egg quantity of Victoria Sponge mixture (see page 10)
- 700g (1½lb) white sugarpaste
- brown, red, green and yellow food colourings
- ½ x quantity of buttercream icing (see page 314)
- cornflour to dust
- sugar flowers, dolly mixtures and butterfly decorations

NUTRITIONAL INFORMATION

Per slice 433 cals; 10g fat (of which 6g saturates); 87g carbohydrate; 0.3g salt

1 Preheat the oven to 190°C (170°C fan oven) mark 5. Grease a 900g (2lb) food can (for the stalk) and a 1.1 litre (2 pint) pudding basin (for the cap) and base-line with baking parchment. It doesn't matter how big the basin is, as long as it holds at least 1.1 litres (2 pints). A wide, shallow cake makes a better-looking toadstool.

2 Make the cake mixture according to the instructions on page 10. Half-fill the food can and put the remaining mixture into the pudding basin. Bake for about 30 minutes for the 'stalk' in the food can and 40 minutes for the 'mushroom cap' in the pudding basin. Transfer both to a wire rack and leave to cool.

3 Take 350g (12oz) sugarpaste. Colour a walnut-sized piece with brown food colouring and the rest red. Colour 125g (4oz) green and leave the remaining 225g (8oz) white. Roll out the green icing and cut into a kidney shape as a 'grass' base. Fix to a large rectangular cake board with a little water. Unmould the cakes and peel off the lining paper. Using the food can that the stalk was baked in as a template, cut a semicircle from one side of the grass.

4 Reserve 50g (2oz) white icing. Colour the rest yellow and roll out into a long oblong to fit the stalk. Trim the edges. Spread buttercream thinly around the stalk cake then, holding the cake by the ends, set it at one end of the icing. Roll up the icing around the stalk and press the seam together. With a dab of buttercream, fix the stalk upright in the cut-out semicircle in the green icing. Spread the top with buttercream.

5 Roll out the red icing to fit the mushroom cap. Set the cake flat on the worksurface. Cover the upper surface thinly with buttercream. Lay the red icing over the cake. Smooth in place and trim around the base. Dust the worksurface lightly with cornflour and carefully turn the cake upside down.

6 Colour the remaining buttercream dark brown. Insert a small, fluted nozzle into a piping bag, then fill the bag with the buttercream. Mark a circle in the centre of the base of the mushroom cap, where the stalk will fit. Pipe lines of buttercream radiating from this, to look like the gills of a toadstool. Cover the sponge and red icing join. Turn the cake the right way up and set on top of the stalk.

7 Roll out the reserved white icing and the brown icing. Cut the white icing into dots. Arrange on top of the toadstool, using a little buttercream to fix them. Cut the brown icing into windows and a door and fix to the stalk in the same way. Decorate the 'grass' with sugar flowers, sweets and butterflies.

Classic Christmas Cake

Preparation Time
30 minutes, plus three days'
soaking
Cooking Time
about 4 hours, plus cooling

- 500g (1lb 2oz) sultanas
- 400g (14oz) raisins
- 150g (5oz) each Agen prunes and dried figs, roughly chopped
- 200g (7oz) dried apricots, roughly chopped
- zest and juice of 2 oranges
- 200ml (7fl oz) hazelnut liqueur, such as Frangelico Hazelnut Liqueur, plus extra to drizzle
- 250g (9oz) unsalted butter, softened, plus extra to grease
- 150g (5oz) each dark muscovado and light soft brown sugar
- 200g (7oz) plain flour, sifted
- 1 tsp ground cinnamon
- 1 tsp mixed spice
- ¼ tsp ground cloves
- ¼ tsp freshly grated nutmeg
- pinch of salt
- 4 large eggs, beaten
- 100g (3½oz) toasted blanched hazelnuts, roughly chopped
- 40g (1½oz) toasted pinenuts
- 1 tbsp brandy (optional)

ROYAL ICING – TO COVER A 23CM (9 INCH) CAKE

Preparation 30 minutes, plus
24 hours' drying
Cooking time 3-4 minutes, plus
cooling

- 4 tbsp apricot jam
- icing sugar, sifted, to dust
- 450g packet ready-to-roll marzipan
- vegetable oil to grease
- 500g packet royal icing sugar

Cuts into 24 slices

DECORATION
- 150g (5oz) glacier mint sweets
- 75cm (30 inches) silver ribbon, 2cm wide
- silver candles

NUTRITIONAL INFORMATION
Per slice (un-iced)
375 cals; 14g fat (of which 6g saturates); 56g carbohydrate; 0.4g salt
Per slice (iced)
569 cals; 17g fat (of which 6g saturates); 100g carbohydrate; 0.2g salt

1 Put the fruit into a non-metallic bowl and stir in the orange zest and juice and the hazelnut liqueur. Cover and leave to soak overnight or, preferably, up to three days.

2 Preheat the oven to 140°C (120°C fan oven) mark 1. Grease a 23cm (9 inch) cake tin and double-line with greaseproof paper, making sure the paper comes at least 5cm (2 inches) above the top of the tin. Grease the paper lightly. Then wrap a double layer of greaseproof paper around the outside of the tin, securing with string – this will stop the cake burning.

3 Using a hand-held electric mixer, beat together the butter and sugars in a large bowl until light and fluffy – this should take about 5 minutes.

4 In a separate bowl, sift together the flour, spices and salt. Beat 2 tbsp of the flour mixture into the butter and sugar, then gradually add the eggs, making sure the mixture doesn't curdle. If it looks as if it might be about to, add a little more flour.

5 Using a large metal spoon, fold the remaining flour into the mixture, followed by the soaked fruit and the nuts. Tip into the prepared tin and level the surface. Using the end of the spoon, make a hole in the centre of the mix, going right down to the base of the tin – this will stop the top of the cake rising into a dome shape as it cooks. Bake for 4 hours or until a skewer inserted into the centre comes out clean. Cover with foil if it is browning too quickly. Leave to cool in the tin for 10 minutes, then turn out on to a wire rack, keeping the greaseproof paper wrapped around the outside of the cake, and leave to cool completely.

6 To store, leave the cold cake in its greaseproof paper. Wrap a few layers of clingfilm around it, then cover with foil. Store in a cool place in an airtight container. After two weeks, unwrap the cake, prick all over and pour 1 tbsp of hazelnut liqueur over it, or brandy if you prefer. Rewrap and store as before. Ice up to three days before serving (see right).

Icing the cake

1 Gently heat the jam in a pan with 1 tbsp water until softened, then press through a sieve into a bowl to make a smooth glaze. Put the cake on a board and brush the top and sides with the glaze.

2 Dust a rolling pin and the worksurface with a little icing sugar and roll out the marzipan to a round about 15cm (6 inches) larger than the cake. Position on the cake and ease to fit around the sides, pressing out any creases. Trim off the excess around the base. Leave to dry for 24 hours.

3 Preheat the oven to 180°C (160°C fan oven) mark 4. Line a baking sheet with foil and brush lightly with oil. Unwrap the mints and put pairs of sweets on the baking sheet about 1cm (½ inch) apart, leaving 5cm (2 inches) of space between each pair, to allow room for them to spread as they melt. Cook for 3–4 minutes until the sweets have melted and are just starting to bubble around the edges. Leave to cool on the foil for 3–4 minutes until firm enough to be lifted off. Use kitchen scissors to snip the pieces into large slivers and shards.

4 Wrap the ribbon around the bottom edge of the cake. Put the icing sugar in a bowl and make up according to the pack instructions. Using a small palette knife, spread the icing over the top of the cake, flicking it into small peaks as you go. Then tease the edges of the icing down the sides of the cake to form 'icicles'.

5 While the icing is still soft, push the mint shards into the top of the cake and insert the silver candles. Leave the cake to dry. Light the candles and serve.

Cuts into 12 slices

Instant Iced Christmas Cake

Preparation Time
15 minutes

- 3 medium egg whites
- 750g (1lb 11oz) icing sugar
- 20.5cm (8 inch) round fruit cake

DECORATION
- festive cookie cutter (we used a 7.5cm/3in star)
- gold or silver balls
- edible glitter
- decorations on wires (optional)
- ribbon

NUTRITIONAL INFORMATION
Per slice 489 cals; 8.0g fat (of which 1.7g saturates); 107g carbohydrate; 0.3g salt

1 Using a freestanding electric mixer or hand-held electric whisk, whisk the egg whites and sugar together to make the icing. Start on a low speed and work up to the maximum setting, until the mixture becomes thick, fluffy and holds a shape.

2 Put the fruit cake (covered in marzipan or not, depending on taste) on a cake board or stand. Using a palette knife, spread the icing over the cake, swirling as you go, to give a textured effect.

3 Position the cookie cutter in the centre of the top of the cake, then pour in gold or silver balls to give an even covering, making sure they spread right to the edges of the cutter. Carefully lift off the cutter (you may need to rescue a few balls).

4 Sprinkle edible glitter over the surface of the cake then, if you like, press decorations around the edges. Wrap a ribbon around the sides. And that's it!

Baking Know-How

BAKING EQUIPMENT

Not much in the way of specialist equipment is needed for baking, although one or two items in particular, such as a food processor and electric whisk, will make life much easier. Remember that kitchen equipment is subject to a great deal of wear and tear, so look for good-quality items. Below are the essentials when baking.

Scales Accurate measurement is essential when following most baking recipes. The electronic scale is the most accurate and can weigh up to 2kg (4½lb) or 5kg (11lb) in increments of 1–5g. Buy one with a flat platform on which you can put your bowl or measuring jug. Always set the scale to zero before adding the ingredients.

Measuring jugs, cups and spoons Jugs can be plastic or glass, and are available, marked with both metric and imperial, in sizes ranging from 500ml (18fl oz) to 2 litres (3½ pints), or even 3 litres (5¼ pints). Measuring cups are bought in sets of ¼, ⅓, ½ and 1 cups. A standard 1 cup measure is equivalent to about 250ml (9fl oz). Measuring spoons are useful for the smallest units and accurate spoon measurements go up to 15ml (1 tbsp). These may be in plastic or metal and often come in sets attached together on a ring.

Mixing bowls Stainless steel bowls work best when you are using a hand whisk, or when you need to place the bowl into a larger bowl filled with iced water for chilling down or to place it over simmering water (when melting chocolate, for example). Plastic or glass bowls are best if you need to use them in the

microwave. Bowls with gently tapered sides – much wider at the rim than at the base – will be useful for mixing dough.

Mixing spoons For general mixing, the cheap and sturdy wooden spoon still can't be beaten. The spoon should be stiff, so that it can cope with thick mixtures such as dough. In addition, a large metal spoon for folding ingredients together is also an invaluable item to have.

Other useful items These include spatulas, fine sieve, wire whisks, pastry brush, rolling pin, graters (fine and coarse), tape measure and paint brushes (for cake decorating).

BAKEWARE

As well as being thin enough to conduct heat quickly and efficiently, bakeware should be sturdy enough not to warp. Most bakeware is made from aluminium, and it may have enamel or non-stick coatings. A newer material for some bakeware is flexible, oven-safe silicone. It is safe to touch straight from the oven, is inherently non-stick and is also flexible – making it a lot easier to remove muffins and other bakes from their pans than it used to be.

Baking trays/Baking sheets Shallower than a roasting tin, these have many uses in baking. Choose ones that are large (but which fit comfortably in your oven) to avoid having to bake in batches. Buy the best you can afford.

Baking dishes Usually ceramic or Pyrex, you should have them in several sizes, ranging from 15–23cm (6–9 inch) to 25.5–35.5cm (10–14 inch).

Blenders Less versatile than food processors, but perfect for certain tasks, such as puréeing fruit. The traditional jug blender is great but some cooks prefer a 'stick' blender, which can be used directly in a pan, bowl or jug.

Freestanding mixers These powerful machines are particularly useful for bread-making and lengthy whisking, but they take up quite a lot of space on the worksurface.

Hand-held electric mixers and whisks Useful for creaming together butter and sugar in baking and for making meringues. They don't take up a lot of space and can be packed away easily.

Cake tins Available in many shapes and sizes, tins may be single-piece, loose-based or springform.

Loaf tins Available in various sizes, but one of the most useful is a 900g (2lb) tin.

Pie tins You should have both single-piece tins and loose-based tins for flans and pies.

Muffin tins These come in various sizes and depths and are available in both aluminium and silicone. If you make a lot of muffins and cupcakes it's worth investing in different types.

ELECTRICAL EQUIPMENT

Food processor Perfect for making breadcrumbs or pastry or for chopping large quantities of nuts. Most come with a number of attachments – dough hooks, graters, slicers.

Bread machines Kneading bread by hand doesn't take much time and effort, but bread machines are useful for making and baking bread if you have limited time and want to get on with something else. Doughs can also be prepared by the machine and then shaped and baked in the oven.

Ice-cream makers Even if you make ice cream only a few times a year, investing in a good machine will save lots of time and produce better results than an inferior model. The type with two freezing tubs enables you to make two flavours at once, or a larger quantity of a single flavour. A multi-speed ice-cream maker will make ice cream quickly and allow you to make other frozen desserts such as frozen yogurts and smoothies.

CAKE- AND BISCUIT-MAKING TECHNIQUES

Successful cake-making

The key to successful baking lies in using good-quality ingredients at the right temperature, measuring them accurately (using scales and measuring spoons) and following recipes very carefully. Weigh out all the ingredients before you start, using either metric or imperial measures, never a combination of the two. Check that all storecupboard ingredients to be used are well within their 'use-by' date. See also pages 308–311.

INGREDIENTS

FAT Unsalted butter gives the best results in most recipes. Margarine can be substituted in many recipes, although it doesn't lend such a good flavour, but low-fat 'spreads', with their high water content, are not suitable. For most cake recipes, you need to use the fat at room temperature. If necessary you can soften it, cautiously, in the microwave.

EGGS Eggs should also be used at room temperature; if taken straight from the fridge they are more likely to curdle a cake mixture. Make sure you use the correct size – unless otherwise stated, medium eggs should be used in all the recipes. A fresh egg should feel heavy in your hand and will sink to the bottom of the bowl or float on its side when put into water. Older eggs, over two weeks old, will float vertically.

SUGAR Golden caster sugar is generally used for cakes, but for a richer colour and flavour, light or dark muscovado sugars can be substituted. Icing sugar is ideal for icings, frostings and buttercreams.

FLOUR Self-raising white flour is used in most cake recipes, as it provides a raising agent, whereas plain white flour is generally used for biscuits and cookies. Plain or self-raising wholemeal flour can be substituted, although the results will be darker and denser and nuttier in flavour. Half white and half wholemeal makes a good compromise if you want to incorporate extra fibre. If you sieve it before use, tip the bran left in the sieve into the bowl.

NUTS Some nuts can be bought ready-prepared, others need preparation. After nuts have been shelled, they are still coated with a skin, which, although edible, tastes bitter. This is easier to remove if the nuts are blanched or toasted. To blanch, put the shelled nuts in a bowl and cover with boiling water. Leave for 2 minutes, then drain. Remove the skins by rubbing the nuts in a teatowel or squeezing between your thumb and index finger.

Toasting also improves the flavour. Preheat the oven to 200°C (180°C fan oven) mark 6. Put the shelled nuts on a baking sheet in a single layer and bake for 8–15 minutes until the skins are lightly coloured. Remove the skins by rubbing the nuts in a teatowel. Unless you want very large pieces, the easiest way to chop nuts is to put the cold, skinned nuts in a food processor and pulse at 10-second intervals. Or, place a chopping board on a folded teatowel on the worksurface and use a cook's knife to chop to the size of coarse breadcrumbs. Only chop about 75g (3oz) of nuts at a time. Store in an airtight container for up to two weeks. To slice nuts, put them on a board and, using a cook's knife, carefully slice the nuts as thinly as

Nuts: blanching, toasting and cutting

Cake-making methods

required. To make slivers, carefully cut the slices to make narrow matchsticks.

METHODS
A variety of cakes can be prepared using three basic techniques: creaming (Victoria Sponge, page 10), all-in-one (Sticky Lemon Polenta Cake, page 27) and whisking (Whisked Sponge, page 13). These straightforward basic recipes can be adapted in several ways.

CAKE TINS
To ensure successsful home baking, check that you have the correct cake tin – the cake tin sizes quoted in the recipes refer to the base measurement – and line the tin properly where necessary. Allow at least 15 minutes to heat the oven to the correct oven temperature.

LINING TINS
Always line your cake tin with greaseproof paper – this will help to stop the cake sticking to the sides of the tin or burning (use baking parchment for roulades and meringues). Lightly grease the tin first to help keep the paper in place. Apply the butter with a small piece of greaseproof paper. Don't thickly grease the tin, as this will 'fry' the edges of the cake.

Square tin
1 Cut out a square of greaseproof paper slightly smaller than the base of the cake tin. Cut four strips each about 2cm (¾ inch) wider than the depth of the tin and fold up one of the longest edges of each strip by 1cm (½ inch).

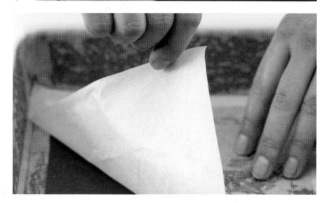

Lining a square tin

2 Lightly grease the tin with butter, making sure it is coated on all sides and in the corners.

3 Cut one strip to the length of the side of the tin and press into place in one corner and then along the length of the strip, with the narrow folded section sitting on the base. Continue, cutting to fit into the corners, to cover all four sides.

4 Lay the square on the base of the tin, then grease the paper, taking care not to move the side strips.

Lining a round tin

Round tin
1 Put the tin on a sheet of greaseproof paper and draw a circle around its circumference. Cut out the circle just inside the drawn line.

2 Cut a strip or strips about 2cm (¾ inch) wider than the depth of the tin and fold up one long edge of each strip by 1cm (½ inch). Make cuts, about 2.5cm (1 inch) apart, through the folded edge of the strip(s) up to the fold line.

3 Lightly grease the tin with butter, making sure it is completely coated.

4 Press the strip(s) on to the sides of the tin so that the snipped edge sits on the base.

5 Lay the circle in the bottom of the tin and grease the paper.

Swiss roll tin
Use this method for a Swiss roll or any other shallow baking tin.

1 Lightly grease the tin with butter, making sure it is completely coated.

2 Cut a piece of baking parchment into a rectangle 7.5cm (3 inch) wider and longer than the tin. Press it into the tin and cut at the corners, then fold to fit neatly. Grease all over.

Loaf tin
1 Lightly grease the tin with butter, making sure it is completely coated.

SHAPED TINS
♦ Round and square are the traditional shapes for cake tins, but tins come in many different shapes, including numerals, and can be either purchased or hired from cake decorating shops. The advantage of these tins is that they give more scope for matching the cake to the occasion.
♦ To line a shaped tin, follow the instructions for a round tin, above.

2 Cut out a sheet of greaseproof paper to the same length as the base and wide enough to cover both the base and the long sides. Press it into position, making sure that it sits snugly in the corners.

3 Now cut another sheet to the same width as the base and long enough to cover both the base and the ends of the tin. Press into place. Grease the paper all over.

Lining a loaf tin

Making roulades

Liners

Reusable, non-stick, silicone baking mats and liners are widely available and, as there is no need to grease them, they reduce the fat in your baking. Look out also for silicone muffin trays and cupcake moulds.

MAKING ROULADES

A roulade is made from a very light cake mixture and does not contain flour. It remains very soft when baked, and can therefore be easily rolled around a layer of filling such as jam and cream (see Black Forest Roulade, page 46).

MAKING CUPCAKES AND MUFFINS

Cupcakes and muffins are two members of the same family: individual cakes, usually based on a mixture made with self-raising flour, baked in bun tins or muffin pans, so that it rises and sets to an airy texture. The secret to really light, fluffy muffins is a light hand. Be sure to sift the flour and stir the mixture as little as possible; it's ok if it looks a little lumpy. Over-mixing will give tough, chewy results.

MAKING CHEESECAKES

A cheesecake is more of a deep tart than a cake. It is essentially a rich flavoured mixture of eggs, cream and full- or low-fat soft cheese, curd cheese or cottage cheese – set on a buttery biscuit, sponge or pastry base. Cheesecakes are either baked to cook and set the filling, or uncooked and set with gelatin. Use a spring-release cake tin to make the cake easier to unmould.

When baking cheeesecakes, watch the temperature – too high a heat can cause the top to crack (see page 309).

The mixture for an uncooked cheesecake is poured on to a biscuit crumb base that has been pressed into a flan tin, then chilled until firm. The whole cheesecake is then chilled to set.

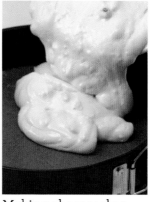

Making cupcakes and muffins   Making cheesecakes

Testing sponges

Testing fruit cakes

BAKING THE CAKE

Bake the cake mixture as soon as you have made it, as the raising agents will start to react straight away. Once the cake is in the oven, resist the temptation to open the door – a sudden gush of cold air will make a part-baked cake sink. Instead, wait until the cooking time is almost up before testing. If your cake appears to be browning too quickly, cover the top loosely with greaseproof paper towards the end of cooking.

Apart from very light sponges, all cakes are best left to stand in their tin for 5–10 minutes after baking to firm up slightly.

TESTING CAKES

Ovens vary and the time given in the recipe might be too short or too long to correctly cook what you are baking. So always test to ensure a successful result.

COOLING CAKES
◆ Round and square are the traditional shapes for cake tins, but tins come in many different shapes, including numerals, and can be either purchased or hired from cake decorating shops. The advantage of these tins is that they give more scope for matching the cake to the occasion.

◆ To line a shaped tin, follow the instructions for a round tin, above.

Testing sponges
1 Gently press the centre of the sponge. It should feel springy. If it's a whisked cake, it should be just shrinking away from the sides of the tin.

2 If you have to put it back into the oven, close the door gently so that the vibrations don't cause the cake to sink in the centre.

Testing fruit cakes
1 To test if a fruit cake is cooked, insert a skewer into the centre of the cake, leave for a few moments, then pull it out. If it comes away clean, the cake is ready.

2 If any mixture sticks to the skewer, the cake is not quite done, so put the cake back in the oven for a few more minutes, then test again with a clean skewer.

STORING CAKES
With the exception of rich fruit cakes and gingerbread, most cakes are best enjoyed freshly baked. If storing is necessary, use a cake tin or large plastic container. Make sure that the cake is completely cold before you put it into the container. If you haven't a large enough container, wrap the cake in a double layer of greaseproof paper and overwrap with foil. Avoid putting rich fruit cakes in direct contact with foil – the fruit may react with it. Never store a cake in the same tin as biscuits, as the biscuits will quickly soften.

Most cakes, particularly sponges, freeze well, but they are generally best frozen before filling and decorating. If freezing a finished gâteau, open-freeze first, then pack in a rigid container.

Successful biscuit-making

As with cake-making, the key to successful biscuit-making is to accurately weigh the ingredients and follow the recipe carefully. See also page 311.

METHODS

The main techniques in biscuit making are: creaming, the all-in-one method, rolled, refrigerator biscuits (form the mixture into a roll, chill until firm, then cut into slices), whisked, melted, moulded, and piped.

baking sheets

Use a shiny-based baking sheet; a darker-coloured sheet will absorb a greater amount of heat and can therefore burn the undersides of the biscuits.

baking biscuits

For hints on baking the perfect biscuits and cookies, see page 311. Once baked, biscuits, with their high sugar content, will seem very soft. They should be left on the baking sheet for a few minutes before transferring to a wire rack.

storing biscuits

Most biscuits are best enjoyed freshly baked. However, if storing, never put in the same tin as a cake, and preferably not with other types of biscuits, as they quickly soften and absorb other flavours.

Crushing biscuits for cheesecake bases

Crush the biscuits to a fine powder in a food processor. (Alternatively, put them into a plastic bag and crush with a rolling pin.)

FILLING BISCUITS

Cream filling:
To sandwich about 18 biscuits, cream 50g (2oz) butter until soft, then beat in 75g (3oz) sifted icing sugar. Mix well and soften by adding a few drops of orange juice or vanilla extract until the mixture is of a firm, spreadable consistency. Spread the mixture on to the flat side of a biscuit and gently press a second biscuit on top to make a sandwich.

Chocolate filling:
To fill about 18 biscuits, cream 50g (2oz) butter until soft, then add 75g (3oz) icing sugar and 2 tsp cocoa powder. Mix well and add a few drops of milk to soften if necessary.

Toffee filling:
Spread dulce de leche over one biscuit and top with another. Roll the edges in desiccated coconut, if you like.

Filling biscuits

Dos and don'ts of cake and biscuit-making

HOW TO MAKE PERFECT CAKES

◆ Weigh out all the ingredients carefully before starting the recipe, so that you have everything to hand when you begin to make the cake.

◆ Always work in metric or imperial – never mix the two measurements.

◆ Check that you have the correct cake tin for the job. The tin sizes quoted in this book refer to the base measurement of the tin.

◆ Always line the tin properly where necessary.

◆ Allow the oven to preheat to the correct temperature.

◆ Try not to be heavy-handed – when folding in flour, use light strokes so the air doesn't get knocked out.

◆ Don't let a cake mixture sit around once you've made it: pop it straight into the cake tin and into the oven, otherwise the raising agents will start to react.

◆ After it has come out of the oven, leave the cake in the tin to cool for 10 minutes and then turn out on to a wire rack to cool completely.

◆ Let the tins cool completely before washing them in warm, soapy water with a non-abrasive sponge.

WHAT WENT WRONG?

THE BROWNIES ARE DRY AND CRUMBLY
◆ The brownie was cooked for too long. Test with a skewer – a little of the mixture should cling to it.
◆ The oven temperature was too high.

THE BROWNIES HAVE A THICK CRUST
◆ There is too much sugar in proportion to the other ingredients.

THE FLAPJACKS ARE GREASY
◆ Too much butter in proportion to other ingredients.

HOW TO MAKE PERFECT CHEESECAKES

♦ When making cheesecakes, bring eggs and cream cheese to room temperature before using.

♦ Use good-quality cream cheese for the best results.

♦ Cream cheese will give richer-tasting cheesecakes.

WHAT WENT WRONG?

THE CHEESECAKE IS DRY
♦ The cheesecake was over-baked.

CRACK IN THE SURFACE OF THE CHEESECAKE
♦ The cheesecake was over-baked.
♦ The cheesecake was cooled too quickly – leave to cool in a switched-off oven with the door ajar.

THE CHEESECAKE CENTRE IS STILL RUNNY
♦ The cheesecake was under-cooked.
♦ The oven temperature was too low.

THE CHEESECAKE IS GRAINY IN TEXTURE
♦ The cheesecake was over-baked.
♦ The oven temperature was too high.

HOW TO MAKE PERFECT TRAYBAKES

◆ If you don't have the size traybake tin specified in a recipe, find a similar one that has sides that add up to the same amount.

◆ Be careful not to overcook traybakes. They are ready when they are golden brown, but will not be set firm when they come out of the oven.

◆ Brownies should always be slightly under-cooked to ensure their distinctive soft and squidgy texture – a skewer inserted into the centre should still have a little mixture clinging to it.

◆ Some traybakes (such as flapjacks) are soft mixtures when hot and firm up when cold (especially when made with golden syrup or honey), so it is essential to mark the cooked bake into squares or bars while it is hot. Leave to cool completely in the baking tray before turning out of the tin.

◆ Remove carefully, using a spatula or palette knife, as some bakes can be a little crumbly.

◆ Some traybakes have a more 'cakey' mixture (they contain a larger amount of flour and some eggs) and can be made with two different layers of mixture or an iced topping. Leave to cool before cutting.

Most traybakes keep well for several days, or longer, if stored in an airtight tin.

WHAT WENT WRONG?

THE CHEESECAKE IS DRY
◆ The cheesecake was over-baked.

CRACK IN THE SURFACE OF THE CHEESECAKE
◆ The cheesecake was over-baked.
◆ The cheesecake was cooled too quickly – leave to cool in a switched-off oven with the door ajar.

THE CHEESECAKE CENTRE IS STILL RUNNY
◆ The cheesecake was under-cooked.
◆ The oven temperature was too low.

THE CHEESECAKE IS GRAINY IN TEXTURE
◆ The cheesecake was over-baked.
◆ The oven temperature was too high.

HOW TO MAKE PERFECT COOKIES AND BISCUITS

◆ Don't over-flour the worksurface when rolling out – it can make biscuits too dry.

◆ Be aware that re-rolled dough can result in tougher cookies.

◆ Use a shiny-based baking sheet.

◆ Don't overcrowd the biscuits on the baking sheet or in the oven – air needs to circulate all around them. If you are baking more than one sheet, make sure they are on shelves at least 20.5cm (8 inch) apart and be prepared to have them bake at different speeds. Watch them closely for uneven cooking.

◆ Turn the baking sheet(s) around once or twice during baking. Most ovens get hotter in some places than in others, and this can cause uneven cooking.

◆ Leave biscuits to set for 1 minute on the baking sheet once out of the oven, then transfer immediately to a wire rack (but see below). If left on the sheet the hot baking sheet will continue to cook them, and steam will build up underneath, which can make the bases soggy. Some biscuits, however (particularly those made with syrup), need to be left on the baking sheet to firm up a little before they are transferred to a rack. Put the biscuits on a fairly fine-meshed rack if at all possible. If possible, raise the rack by putting it on supports so that it is at least a few centimetres higher than the worksurface it's resting on: the more air circulating underneath, the crisper the bases will be.

◆ Start testing biscuits slightly before you expect them to be cooked. And watch them very closely during the final minutes, as they can go from perfect to overcooked in a matter of only a few seconds.

◆ Cool biscuits completely before storing.

WHAT WENT WRONG?

THE BISCUITS ARE TOUGH
◆ They have been over-baked.
◆ The dough was over-worked when the flour was added.

THE BISCUIT MIXTURE SPREADS WHEN BAKING
◆ Too much sugar or fat in the recipe.
◆ Too much air was beaten into the butter.
◆ The dough was under-chilled before baking.

THE BISCUITS HAVE A CAKE-LIKE TEXTURE
◆ There is too much flour in proportion to the other ingredients.
◆ The oven temperature was too high.

ICING AND DECORATING

Filling and topping cakes

To make sponge cakes even tastier, they can be split and filled with jam, cream or buttercream. Icings complete a special-occasion cake and are especially good when covering home-made almond paste.

Splitting and filling a cake

1 Leave the cake to cool completely before splitting. Use a knife with a shallow thin blade, such as a bread knife, a ham knife, or a carving knife. Cut a notch from top to bottom on one side so you will know where to line the pieces up.

2 Cut midway between top and bottom, about one-third of the way through the cake. Turn the cake while cutting, taking care to keep the blade parallel with the base, until you have cut all the way around.

3 Cut through the central core and lift off the top of the cake.

4 Warm the filling slightly to make it easier to spread, then spread on top of the base, stopping 1cm (½ inch) from the edge. Add the top layer of cake.

Basic icings and frostings

There are lots of options for covering cakes, depending on the finish you require. Royal and glacé icings are the classics. Almond paste, followed by a layer of ready-to-roll icing (sugar paste) is popular, as is buttercream or apricot glaze.

GLACÉ ICING

To make 225g (8oz), enough to cover 18 fairy cakes, you will need: 225g (8oz) icing sugar, a few drops of vanilla or almond flavouring (optional), 2–3 tbsp boiling water, food colouring (optional).

1 Sift the icing sugar into a bowl. Add a few drops of flavouring, if you like.

2 Using a wooden spoon, gradually stir in enough water until the mixture is the consistency of thick cream. Beat until white and smooth and the icing is thick enough to coat the back of the spoon. Add colouring, if you like, and use immediately.

Splitting and filling a cake

Variations

◆ Orange or lemon: Replace the water with strained orange or lemon juice.

◆ Chocolate: Sift 2 tsp cocoa powder with the icing sugar.

◆ Colour: Add a few drops of liquid food colouring, or use food colouring paste for a stronger colour.

note
Food colourings are available in liquid, paste or powder form.

Add minute amounts with the tip of a cocktail stick until the desired colour is achieved.

ROYAL ICING
Royal icing can also be bought in packs from supermarkets. Simply add water or egg white to use.

To make 450g (1lb), enough to cover the top and sides of a 20.5cm (8 inch) cake, you will need:
2 medium egg whites, ¼tsp lemon juice, 450g (1lb) icing sugar, sifted, 1 tsp glycerine.

1 Put the egg whites and lemon juice into a clean bowl. Stir to break up the egg whites. Add sufficient icing sugar to mix to the consistency of unwhipped cream. Continue mixing and adding small quantities of icing sugar until the desired consistency is reached, mixing well and gently beating after each addition. The icing should be smooth, glossy and light, almost like a cold meringue in texture, but not aerated. Do not add the icing sugar too quickly or it will produce a dull heavy icing. Stir in the glycerine until well blended. (Alternatively, for large quantities of royal icing, use a food mixer on the lowest speed, following the same instructions as before.)

2 Allow the icing to settle before using it; cover the surface with a piece of damp clingfilm and seal well, excluding all the air.

3 Stir the icing thoroughly before use to disperse any air bubbles, then adjust the consistency if necessary by adding more sifted icing sugar.

APRICOT GLAZE
To make 450g (1lb), you will need:
450g (1lb) apricot jam, 2 tbsp water.

1 Put the jam and water into a saucepan and heat gently, stirring occasionally, until melted. Boil the jam rapidly for 1 minute, then strain through a sieve.

2 Using a wooden spoon, rub through as much fruit as possible. Discard the skins left in the sieve.

3 Pour the glaze into a clean, hot jar, then seal with a clean lid and cool. Store in the fridge for up to two months. You only need 3–4 tbsp apricot glaze for a 23cm (9 inch) cake, so this quantity will glaze 6–7 cakes.

ALMOND PASTE
To make 450g (1lb) almond paste, enough to cover the top and sides of an 18cm (7 inch) round cake or 15cm (6 inch) square cake, you will need:
225g (8oz) ground almonds, 125g (4oz) golden caster sugar, 125g (4oz) sifted golden icing sugar, 1 large egg, 2 tsp lemon juice, 1 tsp sherry, 1–2 drops vanilla extract.

1 Put the ground almonds and sugars into a bowl and stir to combine. In another bowl, whisk together the remaining ingredients, then add to the dry ingredients.

2 Stir well to mix, pounding gently to release some of the oil from the almonds. Knead with your hands until smooth, then cover until ready to use.

note
If you wish to avoid using raw egg to bind the almond paste, mix the other liquid ingredients with a little water instead.

FONDANT ICING

To make 500g (1lb 2oz), enough to cover the top and sides of an 18cm (7 inch) round cake or 15cm (6 inch) square cake, you will need:
500g (1lb 2oz) golden icing sugar, plus extra to dust, 1 medium egg white, 2 tbsp liquid glucose, warmed, 1 tsp vanilla extract.

Whiz the icing sugar in a food processor for 30 seconds, then add the egg white, glucose and vanilla extract and whiz for 2–3 minutes until the mixture forms a ball.

VANILLA FROSTING

To make about 175g (6oz), enough to cover the top and sides of an 18cm (7 inch) cake, you will need:
150g (5oz) icing sugar, 5 tsp vegetable oil, 1 tbsp milk, a few drops of vanilla extract.

Sift the icing sugar into a bowl and, using a wooden spoon, beat in the oil, milk and vanilla extract until smooth.

COFFEE FUDGE FROSTING

To make 400g (14oz), enough to cover the top and sides of a 20.5cm (8 inch) cake, you will need:
50g (2oz) unsalted butter, 125g (4oz) light muscovado sugar, 2 tbsp single cream or milk, 1 tbsp coffee granules, 200g (7oz) golden icing sugar, sifted.

1 Put the butter, muscovado sugar and cream or milk into a pan. Dissolve the coffee in 2 tbsp boiling water and add to the pan. Heat gently until the sugar dissolves, then bring to the boil and boil briskly for 3 minutes.

2 Remove from the heat and gradually stir in the icing sugar. Beat well with a wooden spoon for 1 minute until smooth.

3 Use the frosting immediately, spreading it over the cake with a wet palette knife, or dilute with a little water to use as a smooth coating.

Variation

Chocolate fudge frosting: Omit the coffee. Add 75g (3oz) plain chocolate, in pieces, to the pan with the butter at the beginning of step 1.

AMERICAN FROSTING

To make 225g (8oz), enough to cover the top and sides of a 20.5cm (8 inch) cake,
1 large egg white, 225g (8oz) golden caster or granulated sugar, pinch of cream of tartar.

1 Whisk the egg white in a clean bowl until stiff. Put the sugar, 4 tbsp water and the cream of tartar into a heavy-based pan.

Heat gently, stirring, until the sugar has dissolved. Bring to the boil, without stirring, and boil until the sugar syrup registers 115°C on a sugar thermometer.

2 Remove from the heat and, as soon as the bubbles subside, pour the syrup on to the egg white in a thin stream, whisking constantly until thick and white. Leave to cool slightly.

3 When the frosting begins to turn dull around the edges and is almost cold, pour quickly over the cake and spread evenly with a palette knife.

SEVEN-MINUTE FROSTING

To make about 175g (6oz), enough to cover the top and sides of an 18cm (7 inch) cake, you will need:
1 medium egg white, 175g (6oz) caster sugar, 2 tbsp water, pinch of salt, pinch of cream of tartar.

1 Put all the ingredients into a heatproof bowl and whisk lightly using an electric or hand whisk.

2 Put the bowl over a pan of hot water, making sure the base of the bowl doesn't touch the water, and heat, whisking continuously, until the mixture thickens sufficiently to stand in peaks. This will take about 7 minutes.

3 Pour the frosting over the top of the cake and spread with a palette knife.

BUTTERCREAM

To cover the top of a 20.5cm (8 inch) cake, you will need:
75g (3oz) unsalted butter, 175g (6oz) icing sugar, sifted, a few drops of vanilla extract, 1–2 tbsp milk.

1 Soften the butter in a mixing bowl, then beat until light and fluffy.

2 Gradually stir in the remaining ingredients and beat until smooth.

Variations

◆ Citrus: Replace the vanilla with a little grated orange, lemon or lime zest, and use some of the fruit's juice in place of the milk.

◆ Chocolate: Blend 1 tbsp cocoa powder with 2 tbsp boiling water. Cool, then add to the mixture in place of the milk.

◆ Colour: For a strong colour, use food colouring paste; liquid colouring gives a paler effect.

EASIEST ICING

To make 675g (1½lb), enough to cover a 20.5cm (8 inch) almond paste-covered cake, you will need: 3 medium egg whites, 2 tbsp lemon juice, 2 tsp glycerine, 675g (1½lb) icing sugar, sifted.

1 Put the egg whites into a large bowl and whisk until frothy. There should be just a layer of bubbles across the top. Add the lemon juice, glycerine and 2 tbsp icing sugar and whisk until smooth.

2 Whisk in the rest of the sugar, a little at a time, until the mixture is smooth, thick and forming soft peaks.

3 Using a palette knife, smooth half the icing over the top and sides of the cake, then repeat using the remaining icing to cover. Run the knife around the sides to neaten, then use the tip to make peaks all over the top. Leave to dry in a cool place for at least 48 hours.

CHOCOLATE GANACHE

To make 225g (8oz), enough to cover an 18cm (7 inch) round cake, you will need: 225g (8oz) good-quality plain dark chocolate (with 60–70 per cent cocoa solids), chopped into small pieces, 250ml (9fl oz) double cream.

1 Put the chocolate into a medium heatproof bowl. Pour the cream into a small heavy-based pan and bring to the boil.

2 Immediately pour the cream on to the chocolate and stir gently in one direction until the chocolate has

melted and the mixture is smooth. Set aside to cool for 5 minutes.

3 Whisk the ganache until it begins to hold its shape. Used at room temperature, the mixture should be the consistency of softened butter.

note

Use ganache at room temperature as a smooth coating for special cakes, or chill it lightly until thickened and use to fill meringues, choux buns or sandwich cakes.

Variations

These are all suitable for a sauce made with 225g (8oz) chocolate:

◆ Milk or single cream: Substituted in whole or in part for the water.

◆ Coffee: Stir in 1 tsp instant coffee or a shot of espresso when melting the chocolate.

◆ Spices: Add a pinch of ground cinnamon, crushed cardamom seeds or freshly grated nutmeg to the melting chocolate.

◆ Vanilla extract: Stir in ¼ tsp vanilla when melting the chocolate.

◆ Rum, whisky or Cognac: Stir in about 1 tsp alcohol when melting the chocolate.

◆ Butter: Stir in 25g (1oz) towards the end of heating.

Icing and frosting cupcakes

The icing on cupcakes is now almost as important as the cake underneath. Icing helps keep the cake softer for longer (as long as the cakes are kept in their paper cases) and allows you to theme and decorate your cupcakes as desired.

Piping icing on to cupcakes

Many cupcake bakeries have developed a signature swirl of buttercream icing – practise and soon you'll have your own. Half-fill the piping bag with buttercream or frosting and hold the bag vertically as you pipe, squeezing gently from the top.

Spreading

Start by gently brushing the top of the cooled cupcake with your finger or a brush to remove crumbs. Dollop a generous amount of buttercream or frosting on to the cake (it takes more than you might think) and gently spread the icing to the sides of the cake with a palette or butter knife for a smooth look. Alternatively, push the icing into a swirl or points with your spatula or knife.

Filling cupcakes

Before icing it, you can easily fill your cupcake with extra icing, buttercream or smooth jam. Insert a plain nozzle (not too fine) into a piping bag, half-fill the bag with the chosen filling and push the nozzle down through the top into the centre of the un-iced cake (alternatively, hollow out some of the cake with a small knife first). Squeeze in some mixture, then ice as normal. It's worth cutting your first filled cake in half vertically to check how much filling you have managed to get into the cupcake.

Flooding cupcakes

Use a little less cake mixture when baking the cupcakes, so that when baked they don't quite reach the top of their cases. Spoon some glacé icing on top of the cooled cakes so that it floods out to the sides of the cases. Decorate with feathering, sprinkles, dragees, gold leaf or other decorations as desired.

Covering with sugarpaste

Covering cupcakes with sugarpaste works best if the baked cupcakes are flat – if they have peaked during baking, then trim to flatten. Next, simply roll out some sugarpaste in the desired colour, to a thickness of 5mm (¼ inch). Measure the top of the cupcakes, then cut out circles of sugarpaste to match. Spread a thin layer of buttercream over the cupcake, then secure the sugarpaste circle in place.

If you don't want to completely cover the tops with sugarpaste, cut out smaller shapes of the sugarpaste – hearts always look nice. Leave to dry completely on baking parchment. Position the sugarpaste shapes on buttercreamed cupcakes (the decorations should be stiff enough to stand up).

BREAD-MAKING TECHNIQUES

Baking bread is one of the greatest pleasures of the kitchen, and one of the simplest. Simple loaves provide the foundation for further experimentation, so they are the best place to start with bread-making (see White Farmhouse Loaf, page 230). See also pages 320–21.

Ingredients

The basic ingredients for bread-making are very simple, but you can also experiment with flavourings. Savoury doughs can be enhanced with cheese, fresh herbs, olives or sun-dried tomatoes, for example; while sweet doughs are enriched with dried fruits, nuts, vanilla sugar, or scented spices like cinnamon and nutmeg.

YEAST Yeast is available in a number of different forms, which are interchangeable in recipes providing that the method is adjusted accordingly. As a rough guide, 15g (½oz) fresh yeast, a 7g sachet (2 tsp) fast-action (easy-blend) dried yeast, or 1 tbsp ordinary dried yeast is enough to rise 700g (1½lb) flour. In general, if you add more than this, the dough will not rise any higher and the bread is likely to have an unpleasant yeasty taste. However, if the dough is enriched with fruit, sugar, butter or nuts, the rise is more difficult and you will usually need more yeast – be guided by the recipes. Fast-action dried yeast, also called easy-blend dried yeast, is now the most readily available dried form. It is sprinkled directly into the flour and the liquid is mixed in afterwards. After kneading, the dough can be shaped straightaway and only requires one rising. However, for enriched doughs – particularly heavily fruited ones – better results are obtained if the dough is given the traditional two rises. Always make sure you adhere to the 'use-by' date on the pack; fast-action dried yeast won't work if it is stale. Traditional dried yeast needs sugar to activate it. If using milk as the liquid, the natural sugars present in the milk will be enough; if using water, you will need to add a pinch of sugar. To use traditional dried yeast, blend it with the warm liquid (see opposite), adding a pinch of sugar if needed, and leave it in a warm place for about 15 minutes until a frothy head develops. This shows that the yeast is active. If it refuses to froth, then it is probably past its 'use-by date'; discard and begin again with a fresh pack of yeast. Fresh yeast is a living organism and must be handled in the right way in

Leaving the dough to rise

order to work effectively. It is available from some healthfood shops, bakers and supermarkets. It should be firm, moist and creamy coloured with a good 'yeasty' smell. If it is dry and crumbly with brown patches, it is probably stale and won't work effectively. When you buy fresh yeast it is alive, but inactive. Only when it is mixed with a warm liquid does it become active and release the gases that make the dough rise. Fresh yeast is easy to use: simply blend with a little of the liquid specified in the recipe, add the remaining liquid, then mix into the flour. Fresh yeast will stay fresh for about three days if stored in the fridge, or it can be frozen for up to three months.

Sourdough starter is a traditional method that has regained popularity. A mixture of yeast, flour and water is left to ferment for several days and then added to the dough. A sourdough starter produces a close-textured loaf with a distinctive flavour. If you make bread regularly, a sourdough starter is a convenient way of leavening. Simply blend 15g (½oz) fresh yeast (or 1 tsp dried yeast) with 450ml (¾ pint) warm water and about 225g (8oz) strong plain white flour or enough to make a thick pourable batter. Cover the bowl with a damp cloth and leave at room temperature for 3–5 days to ferment and develop the sourdough flavour. Use 125ml (4fl oz) starter to replace each 15g (½oz) fresh yeast called for in a recipe, then make the bread in the usual way. To store, keep it in the fridge and use within 1 week. Sourdough starter keeps well but must be 'refreshed'. Keep the starter covered in the fridge and whisk in a handful of flour and a small cup of water every day – this provides fresh nutrients for the yeast and aids its leavening properties.

LIQUID No matter which variety of yeast you are using, the liquid should be just warm or tepid, that is at a temperature of 43°C, which will feel slightly warm to the fingertips. If it is too hot it could kill the yeast; if too cold the yeast will not begin to work. Milk gives bread a slightly softer texture than water. You should always regard any quantity of liquid specified in a recipe as a guide because flour absorbency varies according to the type of flour, and from brand to brand.

FLOUR Various flours are used for bread-making. Strong flours give better results because they have a higher proportion of protein, which helps the formation of gluten – the substance that stretches the dough and traps in air as it cooks, to give bread its characteristic airy texture. Ordinary plain flour produces a close-textured crumbly loaf. Strong white bread flour is ideal. If possible, use unbleached white flour, which has not been chemically treated to whiten it. Strong wholemeal bread flour is ground from the whole wheat kernel and has a coarser texture than white flour, with a fuller flavour and more nutrients; it is also an excellent source of fibre. This flour lends a distinctive flavour, but it is best used with some strong white flour to obtain a good textured loaf. Bread made with 100% wholemeal flour has a heavy, dense texture. Strong brown bread flour has a percentage of the bran removed and therefore has a finer texture than wholemeal flour. Stoneground flour takes its name from the specific grinding process – between stones – which heats the flour and gives it a slightly roasted, nutty flavour. Both stoneground wholemeal and brown flours are available. Granary flour is a strong brown flour, with added malted wheat flakes, which give it a distinctive flavour. Rye flour makes a dark,

close-textured bread with plenty of flavour. As it is low in gluten, it must be mixed with a strong white flour for best results.

SALT An important ingredient in breads because it controls fermentation, strengthens gluten and improves the flavour. However, it also slows down the action of yeast, so don't add too much. Be guided by the amount specified in the recipe.

FAT Some recipes call for a little fat to be rubbed into the flour before the yeast is added. This improves the keeping quality of the bread and imparts extra flavour, but too much fat will slow down the action of the yeast.

Mixing and kneading the dough

Some recipes recommend warming the flour and mixing bowl in advance. If using fresh or 'ordinary' dried yeast, or if you are working in a cold room, this helps to speed things up a little, but otherwise it isn't necessary.

After mixing the yeast and liquid into the dry ingredients, vigorous kneading is required to strengthen the gluten in the flour, make the dough elastic and ultimately to achieve a good rise. If you omit this stage, the dough will not rise. There is nothing difficult about kneading and, contrary to popular belief, it doesn't take long – 10 minutes should be enough. Turn the dough on to a floured surface, fold it firmly towards you, then quickly and firmly push it down and away from you with the heel of your hand.

Give it a quarter turn and continue kneading until the dough feels elastic and smooth: it shouldn't be sticky. As an alternative to kneading by hand, you can use a large mixer with a dough hook attachment.

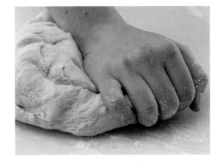
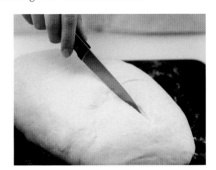

Mixing and kneading the dough

Baking in a bread machine

BREAD MACHINES

Bread machines can make doughs for all kinds of shaped breads. They knead, prove and bake, but models vary. Most will bake different sizes of loaf as well as different breads; some have a 'beep' function to tell you when to add other ingredients during the dough cycle. Most allow you to select the crust colour, and some have a timer so that you can set the machine to bake bread ready for a selected time, such as first thing in the morning. See also page 321.

RISING

Put the kneaded dough into a clean bowl and cover with a clean teatowel, an oiled plastic bag or oiled clingfilm to prevent a skin forming. Leave in a warm place until the dough has doubled in size and springs back when pressed. The time it takes for the dough to rise will depend on the ambient temperature. If the bowl is near a warm oven or in an airing cupboard, rising can take just 30 minutes; at cooler temperatures it may take well over an hour. Don't be tempted to put it somewhere hot to speed things up; you will end up with a badly shaped, uneven-textured loaf, or you could even kill the yeast. For a slower rise, leave the dough in the fridge overnight, then bring it to room temperature in the morning before shaping.

KNOCKING BACK AND PROVING

The risen dough is 'knocked back' (kneaded) to smooth out any air pockets. Just 2–3 minutes kneading is sufficient before shaping. Leave the shaped dough once again in a warm place until it has doubled in size and springs back when pressed. This proving stage is quicker than the first rising.

SHAPING BREAD

The shape and size of bread can be varied almost endlessly after the first rise. After the second rising, the dough is ready to bake. Understanding the basics will ensure success. The simplest way to shape a loaf is to roll the dough into a ball, flatten it slightly and put on a baking sheet. Alternatively, shape the dough as follows:

Long loaves After knocking back, cut the dough into pieces, each weighing about 200g (7oz). Roll one piece until it is about 40.5cm (16 inch) long. Transfer to a baking sheet, seam-side down. Repeat with the remaining pieces. Cover with oiled clingfilm and leave to prove (rise) for 30 minutes. Slash 3–4 times before baking.

Traditional tin loaf Flatten the dough to an oblong,

Shaping bread

the length of the dough, but three times as wide. Fold this in three, then put into the tin, to two-thirds fill it.

Cottage loaf Cut off one-third of the dough. Shape both pieces into rounds and put the smaller one on top of the larger round. Push the handle of a wooden spoon down through the middle.

Plait Divide the dough into three equal-sized pieces. Roll each piece into a long sausage, then pinch these together at one end and plait loosely. Pinch the other ends together firmly.

Twist Divide the dough into two equal-sized pieces. Roll each piece of dough into a long sausage. Hold one end of the two pieces of dough together and twist. Dampen the ends and tuck under.

Baton Shape the dough into a long sausage with tapering ends about 20.5cm (8 inch) long.

Rings Take a piece of dough and form into a long sausage. Bend it round to form a ring, then dampen the ends and mould them together.

Simple rolls After knocking back, cut the dough into even pieces, each about 40g (1½oz). Roll each piece with the palm of your hand on a lightly floured surface to make a ball. Place on a greased baking sheet, seam-side down, and press down slightly. Cover with clingfilm and leave to prove for 30 minutes before baking.

Knots Shape each piece of dough into a long sausage, then tie into a knot.

FINISHES
As well as glazing the dough before baking (see below), other finishes can add interest, variety and extra fibre. Lightly sprinkle the surface of the dough with seeds, such as poppy, caraway, fennel or sesame, or try barley or wheat flakes on wholemeal bread.

BAKING THE BREAD
Bread is baked in a hot oven to kill the yeast and halt its action.

If the bread shows signs of browning too quickly, cover with foil. When cooked, the bread should be well risen, firm to the touch and golden brown; if you turn it over and tap it on the bottom the loaf should sound hollow. To crisp the crust of large loaves all

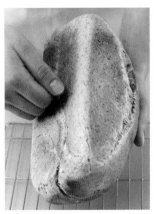
Topping bread

Cooling bread on a rack

over, return them to the oven upside down for about 10 minutes. Always remove bread from the tins before transferring to wire racks to cool.

STORING BREAD
Bread with a high fat or sugar content should keep well for 3–4 days, but other home-made bread stales quite quickly. It is best stored in a dry, well-ventilated bread bin, not the fridge, and eaten the day it is made.

Bread freezes well for a relatively short time, up to 1 month, after which the crust begins to deteriorate and lift off. Frozen or slightly stale bread can be freshened in a warm oven.

Quick yeastless breads, leavened with baking powder or bicarbonate of soda rather than yeast, tend to stale quickly. They are invariably at their best eaten fresh and warm from the oven.

GLAZING
Glazing bread before baking gives an attractive finish.
- For a golden, shiny effect, brush with beaten egg or egg beaten with a little water or milk.
- For a crusty finish, brush with salted water, made by dissolving 2 tsp salt in 2 tbsp water.
- For a soft golden crust, brush with milk. Some breads and yeast buns are glazed after baking with warm honey or syrup.
- The dough was under-proved.

Dos and don'ts of bread-making

HOW TO MAKE PERFECT BREAD

◆ Make sure shaped dough has risen sufficiently – usually to double.

◆ Always oil or flour the loaf tin, or baking sheet, to prevent sticking.

◆ Make sure the oven is at the correct temperature before baking.

◆ Bake on a preheated ceramic baking stone (from good kitchen shops) if possible, even if the bread is in a loaf tin. The heat of the stone will give the bread a crisp base.

◆ If baked bread is left for too long either in the loaf tin or on the baking sheet, steam will gather and, as a result, the underneath will start to become soggy. To prevent this, always remove the loaf immediately and put it on a wire rack. Then leave it to cool completely before slicing, as you like.

WHAT WENT WRONG?

THE LOAF HASN'T RISEN PROPERLY
- Not enough liquid was added during mixing.
- Too much salt or sugar was added during mixing.
- The yeast was stale.
- The liquid was too hot and killed the yeast.
- The second proving wasn't long enough.
- The second proving was too long causing it to collapse during baking.

THE BREAD IS CAKE-LIKE OR OVER-DENSE
- The dough wasn't kneaded for long enough.
- The dough was under-proved.
- Too much salt was added.
- Too much fat was added.
- Not enough, or too little, liquid was added.

THE BREAD HAS HOLES IN IT
- The dough wasn't knocked back sufficiently.
- The dough was over-proved.

THE BREAD HAS A CRACKED CRUST
- The oven was too hot.
- The dough was under-proved.

DOS AND DON'TS OF MACHINE-BAKED BREAD

- Use recipes that have been designed for bread machine use only, as conventional bread recipes use different quantities of ingredients and are not converted easily.

- Measure out all the ingredients carefully, as exact quantities are essential for a perfect loaf.

- Always follow the bread machine instructions carefully; it is essential that the ingredients go into the machine in the order stated, as the yeast must not come into contact with the liquid until the machine begins to mix.

- Avoid lifting the lid during the rising and baking cycles, as this may cause the loaf to sink.

- The loaf is best removed from the machine as soon as it is baked, otherwise it will become soggy.

PASTRY-MAKING TECHNIQUES

The art of making good pastry lies in paying careful attention to the recipe and using the correct proportion of fat to flour. It is important to 'rest' pastry before baking, as it gets stretched during shaping and if not allowed to 'rest' and firm up, it may shrink away from the sides of the tin during baking.

Ingredients

FLOUR For most pastries, plain flour works best, as it gives a light, crisp result. Self-raising flour would produce a soft spongy pastry. Wholemeal flour gives a heavier dough, which is more difficult to roll. For wholemeal pastry, it is therefore preferable to use half wholemeal and half white flour. Puff pastry is usually made with strong plain (bread) flour as this contains extra gluten to strengthen the dough, enabling it to withstand intensive rolling and folding. A little lemon juice is usually added to puff pastry to soften the gluten and make the dough more elastic.

FAT Traditionally, shortcrust pastry is made with a mixture of lard (for shortness) and either butter or margarine (for flavour). However, it is now more often made with a mixture of white vegetable fat and butter or margarine, or all butter for a rich flavour. If margarine is preferred, it should be the hard, block type rather than soft-tub margarine.

LIQUID Care must be taken when adding the liquid to a pastry dough: too much will result in a tough end result; too little will produce a crumbly pastry, which is difficult to handle. Use chilled water and add just enough to bind the dough. Egg yolks are often used to enrich pastry.

QUANTITIES

Tart tins vary in depth, which affects the quantity of pastry needed. The following quantities are approximate.

Tart tin size	Pastry
18cm (7 inch)	125g (4oz)
20.5cm (8 inch)	175g (6oz)
23cm (9 inch)	200g (7oz)
25.5cm (10 inch)	225g (8oz)

Using pastry

A light touch and a little care with rolling and lifting your prepared dough will ensure your pastry case or pie crust is crisp and perfect. Take your time for the best results.

LINING TART AND PIE TINS

1 Working carefully, roll out chilled dough on a floured surface to make a sheet at least 5cm (2 inch) larger than the tart tin or pie dish. Roll the dough on to the rolling pin, then unroll it on to the tin, covering it completely with an even overhang all round. Don't stretch the dough.

2 Lift the hanging dough with one hand while you press it gently but firmly into the base and sides of the tin. Don't stretch the dough while you're pressing it down.

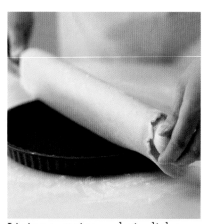

Lining tart tins and pie dishes

Baking blind

Topping

Sealing

Finishing

3 For a tart case, roll the rolling pin over the tin and remove the excess dough for later use. For a pie dish, ensure the pastry covers the lip of the dish.

4 Push the dough into and up the sides of the tin or dish, so that the dough rises a little over the edge.

BAKING BLIND
Cooking the pastry before filling gives a crisp result.

1 Preheat the oven according to the recipe. Prick the pastry base with a fork. Cover with foil or greaseproof paper 8cm (3¼ inch) larger than the tin.

2 Spread baking beans on top. Bake for 15 minutes. Remove the foil or paper and beans and bake for 5–10 minutes until light golden.

TOPPING
Covered pies need a lid of equal thickness to the base.

1 Roll out the pastry on a floured surface to about 2.5cm (1 inch) larger than the baking tin or dish. Roll on to the rolling pin, then unroll over the pie with an even overhang.

2 Using a small knife, cut off the overhang just outside the rim.

SEALING
1 Using your thumb and index finger, pinch the base and top of the pastry dough all the way round the rim. You don't need to squeeze hard, just firmly enough to stick them together. If the pie has no base, just press the top down on the rim of the tin or dish.

2 Use a fork to make decorative fluting marks on the rim – simply press all around the edge of the pie with the back of a floured fork. (See also below.)

FINISHING
1 If you want to make decorations for the pie using leftover pastry, cut them out using pastry cutters and put them in place, using a little water to stick them to the pastry. For pastry leaves, cut neat strips from the pastry trimmings, then cut these on the diagonal into diamonds, to shape leaves. Use the back of the knife to mark veins and pinch one end to form a stem.

2 Brush the top of the pastry with beaten egg if you wish. Cut two slits in the top of the pie using a small, sharp knife to let the steam escape during baking.

Dos and don'ts of pastry-making

How to make perfect shortcrust, pâte sucrée and puff pastry

◆ Work in a cool kitchen.

◆ Always use chilled water and butter whenever specified.

◆ It helps to chill the bowl too, if your hands are very warm.

◆ Use good-quality butter for tastier pastry.

◆ Use your fingertips when rubbing in.

◆ Avoid over-handling the pastry or it will become heavy.

◆ Don't over-flour the worksurface, as it will make your pastry too dry.

◆ Allow pastry to relax for easier rolling out.

◆ To stop it collapsing, chill the pastry well before putting in the oven.

SHORTCRUST PASTRY – WHAT WENT WRONG?

THE TART EDGES ARE UNEVEN/SHRUNKEN
◆ It wasn't chilled thoroughly before baking.
◆ Too much water was added at the mixing stage.
◆ The oven temperature wasn't hot enough.
◆ The pastry was over-stretched when rolling and lining.

THE PASTRY IS TOUGH
◆ The fat wasn't rubbed in properly.
◆ Too little fat.
◆ Too much water was added during mixing.
◆ The pastry was kneaded too much, which over-developed the gluten.

THE PASTRY IS SOFT AND CRUMBLY
◆ Too much fat was added.
◆ Too little water was added.
◆ The pastry has blistered
◆ The fat wasn't rubbed in properly.
◆ Too much water was added.

THE PASTRY IS GREASY
◆ It was overcooked.
◆ It was overworked.

PUFF PASTRY – WHAT WENT WRONG?

THE PASTRY HASN'T RISEN
- The butter broke through the pastry when rolled.
- The pastry was rolled and folded too many times.

THE PASTRY ISN'T FLAKY
- Butter not cool enough when used.
- Insufficient resting and chilling.
- Over-heavy rolling.

FAT HAS RUN OUT DURING BAKING
- The oven was too cool.
- The ends of the pastry were not sealed.

THE PASTRY IS OILY
- The pastry was over-baked.
- The pastry was not properly chilled.

THE PASTRY IS TOUGH
- Too much water was added at the first stage.

PÂTE SUCRÉE – WHAT WENT WRONG?

THE PASTRY IS TOUGH
- The pastry was overworked when the dough was brought together.
- The pastry was overcooked.

THE PASTRY IS OILY
- The butter was too warm.

How to make perfect choux pastry

This soft pastry is usually spooned or piped and is excellent for making cream-filled buns, profiteroles and savouries. It contains a lot of water and so it puffs up beautifully and is wonderfully light and airy.

◆ Before you start, have all the ingredients carefully measured and in place.

◆ Tip in all the flour at once, then leave the mixture to cool before beating in the eggs gradually.

◆ Use a dampened baking sheet (the steam will help the pastry to rise), and don't open the oven door for the first 20 minutes of baking, as the cold air will make the pastry sink.

CHOUX PASTRY – WHAT WENT WRONG?

THE MIXTURE IS TOO SOFT
◆ Insufficient cooking of flour before adding the egg.
◆ Insufficient beating after addition of egg.

THE PASTRY HASN'T RISEN ENOUGH DURING BAKING
◆ Not enough egg was beaten into the mixture.
◆ The mixture was too warm when the egg was added.
◆ The oven was too cool.
◆ The mixture was under-cooked.
◆ The mixture wasn't beaten enough.
◆ The oven door was opened before the pastry had set.

THE PASTRY HAS SUNK
◆ Insufficient baking, which can sometimes be remedied by returning the pastry to the oven.

FILO PASTRY – WHAT WENT WRONG?

THE PASTRY CRACKS WHEN ROLLED
◆ The pastry became too dry. Brush with oil or melted butter. Keep the rest of the pastry covered with a damp teatowel while assembling.

How to work with filo pastry

Making filo pastry is time-consuming, but ready-made filo is an excellent alternative. The delicate sheets of pastry are usually brushed with butter, then layered and filled to create crisp, golden treats.

◆ Filo pastry is often sold frozen; if you plan to put it into the freezer at home, get it home quickly so that it doesn't thaw.

◆ Thaw it completely before you start to work with it, otherwise it can crack or crumble. The best way to do this is to leave it to thaw overnight in the fridge.

◆ As you work, cover the unused sheets with a clean damp teatowel, to prevent them from drying out.

FILO PASTRY – WHAT WENT WRONG?

THE PASTRY CRACKS WHEN ROLLED
◆ The pastry became too dry. Brush with oil or melted butter. Keep the rest of the pastry covered with a damp teatowel while assembling.

Shortcrust Pastry
MAKES 225G (8OZ)
PREPARATION
10 minutes, plus chilling

- 225g (8oz) plain flour, plus extra to dust
- pinch of salt
- 125g (4oz) unsalted butter, or half white vegetable fat and half butter, cut into pieces

PER 25G (1OZ)
110 cals; 6g fat (of which 3g saturates); 12g carbohydrate; 0.6g salt

1 Sift the flour and salt into a bowl, add the fat and mix lightly. Using your fingertips, rub the fat into the flour until the mixture resembles fine breadcrumbs.

2 Sprinkle 3–4 tbsp cold water evenly over the surface and stir with a round-bladed knife until the mixture begins to stick together in large lumps. If the dough seems dry, add a little extra water. With one hand, collect the dough together to form a ball.

3 Knead lightly on a lightly floured surface for a few seconds to form a smooth, firm dough; do not over-work. Form the pastry into a ball, wrap tightly in clingfilm and leave to rest in the fridge for at least 30 minutes before rolling out. (This allows the pastry to 'relax' and prevents shrinkage when it is baked.)

notes
- To make the pastry in a food processor, put the flour and salt in the processor bowl with the butter. Whiz until the mixture resembles fine crumbs, then add the water. Process briefly, using the pulse button, until the mixture just comes together in a ball. Continue from step 3.
- Shortcrust pastry can be stored in the fridge for up to three days, or frozen.

variations
Wholemeal pastry: Replace half the white flour with wholemeal flour. A little extra water may be needed to mix the dough.
Nut pastry: Replace 50g (2oz) flour with finely chopped or ground walnuts, hazelnuts or almonds, adding them to the rubbed-in mixture just before the cold water.
Cheese pastry: Stir in 3–4 tbsp freshly grated Parmesan or 75g (3oz) finely grated Cheddar cheese and a small pinch of mustard powder before adding the water.

Herb pastry: Stir in 3 tbsp finely chopped fresh herbs, such as parsley, sage, thyme or rosemary, before adding the water.

Sweet Shortcrust Pastry
MAKES 125G (4OZ)
PREPARATION
10 minutes, plus chilling

- 125g (4oz) plain flour, plus extra to dust
- pinch of salt
- 50g (2oz) unsalted butter, at room temperature, cut into pieces
- 2 medium egg yolks
- 50g (2oz) caster sugar

PER 25G (1OZ)
110 cals; 6g fat (of which 4g saturates); 14g carbohydrate; 0.5g salt

1 Sift the flour and salt into a mound on a clean surface. Make a large well in the centre and add the butter, egg yolks and sugar.

2 Using the fingertips of one hand, work the sugar, butter and egg yolks together until well blended.

3 Gradually work in all the flour to bind the mixture together.

4 Knead the dough gently on a lightly floured surface until smooth, then wrap in clingfilm and leave to rest in the fridge for at least 30 minutes before rolling out.

note
This pastry can be stored in the fridge for up to three days, or frozen.

Rich Shortcrust Pastry
MAKES 225G (8OZ)
PREPARATION
10 minutes, plus chilling

◆ 125g (4oz) plain flour, plus extra to dust
◆ pinch of salt
◆ 75g (3oz) unsalted butter or block margarine and lard, diced
◆ 1 tsp caster sugar
◆ 1 medium egg, beaten

PER 25G (1OZ)
120 cals; 5g fat (of which 2g saturates); 13g carbohydrate; 0.5g salt

1 Put the flour and salt into a bowl. Rub the fat into the flour until the mixture resembles fine breadcrumbs. Stir in the sugar.

2 Add the egg, stirring with a round-bladed knife until the ingredients begin to stick together in large lumps.

3 With one hand, collect the mixture together and knead lightly for a few seconds to give a firm, smooth dough. Form into a ball, wrap tightly in clingfilm and chill for 1 hour before using. Roll out the pastry on a lightly floured surface to make a sheet at least 5cm (2 inch) larger than the tart tin or pie dish.

Choux Pastry
MAKES A 2-EGG QUANTITY
PREPARATION
10 minutes

◆ 65g (2½oz) plain flour
◆ pinch of salt
◆ 50g (2oz) unsalted butter
◆ 2 medium eggs, lightly beaten

PER 25G (1OZ)
50 cals; 4g fat (of which 2g saturates); 3g carbohydrate; 0.4g salt

1 Sift the flour and salt on to a large sheet of greaseproof paper.

2 Pour 150ml (¼ pint) cold water into a medium pan, add the butter and melt over a low heat. Increase the heat and bring to a rolling boil.

3 Take off the heat, immediately tip in all the flour and beat vigorously, using a wooden spoon. Continue beating until the mixture is smooth and leaves the sides of the pan to form a ball; do not over-beat. Leave to cool slightly, for 1–2 minutes.

4 Gradually add the eggs, beating well between each addition, adding just enough to give a smooth dropping consistency. The choux pastry should be smooth and shiny. Use as required.

note
For a sweeter pastry, add 1 tsp caster sugar with the flour and salt.

ACCOMPANIMENTS

VANILLA ICE CREAM

To serve four to six, you will need:
300ml (½ pint) full-fat milk, 1 vanilla pod, split lengthways, 3 medium egg yolks, 75g (3oz) golden caster sugar, 300ml (½ pint) double cream.

1 Put the milk and vanilla pod into a pan. Heat slowly until almost boiling. Cool for 20 minutes, then remove the vanilla pod. Whisk the egg yolks and sugar together in a large bowl until thick and creamy. Gradually whisk in the milk, then strain back into the pan.

2 Cook over a low heat, stirring with a wooden spoon, until thick enough to coat the back of the spoon – do not boil. Pour into a chilled bowl and leave to cool.

3 Whisk the cream into the custard. Pour into an ice-cream maker and freeze or churn according to the manufacturer's instructions or make by hand (see below). Store in a covered freezerproof container for up to two months. Put the ice cream in the fridge for 15–20 minutes before serving to soften slightly.

Variations

◆ Fruit Ice Cream: Sweeten 300ml (½ pint) fruit purée (such as rhubarb, gooseberry, raspberry or strawberry) to taste, then stir into the cooked custard and churn.

◆ Chocolate Ice Cream: Omit the vanilla and add 125g (4oz) plain chocolate to the milk. Heat gently until melted, then bring almost to the boil and proceed as above.

◆ Coffee Ice Cream: Omit the vanilla and add 150ml (¼ pint) cooled strong coffee to the cooked custard.

MAKING ICE CREAM BY HAND

1 If possible, set the freezer to fast freeze 1 hour ahead. Pour the ice cream mixture into a shallow freezerproof container, cover and freeze until partially frozen.

2 Spoon into a bowl and mash with a fork to break up the ice crystals. Return to the container and freeze for a further 2 hours. Repeat and freeze for another 3 hours.

VANILLA CUSTARD

To serve eight, you will need:
600ml (1 pint) full-fat milk, 1 vanilla pod or 1 tbsp vanilla extract, 6 large egg yolks, 2 tbsp golden caster sugar, 2 tbsp cornflour.

1 Put the milk into a pan. Split the vanilla pod and scrape the seeds into the pan, then drop in the pod. If using vanilla extract, pour it in. Bring to the boil, then turn off the heat and leave to cool for 5 minutes.

2 Put the egg yolks, sugar and cornflour into a bowl and whisk to blend. Remove the vanilla pod from the milk and gradually whisk the warm milk into the egg mixture.

3 Rinse out the pan. Pour the custard back in and heat gently, stirring constantly, for 2–3 minutes. The mixture should thicken enough to coat the back of a wooden spoon in a thin layer. Remove the pan from the heat.

note
For convenience, make the custard up to 4 hours in advance.

If you are not serving the custard immediately, pour it into a jug. Cover the surface with a circle of wet greaseproof paper to prevent a skin from forming, then cover with clingfilm and chill. To serve hot, reheat very gently.

Vanilla custard

Raspberry Coulis and Brandy Butter

RASPBERRY COULIS

To serve four to six, you will need:
225g (8oz) raspberries, 2 tbsp Kirsch or framboise eau de vie (optional), icing sugar to taste.

1 Put the raspberries into a blender or food processor with the Kirsch or eau de vie, if using. Whiz until they are completely puréed.

2 Transfer the purée to a fine sieve, then using a spoon, press and scrape it through the sieve until nothing is left but the pips.

3 Sweeten with icing sugar to taste and chill in the fridge until needed.

Variation

Use different soft fruits and liqueurs. For example, try crème de cassis with blackcurrants or Amaretto with apricots.

CHANTILLY CREAM

To serve eight, you will need:
284ml carton double cream, 1 tbsp golden caster sugar, finely grated zest of 1 orange (optional).

1 Whip the cream with the sugar until it forms soft peaks. Fold in half the grated orange zest, if you like. Cover and chill until needed.

2 Serve the Chantilly cream sprinkled with the remaining orange zest, if you like.

note

Flavour the Chantilly cream with 2 tbsp Grand Marnier to serve with fruity puddings.

BRANDY BUTTER

To serve eight, you will need:
150g (5oz) unsalted butter, at room temperature, 150g (5oz) golden icing sugar, sifted, 3 tbsp brandy.

1 Put the butter into a bowl and whisk to soften. Gradually whisk in the icing sugar, pouring in the brandy just before the final addition. Continue whisking until the mixture is pale and fluffy, then spoon into a serving dish.

2 Cover and chill until needed. Remove from the fridge 30 minutes before serving.

note

For a light, fluffy texture, whisk the brandy butter using an electric mixer just before serving.

CRÈME PÂTISSIÈRE

To make 450ml (¾ pint) you will need:
300ml (½ pint) full-fat milk, 1 vanilla pod, split, or 1 tsp vanilla extract, 3 medium egg yolks, beaten, 50g (2oz) golden caster sugar, 2 tbsp plain flour, 2 tbsp cornflour.

1 Pour the milk into a heavy-based pan. Scrape the vanilla seeds into the milk and add the pod, or add the vanilla extract. Slowly bring to the boil, take off the heat and leave to infuse for 10 minutes. Discard the pod.

2 Whisk the egg yolks and sugar together in a bowl until thick and creamy, then whisk in the flour and cornflour until smooth. Gradually whisk in the hot milk, then strain back into the pan. Slowly bring to the boil, whisking constantly. Cook, stirring, for 2–3 minutes until thickened and smooth. Pour into a bowl, cover the surface with a circle of wet greaseproof paper and leave to cool. Use as a filling for fruit flans and other pastries.

Index